Into the Diaspora Wilderness

Selma Carvalho

Best wishes,

Goa, July 2010

Into the Diaspora Wilderness © by Selma Carvalho
lescarvalhos@yahoo.com
Creative Commons 3.0, non-commercial, attribution. May be copied with
attribution for non-commercial purposes in its entirety.

Co-published by

Goa,1556 Trust, 784, Sonarbhat, Saligão 403511 Goa, India.
http://goa1556.goa-india.org, goa1556@gmail.com +91-832-2409490
http://goa1556.notlong.com
Goa,1556 is an alternative publishing venture, named after the accidental
arrival here of Asia's first Gutenberg-inspired printing press. It aims to give
Goa a voice to help understand itself and articulate its own priorities.
and

BROADWAY PUBLISHING HOUSE

A division of Goa's largest bookshop, Broadway Book Centre, at Ashirwad,
18th June Rd, Panjim 403001, Goa, India Ph +91-832-6647038.
http://broadwaybooksgoa.com

Project coordination by Frederick Noronha, Managing Trustee, Goa,1556.
Cover design by Bina Nayak http://www.binanayak.com
Copy editing by Pamela D'Mello
Printed and bound in India by Rama Harmalkar, 9326102225
Typeset using LyX, http://www.lyx.org
Text set in Times Roman, 10 point.
ISBN 978-93-80739-02-1
First printing: July 2010
Second printing: October 2010
Price (in India): Rs. 345

Contents

A brief introduction		vii
1	Into the Diaspora wilderness	1
I	**Goa**	5
2	An alliance... of sorts	7
3	A quiet rebellion	17
4	The war years	39
5	The red book	47
II	**The Arabian Gulf**	57
6	An illicit past	59
7	The dawn of a new era	67
8	Early arrivals in the Emirates	73
9	The *M.V. Dara*	81
10	Of faith and learning	85
11	Afrik'kar, Dubai'kar, Goem'kar	93

12 Disparate, unequal society	105
13 The Gulfkar	111
14 Saddam's war	121
15 Homeless in Utopia	125
III The New World	**131**
16 Ten thousand lakes	133
17 A land of immigrants	135
18 The exiled intellectual	141
19 Heathendom, Christendom	149
20 The independent Goan	153
21 The student	159
22 The young bride	163
23 Race relations	169
24 Colour of friendship	177
IV A Mighty Empire	**179**
25 My Beautiful Launderette	181
26 Setting sail with the English	185
27 Early days in Uganda	191
28 The Goan man of Kenya	201
29 Emma Gama Pinto	209
30 Expulsion from Malawi	215

Contents

31 Onwards to England	221
32 Freedom fighters in London	229
33 Salubritas et Industria	237
34 Growing up Goan-British	241
35 Love, friendship and farewell	247
A debt of gratitude	253
36 A debt of gratitude	253
37 Notes	257

Dedicated to Helen Gomes and Roque Cardoso,

the quiet heroes of Goan villages.

There is no phenomenon more permanent in the history of mankind than the migration of men from place to place in quest of easier labour and more abundant means of subsistence.

Editorial, *The Times*, June 10, 1864.

A brief introduction

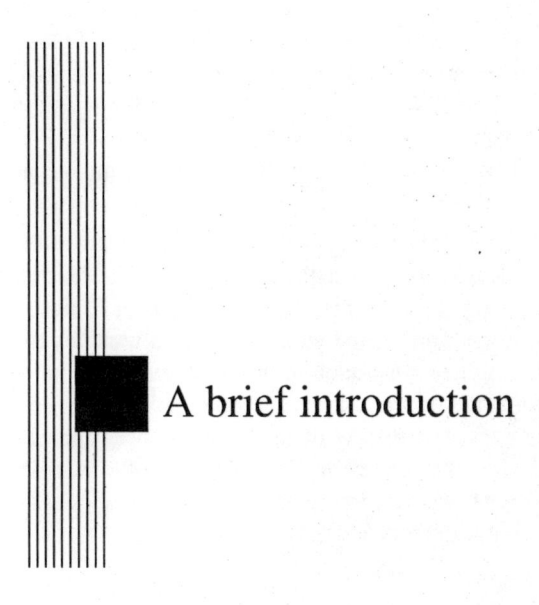

SIR RICHARD BURTON, the 19th century British explorer, tall, reminiscent of swash-buckling pirates, cleaved to memory for his entry into Mecca disguised as a Muslim, wrote: "The man wants to wander, and he must do so, or he shall die."

It is perhaps ridiculous that I begin a book about Goans with a quote from Burton, for upon sailing to Goa on a *pattimar*, a wooden sail boat, circa 1846, he found Goa to be populated by thieves, Christian wife-beaters, negro Robin Hoods and other reprobates. Burton's relentlessly, uncharitable account of Goa, in *Goa and the Blue Mountains*, did not dissuade him from including in his troupe two Goan servants, Valentine Rodrigues and Caetano Andrade, as he set out on his second expedition, almost ten years later, into the interiors of Africa. In typical Burton speak, he describes them as receiving exorbitant wages for doing a bit of everything and nothing well. But leaving aside British stereotypes of Goans, to which I shall return later in the book, Burton does deftly articulate the longings of the human soul; its inextinguishable need to explore, and in this journey of exploration come to a deeper understanding of the self.

A BRIEF INTRODUCTION

By the dawn of the twentieth century, what little was left of Goa's illustrious history as an eastern cultural and economic entrepôt, dissipated into further rack and ruin, reeling as it was from the backlash of Portugal's own financial woes, in the custody of disinterested Portuguese Governor-Generals and the raising of taxes as the only means to balance its trade deficits.

A minuscule section of the Goan population sat indolently in the grandeur of chandeliered reception halls, manacled by the lack of civil liberties and nursing an intellectual ennui, in what poet Armando Menezes described as an "intellectual wilderness"[1] laid waste by the conquistadors. The valve of frustration in this wilderness only temporarily relieved for some by studying in Lisbon or working in Portuguese Africa. For the vast section of the agrarian society, backs bent in paddy fields, it was a very modest life. The lack of infrastructure and industry meant there were few job opportunities besides basic trades such as tailoring, carpentry and masonry.

Within Goa itself, movement was constant. Flooding of low-lying areas, epidemics of flu or cholera, impoverishment after a failed crop, persecution – be it social or religious, a non-agrarian population of bakers, carpenters, tailors meant movement for many people especially for those coming from the hinterlands of Goa. The vagaries of nature and fate prompted a resettlement to more fertile, forested or otherwise yielding land, nearer to fresh water sources and virgin to the extent that settlement was thin. In this, Goa had an unique counterbalance, which made such re-settlements possible and indeed profitable. Complete destitution after a failed crop in the hinterlands with its thick, fertile soil ideal for paddy, could be staved off by a migration to the coastal areas, its abundance of tall, almost dignified, coconuts trees making it possible for populations to sustain themselves.[2] Goans soon ventured further afield, across the border into Poona, Bombay and Calcutta, then across the seas into more alien countries.

Unlike the European explorer who was funded by scientific societies, governments or benevolent benefactors, the Goan's foray into new lands was driven by sheer necessity and his own gumption. Was the Goan an explorer? An intrepid traveler? Or was he just in a very primitive sense, someone who foraged for food in new territory? The reasons for the movement are incidental. If exploration and discovery of virgin land are to be measured by the courage it takes to venture into them, contribute to them and benefit from them, then the Goan's stake as an explorer and early settler must be on par with that of European explorers and settlers, and his journey must be documented with as much rigour.

* * *

The stories of Goans who left its shores are as integral in piecing together our collective identity as those that stayed behind. What were the social and economic forces that drove these Goans to journey far from their homeland, often across an undulating expanse of sea into the interiors of Africa, the arid deserts of the Gulf or the bitter cold of England? What were their lives like in these foreign countries? Did the Goan in them survive at all? Did they cling to the motherland only in memory or did they refuse to sever the umbilical chord, drawing an almost spiritual strength from the culture, language and religion it had engendered and which ultimately favoured their survival in the Diaspora?

My own opinion is that the genesis of the wider Diaspora belongs to that much caricatured and ignored Goan, the *tarvotti*, or seaman. Coming from Nuvem, I am well acquainted with *tarvottis*. Nuvem is known to have many a son-of-the-soil embark on a career at sea.

It is easy to recognise a *tarvotti*. They possess a certain fast-talking bravado which can easily be mistaken for brashness. The agrarian farmer lives in constant fear of the elements. The sea-farer battles them. The Goan's *affaire de coeur* with the sea would inevitably change his psyche from that of a fatalistic victim of uncertainty to one of conquering obstacles. What had life presented to this lot of able-bodied men, muscled by manual labour and matured by an early burden of family responsibility? Most of them were from proud but impoverished "Chardo stock",[3] now living in the *kudds*, seamen's hostels of Bombay while onshore, manipulated by recruiting agents, at the receiving end of a bristling English captain's temper and journeying for months on end on an unpredictable expanse of blue sea. Yet within a few years from the time British India ships started recruiting them, they proved themselves worthy of the sea and all that it wrought unto them. Soon British captains and officers refused to sail without their favourite Goan *boatlers*, or butlers.

These seafarers returned home with larger-than-life stories of strange sightings at sea, smooth sails and storms, jungles and cities, some true, mostly embellished. They elicited in the humble Goan soul an even deeper desire to travel beyond the confines of his own village and engage in a world which seemed endlessly wide, open and beckoning. Inevitably some of them settled around the port areas of the countries where they docked in.

Historical-geographer Clifford Pereira has established that Goan sailors settled around London's dockland areas. There is every possibility that those who plied the busy Bombay-to-Zanzibar and onwards route settled in Zanzibar, operating liquor shops and ice factories.[4] This was a trade Goans engaged in successfully, whether they moved to Poona or Zanzibar. The sea and the Goan are intricately woven. It shaped the Goan and it took him away from Goa. Wherever a port of call gained prominence, fledging Goan communities could be found, be it Mozambique, Mombasa on the east coast of Africa or as far as Cabo Verde on the west coast of Africa.

The early emigrant who travelled to East Africa has profoundly shaped our cultural mores. His impact remains vastly ignored in our questions about identity. He is a curious experiment in defining identity itself. Like all organic entities, identity is subject to Darwinian evolution, building upon chance and circumstance, shaping according to need, absorbing, learning and breaking off from that which is redundant. Defining identity is an exercise in futility, suspended on the continuum of time, trying to preserve it is like holding back the tide. And yet do we really know how identity and its subset culture is transferred, absorbed and preserved by communities? Is it all a product of our environment or is it rooted deeper in our psyche? Do we really understand why we seek comfort in its familiarity or why its conservation is such a strong, driving force?

I have not lived the *Afrik'kar's* story, neither in time nor space. For me it is a fragmentary story taken from the recesses of memory of those who were there and who are now aging, or live only through the yellowed files kept at dusty archives. When the last custodians of the story pass away it will be lost forever unless recorded with the passion it deserves. Throughout this book, Africa weaves in and out of almost every chapter; our understanding of the Diaspora consciousness can only be heightened when examined against a backdrop of this important aspect of history.

Another aspect largely ignored is how deeply our history is contrived by the British Empire. While the Goan in Goa was influenced by the machinery of Portugal's politics, the substantial number of

Goans who worked in British India or British East Africa and the Middle East were impacted by the machinations of the British. Inevitably, a complex relationship between the Goan and the Briton evolved, swinging like a pendulum between racism and respect. Ultimately, Goans would become intermediaries between native populations and the wieldy administration of Empire.

Very often, when the story of the Goan migration is told, it is done from the vantage point of Goa. It is as if Goans went to these countries but somehow remained unaffected by what transpired in these distant lands, as if they existed in a political and cultural vacuum. The reality is, there were transformations taking place every step of the journey, transformations which have inevitably affected the collective Goan psyche.

For a great many people that migrated, new realities became important and our tryst with Portugal receded into the background. These personal and community stories are set against a backdrop of the regional histories and the political frays of adopted countries. The book hopes to demystify the lives of Goans who live abroad, by bringing to the fore the austerity of the circumstances they usually have to contend with; but at the same time it also celebrates their ultimate triumph, achievement and contribution both to Goa and their adopted homelands.

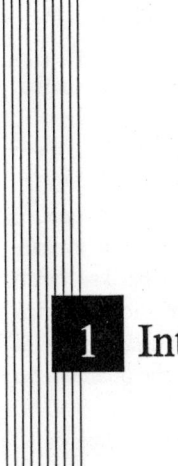

1 Into the Diaspora wilderness

MY MOTHER STOOD on deck in her stylish, sixties dress and waved goodbye to her sari-clad mother and teary-eyed son who had come to Bombay to see her off. The uncertainty of setting forth to a land of which she knew nothing about, save for stories of its blistering heat and dervish-like *shamals,* sand storms, did not weigh heavily on her mind. Her immediate concerns were how to keep comfortable the baby cleaving to her, and how best to hide the unbearable pain of leaving her six year old son behind.

It was June 1968 and much like my mother, over 600 other Indians were setting sail on the British India passenger-liner, *S. S. Dwarka,* from the port of Bombay to the Arabian Gulf. This god-forsaken corner of land, which had sustained neither man nor beast had been brought to life with the discovery of oil.

It looked to be an arduous journey as the ship left port. The monsoons threatening an onslaught to the east and a blistering summer awaiting towards the Strait of Hormuz. The British India line had commissioned four modern D-class vessels – the *Dumra,* the *Dwarka,* the *Dara* and the *Daressa* – to deal with the increased volume of pas-

1. INTO THE DIASPORA WILDERNESS

sengers to the Arabian Gulf. These ships of 5000 gross tons, and deck capacities of over a thousand, plied the Gulf axis between Bombay to Basra, stopping en route in Karachi, Muscat, Dubai, Bahrain and Kuwait, carrying on board all the dreams, hopes and aspirations that stirred in the souls of those setting out for the Gulf.

The lack of good schools in the Gulf region made it a prudent decision not to disrupt my brother's schooling. Like so many parents of that era, my mother left him in the custody of his grandmother. It was a decision she would regret for the child did not flourish without her. She rectified it just a few years later; but now she was faced with the memory of his tear-rimmed eyes and quivering mouth, which could muster just one question as she left: "Are you not taking me with you?" With this dagger firmly embedded in her heart, she boarded the ship.

My mother's recounting of the journey, which lasted five days, is sketchy. She spent most of it trying to find her sea-legs and hold down the serviceable if unvaried meals of rice, chapattis, vegetables and meat. She and my uncle, Bruno Gomes, who accompanied her, were unberthed passengers. They laid their mats and *chadors*, sheets, along the deck, wet and damp from the oncoming spray of water and braced themselves for the journey ahead. She had meticulously packed two tin-trunks with enough clothes to weather a few desert summers, winters and storms. Placed in between the several layers of clothes were cashew nuts, *doce*, a Goan sweet made of chickpeas and coconut, pickles and *chouriço*, spicy sausage for my father who awaited her arrival in Dubai. In her hand-bag as usual was her rosary to ward off evil.

Their first port of call was Oman, then onto Dubai which did not have a port at the time and so her ship dropped anchor mid-sea. With the Arabian Sea lashing huge frothy waves onto the ship, she began the tremulous descent by a rope-ladder into a boat which would ferry her to shore. For possibly the same reasons the Arabs called it the Empty Quarter, my mother called it her endless sea of sand. A frugal line of *barastis*, thatched hutments, dotted the landscape, the stench of goat droppings clung to the hot, humid air and fat, bulbous flies assaulted her face.

My father João Roque Cardoso had arrived in Dubai a year earlier and secured a job with Abdulrahman Al Bahar. He was a tall, handsome man with piercing green eyes inherited from his grandmother Catarina Dias. His chiseled face carried a fierce determination to improve his lot in life. He came

2

from a family of six siblings. His father, Joaquim Santan Purificação Cardoso, a dark, smallish and chronically asthmatic man, operated a *tavern* out of the house. Men would stop by on their way home from the paddy fields for a peg or two of feni, just before nightfall.

To understand why my father left, one has to understand the desultory, isolation of the *vaddo* Murda in the 1960s. For all the things that could occupy a young man's life during the day – fishing in the lake or thatching the roof – there was also the eerie silence of the night. The empty, hollow sense that nothing could germinate in the village which could take one beyond its boundary. Nothing in those dung-floored houses could lead to success. There are others who will argue for the quiet eloquence of rural Goa; the peace, tranquility, self-sustaining village life in which one seeks solitude. That is not what young men with blood coursing through their veins and arrogance flaring in their aquiline noses seek. They seek adventure, dream dreams larger than themselves and seek mythical fortunes in far away lands. Only their instinct tells them these fortunes are not as mythical as everyone says. They see a life beyond their own hemmed-in horizons.

Roque had finished a diploma in Accounting after completing high school and secured a job at Timblo's, paying him the princely sum of Rs 100 per month. The Timblo's of Goa eventually spread the tentacles of their business empire into various fields but their beginnings were in iron-ore mining. Roque's brother-in-law Lenny Gomes arranged a visa for him to Dubai; in 1967 he arrived in the Gulf. His first salary was Gulf Rupees 700 as an Accountant, a not insubstantial increase from his earnings in Goa. Life in Dubai was wrought with all the hardship an under-developed region entails. He worked out of a private home which had been hastily converted into an office.

That summer in 1968, when my mother and I first sailed to the Gulf, my father had rented an Arabic house in anticipation of our arrival. A few rooms huddled around a square open space. Its thatched roof made the installation of an air-condition an impossibility. If nature and the water-supply were on our side, the open space was meant for gardening, a feature typical of traditional Arabic houses. The house overrun with leathery lizards and winged cockroaches, I christened *Xilian Ghor*, the house of lizards. So began my journey into the Diaspora wilderness.

Part I

Goa

2 An alliance... of sorts

> Very few persons are probably aware that in the year 1878 a treaty of commerce was signed at Lisbon between the English and the Portuguese governments in reference to certain matters connected with that relic of Portuguese dominion in the East, the town and dependency of Goa. — *The Times*, September 30, 1884.

AS THE FIRST PEEK of summer spread over Europe thawing the ground with lashings of warm rain, Robert Walpole was in a rather excited state. It was April 1772, and he had just come across information that the all powerful Minister of Portugal, Sebastião José de Carvalho e Melo, better known as the Marquês de Pombal, was to sell off Goa to the Dutch.[1]

Robert Walpole had been appointed envoy extraordinary and Minister Plenipotentiary, a title which more simply meant ambassador to Portugal, setting sail from Portsmouth harbour in the bitter English cold and arriving at Lisbon in January 1772. The 36-year-old ambassador came from good Walpole stock from the county of Norfolk lying to the East of England, which had to its credit produced more

2. AN ALLIANCE... OF SORTS

than its fair share of aristocracy and diplomats. His uncle and namesake had occupied the office as First Minister from 1721-42, generally considered to be Britain's first Prime Minister, and his father Horatio Walpole was a noted diplomat. In the years that followed he would share a taxing but on the whole profitable relationship with the Marquês de Pombal, though on occasion the minister kept him waiting pleading a cold or a bout of indigestion.

Pombal had ridden to power in Portugal in the wake of the cataclysmic earthquake which rocked Lisbon in 1755. Before that, he had weaved in and out of obscurity, brusquely shunned by the aristocracy and described by King John V of Portugal as a man with *cabelos no coração*, a hairy heart, quite corruptible and denied any substantive post during his reign.[2] It was only after King John V died and the line of succession passed on to King Joseph I, that his star was in ascendance. This rise would have a profound effect on Goa. If ever there was a dichotomous personality, on the one hand perceived as the intractable *homme fort du Portugal* and on the other decried as a merciless despot, then Pombal was that man.

Walpole hurriedly dispatched by packet boat a letter to the boyish-looking Secretary of State, the fourth Earl of Rochford,* on this matter of grave importance to the English. If anything, Walpole felt, Portugal should "on many accounts make the offer to Great Britain, her friend and ally."[3]

Pombal had spent several years in England as envoy, during which time he had hardly endeared himself to the English.[4] Upon his rise to power, he had instituted what were perceived to be anti-British policies. The English were already wary of Pombal, when the news of the sale arrived, fearful as they were of an alliance amongst Portugal, Spain and France in renunciation of the Anglo-Portuguese alliance.

As the plot thickened, the Earl of Rochford himself came into possession of a letter by a George Johnstone who claimed that Pombal found, "the annual expense of the settlement of Goa as a public misfortune" and planned to deliver Goa to the Marathas, finally making its way to the French. The only person standing in the way of this negotiation was King Joseph I of Portugal, who would not "indulge a proposition on the subject".[5]

---

*William Nassau de Zuylestein, fourth Earl of Rochford was Secretary of State for the Southern Department of Britain.

8

Was the man much celebrated for bringing to a temporary halt the Inquisition, making subsidised government schooling available in Goa and declaring the equality of all citizens in its colonies despite racial difference,[6] indeed an avaricious minister in King Joseph I's court, seeking to dispose of a burdensome and dispensable Goa without batting an eyelid?

As was the custom in Europe, visiting ambassadors had front-row seats to the taffeta-clad and powdered-wig shenanigans that went on in the circus-like royal courts. Where personal relationships intertwined with political ones to create an entangled web of loyalty and deceit, where dagger and danger lurked behind every smile and, daughters and dominions could be sold to seal liaisons or write off debts. Walpole, the English ambassador, having settled in and now a little better acquainted with the Portuguese court wrote back to Rochford, three months later, repudiating his earlier intelligence:

> "I do not believe a word of it; nor do I think judging by the steps that are taking with respect to Goa, that there is at present any Negotiation any where for the Sale of it... but on the other hand supposing that if a good price could be got for it, that their Ministers would not hesitate parting with it, yet the difficulty would be in estimating its Value."[7]

Estimating Goa's value was a difficult task.

It was a strategic port but its economy was in shambles. The rigours of the Inquisition having driven out what little commerce existed from the Hindu trading community. Pombal had instituted sweeping changes among which was making Viceroys in the colonies defunct and replacing them with Governor-Generals. Dom José Pedro da Camara was earmarked as Governor-General and he, along with António José de Noronha, the Bishop of Halicarnassus, were to journey to Goa the next monsoon to resuscitate the ailing colony. The Bishop of Halicarnassus, of Portuguese lineage, was a controversial figure. He was embroiled in the murky politics of Indo-French and Anglo relations, at any given time playing all parties, and whose legacy remains as sullied and as much a paradox as that of Pombal.

His ability to converse in native languages made him an indispensable diplomat, but he seemed to display little loyalty to any particular party and had been taken prisoner at one point by the English East India Company and jailed in England. His release was secured by the intervention of Portugal, upon which he returned to Goa. But his

2. AN ALLIANCE... OF SORTS

detractors managed to have him jailed at Aguada, later deported to Limoeiro prison in Lisbon, where he spent a good 18 months before being released.

The Lisbon detention proved to be a blessing in disguise for he managed to ingratiate himself into the good graces of Pombal's coterie and got on rather famously with Dom José Pedro da Camara, the designated Governor-General and a former army-man himself. By Walpole's accounts, the Bishop was closely involved in Pombal's plan for the rehabilitation of Goa, which might have included collating population statistics of Goa for it is during the time of Camara's governorship, that the first collation of any statistics† appears.[8] The Bishop confided to Walpole that he wished for nothing more than to spend the rest of his days in Goa, the place of his birth. Camara would only receive an official nomination, almost two years later, when the titular Governor Dom João José de Mello who had looked after the affairs of Goa passed away in January of 1774.‡

As the ship carrying José Pedro da Camara left on the Saturday morning of February 19, 1774, the decline of Goa was very much on the king's mind. At one time, "15, 20 and 30 ships" would return yearly from India to Lisbon "richly laden" with bounty and there was "kept up at Lisbon a General Warehouse of India goods and merchandise for the consumption of almost all Europe"[9].

But the windfall that was once Goa, sustaining even other dominions of the Portuguese in the region, was now clearly on the wane. Whatever trade ensued was largely monopolised by Portuguese officers rather than in the hands of private merchants, irking King Joseph to the point where he intended to annul all laws "relating to the Government of Goa" and set up an entirely new system, much scaled down which would do away with all the accoutrements of stately houses and privileges accorded to officials sent there in keeping with the "diminished revenues of that enfeebled capital."[10]

All these plans might have been prematurely extinguished as King Joseph was ailing in health and his death heralded Pombal's own fall

---

†The population is given as: Goa: 44,588 Bardez: 79,382, Salsette: 78,847 Total: 202,817. Danvers F C, *The Portuguese in India: Being a history of Rise and Decline of their Eastern Empire*, Delhi: B R Publishing, 2006, p 438.

‡Dom João José de Mello passed away in Goa on January 10, 1774 and Dom José Pedro da Camara received his nomination on February 4, 1774. Danvers F C, *The Portuguese in India: Being a history of Rise and Decline of their Eastern Empire*, Delhi: B R Publishing, 2006, 437-38.

from power just three years later, followed by his forced exile to his country house and subsequent death in 1782. The Bishop of Halicarnassus had died in Daugim, Goa, as he desired, in 1776. Governor-General Câmara returned from Goa in 1779 and Walpole who had been ambassador to Portugal all this time left a year later.

It is perhaps a quandary of history how the tiny dominion of Goa remained a Portuguese colony for over four centuries, when all around it a much more powerful colonizer, the English, prevailed. But Goa's story isn't just about colonization and subjugation, of a myriad cultures merging, churning and thrashing about to form synthesis, much like the Arabian Sea which fronts the land on her western shores. Rather, it is one of barter and trade, of negotiation and checkmate, of intrigue and deceit, of courage and cunning. A story contrived by colonization but one that meanders into eventual benefit for a section of Goan society,

For all their time together in the Indian sub-continent, Portugal and England shared an uneasy alliance of sorts, bound by an Anglo-Portuguese Treaty of 1373 which did not prevent them from fighting proxy wars in the region.[§]

Occasionally the British tried to buy Goa. In 1839, they made an offer of £500,000, which the Portuguese turned down.[11] In 1857, rumours once again surfaced that the King of Portugal intended to divest of Goa in order to settle an old debt with the English.[12] Plans were afoot for Goa to be governed by an officer appointed by the Governor-General of India, or more likely become part of the Bombay Presidency. Within days, the Portuguese quelled this rumour, asserting that not only was there no intention of selling Goa but that every effort would be made to strengthen ties with Portugal. The reportage by the *Bombay Telegraph* was understandably grudging: "It seems that the

---

[§]The Portuguese tried to thwart the growth of Bombay which they had ceded to the British, by levying heavy fines. The British in turn took to supplying arms and ammunition to the seafaring Muscati Arabs who had been plaguing Portugal on its East African coast, namely Mombasa. De Souza, T R, Medieval *Goa: A socio-economic history.*Goa: Goa,1556. 2009, p 4.

On September 6, 1799, Richard Wellesley, Earl of Mornington and Governor-General of India, dispatched troops to Goa, on the flimsy pretext of protecting it from an imagined French threat. When no such threat was detected, he nonetheless managed to convince the resident Portuguese Governor, Veiga Cabral, of this shadowy enemy and stationed his troops in Goa, resulting in an uneasy occupation of Goa by the British, that would end only in 1813. Marques P. L, *The British Occupation of Goa*, 1799-1815, Lisbon: British Historical Society of Portugal, 1994.

2. An Alliance... of Sorts

Portuguese have resolved to retain possession of Goa, preferring that it should remain a nursery for cooks and *ayahs*."[13]

Eventually what the British did not acquire through military might, they negotiated through their treaties of commerce. In the Goa Treaty of 1878, ¶ they availed an almost unheard of concession from the Portuguese, to handover the production of salt in Goa and Damão. Both these territories had robust salt producing capabilities and large amounts of salt found its way smuggled into British India, resulting in substantial loss of tax revenue. Britain leaned on Portugal to have the manufacture and sale of salt in Goa and Damão to be over-seen by them and for a certain amount to be "sold" back to the Portuguese at the cost of manufacture. So unpopular was the regulation of salt production and other Custom duties negotiated on spirits and opium, that both Portugal and Britain failed to come to an amicable agreement twelve years later when the treaty came up for renewal.

The greater significance of the Goa Treaty, for Goans at least, were not its salt concessions but rather the conception of the Western India Portuguese Railway. It set in motion the idea of connecting Mormugão port to the town of Hubli, thereon joining Bellary, now part of Karnataka State, and connecting with the Madras Railway Company.[14] It would, for the first time, make Goa accessible by a train route, facilitating the movement of labour and cargo from Goa into British India.

The interest owed to the British through the West of India Guaranteed Portuguese Railway Company was, on one occasion at least, off-set by the money owed by them to the Portuguese for the salt concessions.[15] The winding railway track meanwhile took the sons of the soil away from the very salt of the earth that had paid for it. Ultimately, it was a lesser known outcome of the much earlier Anglo-Portuguese alliance of 1661, forged by the marriage of Catarina da Bragança to Charles II of England, which proved to be of immense benefit to the indigenous Goan. It ensured the protection of Portuguese nationals under British jurisdiction.

The jurisdiction of most relevance to the Goans was Bombay. The island had been ceded to the English by the Portuguese as part of Catarina da Bragança's dowry. Goa's fortunes continued to dwindle but the port of Bombay thrived. In hindsight, it would prove to be a

---

¶The Goa Treaty of 1878 was the result of an Anglo-Portuguese accord concluded in Lisbon in December, 1878.

regrettable miscalculation on the part of the Portuguese. Nonetheless, the relationship between these two colonial powers had become that of benign neighbours by the turn of the 19th century.‖

What made Goans want to leave their familiar Lusitanian, Roman Catholic environment of Goa and seek the patronage of British India? Poona's proximity to Bombay made it a base for a large British garrison. Gently ripped by the Mula-Mutha rivers, it was an Englishman's dream of fine weather, regular boating, cricket grounds and facilities for higher training in mountain warfare. Bands of Goans migrated to Poona to work as cooks for British officers and as carpenters and painters or to operate small general stores, usually wine-shops.[16]

Harold Delamere-Thwaytes, a British officer who served in India from 1909-1935, describes Goan cooks in Poona as "undoubtedly some of the best you could find in the world", their standard of English much higher than anyone else.[17]

Conceição Miguel Gomes, my maternal grandfather, worked as a stores clerk in the British Indian Army at Poona. It is difficult to fathom the aspirations of this tall, feeble-looking, middle-aged man as he toiled in Poona, year after year, for twenty years at a job which in no way rendered him prosperous. His family grew up without him, although his daughter, my mother, frantically clutches at memories of him, his presence palpable and looming large in her life. One thing was clear, his ties were bound to Goa. He never thought of Poona as a permanent residence, he never moved his family to resettle in what to him must have been a transient place.

Other members of my family did settle in Poona. According to the Census of 1881, quite a sizable settlement of Goans was to be found. Of the 3720 Roman Catholics, two-thirds were Goans, their presence made conspicuous by their dress and eating habits.[18] What was once a floating population became permanent; rented houses traded in for tiny row-houses, families mushroomed, burgeoned, and shifted their children as schooling in Poona gained prominence and the prospect of a sustainable income became even more plausible.

At about the same time, Goans were beginning to cluster in Byculla and Parel, the mill towns of Bombay, already squalid, grotty

---

‖ José Nicolau da Fonseca in 1878, wrote: "There is but one telegraph office in Goa, at Pangim, the capital of the country, maintained jointly by the British and Portuguese government, the latter contributing a yearly sum of Rs 160, besides paying £3 monthly as house-rent." Fonseca J N, *Sketch of the City of Goa*, 1878; *Goa, Daman & Diu Gazetteer*, Part 1, 1979.

13

and bursting to the seams. Goans seldom worked in the mills, a few worked in the mill administrative offices, but the two vicinities were home to the workshops of the Great Indian Peninsular Railway and it is here they found sustainable employment, earning a reputation as mechanics adept at "fitting, turning and erecting."[19] The need for cultural familiarity was profound and many others settled in Cavel, Dhobitalao, an enclave of early Roman Catholic converts, when Bombay was part of the Portuguese Empire.

Accommodation was always a problem. Goans found themselves renting box-like, one-room *chawls* if lucky with a tiny *nani* used as a bathing area. These had been speedily erected to house an influx of population into the industrial areas, fronting narrow, dusty roads and jostling for space with street vendors selling fruit and vegetables.

The community was sufficiently rooted and sustained to feel indebted to the British. They were numerous enough to have either officially or unofficially elected community leaders to represent them. This representation on August 15, 1902, sent a congratulatory letter to Lord Knollys, Private Secretary to Edward VII, on the event of King Edward's coronation. João Coutinho, John Godinho, Luis José Pinto, Philip Vincent de Souza, Francisco Xavier Furtado, Aluizio L. Colaço and Ligório José de Lima were some of the signatories, on what looked like a flowery scroll, to thank His Majesty King Edward for:

> "British India has been for a long time the home of adoption, where the sons of Goa under patronage of the British Government, enjoy the same privilege and blessings as Your Majesty's Indian subjects."[20]

Members of my family who had migrated to Bombay made trips back home despairingly yearning for Goa's larger, airy houses and wide open spaces; but they never abandoned Bombay. The bustle of big-city life, the milling crowds, a veritable Babel of language and occupation, the potential for continuous employment, the prospect of good schooling for their children, all had its own allure.

A lifetime could be sustained with annual trips back to Goa but Bombay had become a home in self-imposed exile. When King Edward VII's son and successor, George V, visited Bombay as the King-Emperor at the tail-end of 1911, the Goan community like a good many other communities in Bombay including the Parsees, sponsored a ceremonial arch on the route he was to take through the city.[21] In every way, the Goans of Bombay were part of the great mêlée that was this metropolis, distinct perhaps in the way communities often are, holding on to their own traditions but merging slowly nonetheless and forming the thin thread of nationhood that would eventually become India.

A defining event during the second half of the nineteenth century would forever change the fortunes of Bombay, catapult it to the position it would occupy for the next century, and directly impact the demographics of Goa. The opening of the Suez Canal, a marvel of engineering, almost halved the time it took to travel by sea from Europe to Asia.

Prior to the opening, barely any steamships plied from Bombay Port.[22] Those that did, carried almost their entire cargo in fuel. Most of the vessels docked were light-carrier sailing ships considered to be the best option for the long journey from Bombay to the Cape of Good Hope in Africa and onwards to Europe. The freeing of India's trade from the clutches of the East India Company monopoly, in the eighteenth century, and the opening of the Suez Canal, in the nineteenth century, transformed Bombay Port from a fledgling harbour into the main hub for British India and the Peninsular & Orient steamships.

Exports to Africa rose from 28 lakhs between 1860-70 to 159 lakh rupees by 1900.[23] Uganda and Kenya proved to be a double bounty to the British, a vast potential market for mass-produced European goods and, in return, a virtual cornucopia of raw materials. Uganda Governor Sir John Hathorn Hall (1944-51) once remarked in a report: "contributory cause of idleness (in the African) is to be found in the almost complete absence of consumer goods in the shops, which discourages any sustained effort to earn more money."[24]

The consumerisation of societies which previously had no acquaintance with this concept was essential to the success of Empire but forever changed the social fabric of indigenous populations and in many ways rendered them impotent in their own countries. The Cape Town-Mombasa-Zanzibar-Bombay sea-route, and the trade it commandeered, ultimately motivated Britain's colonization of East Africa. It became part of the Imperial plan to control the entire block of landmass from East Africa, through to the Middle East and India, to protect her trade.

It is Britain's supremacy as a sea-power in the twentieth century, the resultant conquests, trade, business interests and ultimate collapse of its empire, that intertwines with the story of Goans and mirrors the

2. AN ALLIANCE... OF SORTS

trajectory of their travels.

If Goans in Goa were intimately influenced by the Portuguese, in the Diaspora they would engage in a complex and ambivalent relationship with the British; a most tortured and conflicted race who were almost always in turmoil trying to juxtapose their inner sense of justice against their sense of entitlement, their regard for human dignity against their human greed. The Goan relationship with the British has left an indelible mark on our collective psyche.

3 A quiet rebellion

The Government of Portuguese India is preparing to issue a 2,000,000 rupee five per cent internal loan redeemable in 35 years for water, electricity and drainage schemes in Nova Goa. – Reuters, London, November 1928.

The population of Goa according to a census taken in 1921 was 469,494... The emigrant population scattered all over British India, Burma, East Africa and Mesopotamia must number nearly 200,000. – *The Times of India Illustrated Guide to Goa*, 1931.

WHEN THE INTREPID traveller and historian, Graham Sandberg, who had spent a considerable part of his life studying Tibet, visited Goa at the turn of the nineteenth century, it took him twenty-six hours to travel by boat from Bombay to Mormugão.[1] As he neared the rather desolate looking quay with a few "shanty-type" dwellings higher up, a railway station came into view with the warning sign, "*Proibida a entrada*," a clear reminder that here was a closed world and vastly different from British India in many respects. A world gov-

3. A QUIET REBELLION

erned by its own intricate web of relationships between colonizer and indigenous populations, landed gentry and the landless, worshipper and the mediators of worship. All of these relationships would weave a story with its own imprint on the demographics of Goa.

Today, the remnants of the entitlement enjoyed by the Goan elite of the last century come into view for the casual visitor as he turns the corner and embarks on the tarred road leading up to the white-washed, *Igreja do Espírito Santo*, Holy Spirit Church of lower Margão. The splendid homes of Goa's gentry, painted in dark shades of purple or the light pale yellow so reminiscent of the Portuguese era, line the path winding their way past the aging *Hospício*, hospital, leading into central Margão.

It is a small town, almost decrepit, now floundering under the weight of indiscriminate building and inadequate infrastructure, but at one time a bastion of Goa's urban intelligentsia.

Fanning out from Margão, the laterite red soil yields to the more fertile white of agricultural land; rice paddy fields, mango orchards and coconut groves. The visitor chances upon the nearby villages of Navelim, Chandor, Benaulim and Varca dotted by manorial houses, some lying forlornly vacant, others occupied by owners racked with the cost of their upkeep in a post-Liberation Goa. Certainly the machinations of Colonial Goa had heralded privatization of land ownership and empowered a few hundred upper-class Goan families to hold sway over vast estates.

A tour of some of these dwellings[2], inspired by the homes in Portugal, most lying central to the village and its inhabitants and overlooking bougainvillea splashed gardens, reveal the grandeur of a bygone era. Crumbling stripes of paint and wooden beams turned almost to sawdust cannot distort a snapshot of old-world charm preserved in time.

It is typical to have at least two reception halls with vaulted ceilings and enough room to host the bustle of a wedding. An *entrada*, hallway leads to a dining area where a long, narrow wooden table occupies the length of the room. At times, the dining room holds an adjoining small private chapel overlooking a cultivated courtyard of lime, banana, guava or chikoo trees. Previously the kitchen would have a large walk-in larder stocked with dried delicacies of fish, prawn, jack fruit, pickled mango, jams of guava, grains, wines and whatever else was needed to get through the lean monsoon months.

The keys to the larder and other cupboards jiggling from a belt worn around the matronly hips of the female head of the household. By the dawn of the 20th century, Goa had become a *bon vivant* living on borrowed money. There was a huge trade deficit to contend with; in 1908, for instance an import of Rs 61 lakhs was offset against a measly export of Rs 22 lakhs. For a dominion that could boast of nothing more substantial than exports of dry fish, betel nuts, salt, manure, mangoes and manganese, it nonetheless revelled in importing large quantities of wines, butter, silks, sugar, coffee, perfumes and tobacco. Goa's economy was driven by consumption which they could ill-afford, with very little attention paid to industry. In 1908, Goa imported Rs 68,049 worth of industrial machines but ironically imported Rs 1,18,690 worth of hats, Rs 2,76,185 of tobacco and Rs 10,800 of perfumes.

A Goan emigrant returning to celebrate Christmas described the early 20th century redolent lifestyle, in *The Times* of London:

> Our host and hostess were a charming couple who lived on the revenue of their property and had a large house with many rooms to spare. So it was no effort to place a suite of rooms at the disposal of the 'emigrants' as they called us. We for our part may have felt sorry for them living in a tiny town served by a narrow-gauge railway from British India, with its limited shopping facilities and dusty unpaved streets. Christmas dinner proved to be something like a private cabaret, the entertainers being the younger members of the family of our hosts. We sat around a long room and a bottle of vintage wine was opened. A young man gave us a tune on the fiddle and was loudly applauded. Then some of the boys and girls danced to the music of the gramophone. The proceedings followed the same sequence all over again – wine and further toasting, music and dancing and food. What the dishes were I cannot recall at this distance, but they certainly included every type of Goan delicacy, highly spiced sausage, tamarind fish and so on. And of the wines that came around I have no count.[3]

The elite were adequately cocooned in comfort. They were employed in government positions, spoke Portuguese and generally sent their children to prestigious institutes in Lisbon for higher studies.

From the recesses of my own memory, studying in Panjim some twenty-five odd years after Liberation, the Latin quarter of Fontainhas exuded all the grace and charm of Southern Europe. Its narrow alleys thick with town houses, the sounds of a mass drifting down the street, women wearing black mantillas hurrying to the Panjim Church of Our Lady of the Immaculate Conception and music floating from the confines of dark rooms with over sized, carved furniture. Sometimes on a moonlit night, one could still hear a young man, mad with unrequited love, serenade under a balcony for a young lady to show favour.

The *Times of India* guide to Goa, 1931 put it accurately: "In thought, in habit, in dress and in action the Goan is the counterpart of the Latin Catholic of Southern Europe, and except for the complexion can always pass as such."[4] What did the sumptuousness of this lifestyle engender in what was essentially a colony of Portugal, despite its protestations that it was a province?

The writer in his guise as social commentator can at times portray society in shades more astute than the historian who looks at events removed from their urgency. Writing at the turn of the 19th century, Francisco João da Costa, in his column *Notas a lápis* appearing in the daily *O Ultramar*, parodied Goan society's pretensions and vacuity of thought; a lifestyle devoid of any intellectual incisiveness, an incessant preoccupation with the mundane and an ungainly dalliance with all things Portuguese, particularly the language.[5] His unrelenting dissection, although an overstated caricature, caused a furore and earned him the ire of his contemporaries but the popularity of his sardonic writing reflected the grudging acceptance of its veracity. It was concurred by that much celebrated doyen of Goan intelligentsia, José António Ismael Gracias, to be "at the bottom true."[6]

What could a young man returning from higher education in Portugal, exposed to fashionable and current ideologies of Republicanism and individualism, hope to achieve in Goa? Being denied the same rights, his freedom of thought and expression blighted by political restraints and oft times the social censor of a parochial mindset. Bernando Francisco da Costa, uncle to Francisco and founder of *O Ultramar*, within some years of floating this daily in the hope of giving voice to the native Goan, was charged with conspiring against Portugal and exiled to Diu, where he died in 1896.[7]

Goa's hope for autonomy would repeatedly be crushed, until the rise of Dr. António de Oliveira Salazar in 1928 would cause it to fracture prematurely and permanently. In this claustrophobic environment, it is not difficult to imagine an ennui setting in, a malaise born of listlessness, lack of political engagement and the stifling of intellectual curiosity which found an outlet in celebrating the superfluous.

* * *

Just four kilometers to the north of Margão lies the quiet *vaddo* (ward) of Murda-Grande in the village of Nuvem. My paternal great-grandmother, Catarina Dias, moved to Murda in the early 1900s from Shiroda, following the death of her husband, Caitan Piedade Cardoz. Shiroda had been struck by plague and perhaps there was nothing other than destitution for Catarina in Shiroda.

On a broad map of Goa, Murda lies almost diagonal to Shiroda. What made Murda an option? She would have had to cross the serpentine blue of the Zuari river and continue on foot, through a thickly forested area until she reached a patch of land suitable for settlement. Did she just set off wandering in the wilderness until she found her footing?

The topography of Shiroda and Murda is similar. Both areas abound in coconut trees and the possibility of continuing in traditional occupations might have played a role. With the help of her two sons and daughters, Catarina erected a thatched dwelling in Murda. What is clear is that even minor migrations from one area to another greatly improved the quality of life.

Like many a *vaddo* in Salcete, Murda then was an enclave of isolation save for a desolate solitary road, an erratic bus service, a devotion to Christian saints, celebration of their feasts and a love of *tiatr* which might have occasionally taken them away from this pocket of insularity. Despite a cleared settlement of closely huddled houses, it was almost jungle-like with spindly coconut trees, thick oak and reedy cane sprouting everywhere.

Most of the families were related to each other either through marriage, like my parents who are next door neighbours, or by descent. There was even a distinctive whistle which identified a *Mudekar*, a sort of calling card. It was a clan unto itself with an unofficially elected *vaddo* elder. This was a world cut off from the world.

The realities in the villages of Goa, though much romanticised by European journalists like Emile Marini as: "so beloved by the Goanese who live there, and for which Goanese emigrants abroad sigh with nostaliga,"[8] ran afoul of this hyperbole. Damodar Dharmananda Kosambi – renowned Indian mathematician, historian and polymath

3. A QUIET REBELLION

— described it as the "idiocy of village life,"[9] marred by malnutrition, hookworm, apathy, quarrels, violence, litigation and delinquency. Life for the average Goan in its villages was at marked variance with the privilege enjoyed by a few urban elite or landed gentry.

Murda was predominantly home to *mundkars*, tenanted labour. The word, *mundkar*, either refers to a *mund*,[10] an interest-free loan given to a prospective tenant to build a dwelling on the *bhatkar's* (landlord's) property or originates from *mul*, the root of a tree. The one who plants trees and cares for them eventually came to be known as *mundkar*. He was a tenant with very few rights, a casual caretaker of the property who received a token share of the yield from the *bhat* (property) or who cultivated the paddy fields in return for a share of the harvest. I use the word casual for there was another layer of tenants, *tollkars* who had vested in them, a *tolluck*, actual caretaker status. They had a wider net of responsibilities to contend with and in return they enjoyed slightly better privilege in terms of actually living off the land. It was not uncommon for two or three *mundkars* to be attached to large estates, a position which invariably enhanced the status of the *bhatkar*, and one amongst them to be appointed *tollkar*. An *olheiro*, from the Portuguese word overseer, was appointed to supervise harvests, keep track of the yield by making a notation on the trees and estimate the potential of the next yield.

The vast majority of the population in Goa were cultivators of the land, hardened men and women used to being ankle-deep in marshy soil and wrinkled prematurely under the glare of the relentless sun. Some ventured into non-agrarian occupations to become weary-eyed bakers, perpetually hunched carpenters or tailors furiously working the wheel of their Singer machines.

Along the coastal belt in the village of Colvá, for the Catholic *kharvi*, fishing was a common occupation. The word *kharvi* comes from the *kharva* community which had settled along the western coast from Gujarat to Goa, seafarers engaged in fishing. Apart from selling the fresh produce mostly of silver-gilled sardines and mackerels, the families spent long hours filleting, salting and drying it, the smell proprietarily clinging to their skin.

There were also toddy-tappers who tapped the sap of the coconut tree, to be distilled into alcohol. The more prosperous amongst them operated alcohol distilleries in their homes with adjoining taverns. The extended family system as well as the seasonal nature of crop cultivation allowed for two occupations to be taken up simultaneously. Some members of the family tended to bakeries while others cultivated the field.

At home the men wore a *kasti*, a triangular, light cotton loincloth covering the genitals but leaving the buttocks exposed. The *kasti* was more prevalent in the south of Goa, its popularity echoed in the saying "*shastikar kastikar*". On top of this *kasti*, they would wear a *cabaia*, a loose fitting gown, if they needed to venture outdoors. The *cabaia* is thought to be the garment of the upper-class in Goa but it was used more commonly.

In the urban centers men wore the Western pant, but in the villages the *cabaia* was the preferred garment. Just how this came to be the attire is not easily traced for neither a Hindu heritage nor a colonial influence successfully explains the *cabaia*. There is every possibility that it is a vestige of the Islamic influence. Similar attire was prevalent in the royal courts of South India, the word *cabaia* itself borrowed by the Portuguese from the Persian word *qabā*, which describes the dress worn in the Middle East.*

The older women wore a *kapod*, a cotton sari-like wrap. My maternal grandmother, Maria Rita Agustina Santimano from Colvá, a thick-set woman and a staunch Catholic who died with the rosary firmly clutched in her hands, wore a white kapod with an *ole*, a headdress, on her wedding day. This was the wedding dress *du jour* of the proud Chardo caste in the early half of the century. A marriage had been arranged for the young bride of sixteen to a man who had returned from Africa and of whom she knew little, except that he too was of the Chardo caste, coming from a family of *poders* (bakers) in Murda. Within a generation, the *kapod* was replaced with the Western white wedding dress. There was a transitional phase where the white dress was stitched with the material of the traditional *kapod*.

---

*Jan Huyghen van Linschoten, the Dutch merchant, mentions it in 1589, as the dress of the Brahmins. Dalgado S R, (1918) *Glossário Luso-Asiático*, Vol 1, A-L, New Delhi: reprinted by Asian Educational Services, 1988. Linschoten was in the employ of the Portuguese at the time, based in Goa, and allegedly stole their nautical maps which then enabled the Dutch to enter the East Indies.

The Goan *cabaia* made a mid-century comeback thanks to the rebellious streak of a few doctors; Barónio Monteiro, Peregrino Costa, Sales de Veiga Coutinho, José Filipe Menezes and Constâncio Roque Monteiro who together formed the *Liga Económico-Social da India Portuguesa* in the 1930s. This loosely formed association acted as a foil against Western culture and decried the unsuitability of donning on thick Western attire for a tropical climate.

3. A QUIET REBELLION

Choice of attire had become a bone of contention in Goa. It was representative of the wide divide between upper-castes and lower-castes, between urban and rural Goa, between religious sensibilities and indigenous choices.

Western dress was encouraged and expected in the urban centers. The *kasti* and *kapod* were stigmatised as the attire of the uneducated, labouring classes. Marriage proposals from families where women wore a *kapod* were thwarted and social contact with such families was subtly minimised if not curtailed altogether. Such was the condemnation and stigma attached to donning the *kapod* that young Catholic girls even in remote villages took to wearing a dress, gathered at the waist and cascading into a full skirt.

The Church too, played a definitive part in inculcating Western sensibilities. Men arriving for Sunday mass in their *kasti* were denounced from the pulpits and made to stand outside by the priests or cover up their semi-nudity with a towel. Perhaps, the Western *vestido* (dress) and *calção* (pant) proved to be Portugal's most enduring weapon of cultural indoctrination and an expression of our human desire to escape, even if only cosmetically, societal tags of caste and class.

* * *

Marriage for me meant a migration to Vasco. Sitting in a veranda, atop of Mangor Hill, an old-time resident and *ganvkar* educates me about the *ganvkari* of Vasco, yet another entirely different system of land-ownership prevalent in Goa, which predates the arrival of the Portuguese. Students from St. Theresa School walk past us, momentarily distracted from their incessant chatter by the traffic that cuts too close to them. Hardly any of them are from those *ganvkari* families of yore.

Mangor Hill is Vasco's counterpart to Altinho of Panjim. At its foot, the harbour town of Vasco spreads out with the magnificent St. Andrew's Church, framed by a central square of activity. Vasco is now home to Kannadigas, Oriyas and Biharis, one of the most visibly non-Goan towns in Goa. The availability of land and the need for labour has a way of attracting new settlers, who are undoubtedly resented at first but inevitably assimilated.

Life is in a constant flow of migration, settlement and assimilation. The tall, imposing frame of Cruz (name changed) sitting on a wooden chair, both a little weathered by time, nudges my attention back to the *ganvkari* system as he journeys back to his own childhood.

On the lower slopes of Mangor Hill, he recalls about 30 *ganvkari* families as well as a few who had settled in Baina, which rests at the foot of Mangor Hill and looks out to sea. These families, descendants of the original settlers, held the land as part of the *"comunidade de aldeia,"* a joint-custody shared by the community. They were a peaceful *comunidade*, all of them cultivators of the land.

The *ganvkari* would divide amongst themselves whatever revenue accrued from their agrarian enterprise after adequate provisions had been made for the welfare of the village. It was not unusual for *moradores*, the Portuguese word meaning inhabitants or tenants, slightly corrupted to mean *not native* to Vasco, to arrive from the villages of Cansualim and Majordá. Frequent illness caused chronic shortage of labour in the early half of the century. The Chardo caste credentials of these *moradores*, and being cultivators themselves, meant they were gradually but eventually assimilated into Vasco's inner coterie.

Another section of society, fishermen, carpenters and toddy-tappers had settled on the periphery of Vasco. This was essential labour but considered non-*ganvkari*, upholding a social apartheid of sorts. Their occupations and their inherited castes meant they would never be assimilated into the *ganvkari* system.

Cruz gently admonishes me for asking if there were any Brahmins in the area. "There were no Brahmins here, we are all Chardos, I don't know where these Brahmins come from," he shakes his head in disapproval. The conspicuous absence of Brahmins in many South Goa villages such as Velsão, Cansaulim, Majordá, Betalbatim, Colvá, Varca, Carmona, Cuncolim, Assolná and Velim – and the unhealthy rivalry that exists between Chardos and Brahmins – makes caste a reliable tracker of various migrations settling into Goa besides that of occupations.

Despite the egalitarian notions of the *ganvkari* system, by the twentieth century it had been entirely corrupted. Most of the landlords or members of the *comunidade* lived away from the land in the urban centers, showing a distinct lack of interest in the land itself.[11]

Communal land was leased out for cultivation; but the internal rancorous, bickering between landlords was so acute and subversive that it artificially pushed up the price at auctions. Those that actually cultivated the land could rarely show a profit after paying the rent. A layering of status and wealth emerged even amongst those supposed

3. A QUIET REBELLION

to be equal members of the *comunidade*.

Cruz looks at the passing traffic and talks cautiously about the Category A *ganvkar*, who by dint of connivance with vested authorities usurped large tracts of land, with the Category B languishing behind and Category C floundering at the bottom of this hierarchy of material well being. The codification of the *comunidade* privileges into law by the Portuguese through the Charter of Local Usages, 1526, was compiled by taking into confidence Brahmins and other natives.[12] It is highly unlikely that while this company of Portuguese officials and Brahmin natives came together to draw a charter, certain sections of society were not disempowered, either through illiteracy or being unable to mobilise concertedly and leverage their own rights. †

The criss-cross of relationships which emerged between the *bhatkar* and *mundkar*, between *ganvkar* and non-*ganvkar*, between the larger landholders and those endowed with a meager parcel of land, were underpinned by the calcification of the caste system. A strict social, economic and political hierarchical hegemony emerged with the labouring class inevitably being disadvantaged in this chain.

Goa's agrarian society has always been markedly paternalistic, conservative and often chauvinistic. The Catholic *Gauda*, the indigenous tribe of Nuvem, for instance, were all given the family name of the *bhatkar*. A number of them are named Costa, the family name of a prominent *bhatkar* in the area. This was unnervingly similar to the European practice of vesting African slaves on plantations with the slave-owners name, to denote ownership and for the Portuguese to ensure they had been baptized. Was this practice imported to Goa, which in no little part wiped out people's previous identities?

Other inequities which diminished the human spirit prevailed. *Mundkars* could not enter the *bhatkar's* house through the front door or address them by their first names. They could be called upon at short notice to help out in the *bhatkar's* household, especially if there was a wedding or celebration in the family. The position of *mundkar's* wives and daughters was precarious, looked upon as unofficial concubines. Although, even the harshest social commentators would describe the relationship between *bhatkars* and *mundkar* as being gen-

---

† "When at the approach of the rainy season the houses had to be covered with palm leaves to protect the mud walls against the lashing rains, it was the chief *ganvkar's* privileged to begin work on his house first... the dancing girls had to perform first before the house of the chief *ganvkar* and then before the others."[14] Souza T, *Medieval Goa: A socio-economic history*. Goa: Goa,1556, 2009, p 37

erally unobtrusive and cordial, it was nonetheless a relationship based on deference where each member knew his place. The implied threat itself vested power in the *bhatkar* and rendered the *mundkar* powerless. The livelihood of *mundkars* was dependent on the goodwill of the *bhatkar*.

Conflict between *ganvkars* and non-*ganvkars* erupted frequently too. Members of *comunidades* exercised flagrant discrimination against those they perceived to be *"bhailo lok,"* outsiders, even those who might have migrated from just a few kilometers away. Celebration of church feasts was a constant thorn in the flesh of the laity. Maundy Thursday, Good Friday, Easter Sunday and feast days, were considered the prerogative of the *ganvkars*, where non-*ganvkars* were not allowed to participate in the organization or liturgy.

Ganvkars would lead processions wearing the royal-like red of their clan, a visible differentiation between them and the others, an overt act of casteism. Miscegenation between *ganvkars* and non-*ganvkars* was strictly prohibited. Right to *comunidade* membership was inherited through the male off-spring. Education of women was not a priority.

The Portuguese had little incentive to challenge this status quo which was not so different from the manorial privilege enjoyed in Europe by the landed gentry. Indeed power hierarchies are almost endemic in human societies, perhaps the resultant turmoil itself is integral to bringing about evolutionary change in social conditions. Into this fray of social and economic inequity would enter another party, the Church, whose role would be dichotomous and which ultimately would lead to a quiet rebellion in Goa.

* * *

The Catholic Church in Europe has a history of aligning itself with feudal lords who funded wars and crusades, monetarily and with the leasing of peasantry, to recapture the glory of Christendom. Indeed for a large part of medieval European history, the Church is the State and the State is the Church. This feudalization of religion, the Portuguese brought with them onboard their caravels into Goa. *Bhatkars* with large landholdings could be counted on to bequeath money to support the Church's activities in Goa and missions in its other dominions.[13] ‡

---

‡A Senhora Ana de Azavedo, in 1629, donated huge tracts of land to build the

3. A QUIET REBELLION

The native clergy itself was dominated by upper-caste priests, which was not particularly different from what prevailed in Europe where the upper echelons of the Catholic Church was filled with sons of the nobility, accused of sins of pluralism, that is holding more than one post and nepotism, favouring their own. While the Church as an institution upheld the status quo, its dogma heralded change.

Conversions and preferential treatment of the converted spread Christianity in Goa. However, the curious question arises; what forces made the converted Goan implicitly embrace these new Caucasian gods and saints depicted in huge portraits, floating skywards and looking down in admonition? Faith after all requires a certain amount of expectation and promise. The Hindu pilgrims sighted praying at roadside crosses, offering flowers and burning incense and conversely Christians who steadfastly hold onto old Hindu traditions, both speak of a fundamental human condition, that one is not too proud to propitiate other gods if it means a miracle or two could be successfully negotiated.

It is facile to believe that actual conversion took place at the point of imposition or incentive. It was a progression of faith, imbibing it piece by piece, at times synthesising older beliefs with new ideology, at times bartering with a new God who promised miracles abundantly.

An area plagued by frequent epidemics of influenza, cholera and outbreaks of malaria, an agrarian society dependent on the grace of nature, a land where death was frequent and failure familiar; it wouldn't have been too difficult to sell hope. As faith grew, this newly converted population was introduced to the God of Abraham and Moses and, perhaps more impressionably, Jesus Christ the saviour of the downtrodden. However conservative the machinery of the Church was in colluding and upholding an inequitable social order, the central tenet of this religion was equity in the eyes of a monotheistic God.

The French missionary, Reverend Denis Louis Cottineau de Kloguen, drew his *Historical Sketch of Goa* in 1831, on behalf of the Bombay Auxiliary of the Royal Asiatic Society. The Reverend had travelled extensively in India and would write a history of India. He was a keen observer of indigenous populations and had stayed for a while in Goa as a guest at the Archbishop's palace before he

---

parish of Penha da Franca and houses to accommodate the Franciscan monks. Olivinho J F Gomes, *The Religious Orders in Goa*, Goa: Konkani Sorospot Prakashan, 2003, p 79

made his observations. He remarked that the Sudra formed the largest part of the Christian population. They were not as respected as the Chardos and Brahmins but that the situation was changing and that privileges accorded to the other two castes were slowly being conceded to them as well. The Sudra were not admitted to positions of trust but neither were they treated with the same amount of disdain as amongst non-Christian populations in the rest of India. Christianity had made inroads into the blight of caste. The thick barriers were somewhat shaken by compassion and a dogma based on Christian notions of equality. Writing more than a century and half later, Maria Aurora Couto quotes prominent Konkani writer Pundalik Naik in *Goa: A Daughter's Story*: "You sit together in church. Even if there were problems centuries ago, even if caste notions are still there in the Christian psyche and overtly as well, even if subtle distinctions are still there, I still say that your experience is different; all of you participate in everything. You do not have 'no go' areas i.e., areas, for instance, in the temple and other community meeting places where other castes are not free to enter."[14]

This tenet of equality would chip away at a Goan consciousness founded on caste inequities. The notion of egalitarian justice if not in this world then the hereafter, a justice based on the actions of the individual rather than on a measure of his worth by caste, ignited in the Goan that dangerous human emotion which propels one into action. The aspiration to affect the course of his life and to manoeuvre it in a direction of his choosing. To exert his own "free-will," a principle so close to the heart of those disciplined Jesuits who first roamed the hilly plains of Goa in search of "heathen" souls to save.

A relationship with a personal God meant the self was of utmost importance. Even if collectively society wasn't ready to dismantle caste, class, gender and political inequalities, at the individual level the Goan was freed from the burden of divinely attributed inequality.

The *mundkar* no longer wished to bring out a chair when the *bhatkar* came to pluck coconuts from the land he had tended. Instead he nursed a desire to buy the land on which he was a tenant. The young Sudhir lover no longer thought it his fate to be anguished by parental non-consent because of an accident of birth, instead he dreamed of bettering his lot in life and climbing the rungs of respectability. The toddy-tappers of Salcete will often explain the origin of the word, *rendeiro*, which in Portuguese means one who pays rent or dues but in

3. A QUIET REBELLION

Goa is corrupted to mean toddy-tapper. They insist *rendeiros* were the first community in Goa to be taxed for the coconut trees they tapped. Hence the eventual corruption of the word. Even if the veracity of this anecdote cannot be faithfully traced and is embellished to the extent that taxation was wide spread and very much part of the agrarian economy, it does once again speak of the aspiration that resided in the hearts of toddy-tappers. To be treated with dignity, to be seen as equals in their contribution to the economy of Goa; not just converts of the Bhandari caste[§] and burdened by the stigma of their occupation.

Poders (bakers) and *dorjeehs* (tailors) were another aspiring class of people. While the word *poder*, is a corruption of the Portuguese *padeiro*, meaning baker, the word *dorjeeh* comes from *darzi*, in all likelihood adopted from Muslim tailors of Gujarat and Maharashtra who had migrated to Goa;[¶] an indication of how outside influences have shaped Goan occupations. Although *poders* were considered to be largely Chardo, their status within the caste was determined by their wealth. There were *poder-bhatkars*, who in addition to being bakers owned vast tracts of land; but there were others milling at the bottom, living as *mundkars*. They had nothing but aspiration to propel them from the morass of their predicament. They were enterprising and mobile, moving from rural areas and venturing into urban towns and beyond to sell their product.

They re-trained in trades which they previously might not have considered appropriate or below their dignity. In 1916, a memorandum prepared by the British Ministry of Munitions, states its intent to import Indian labour into Britain to help with the World War I effort. Their only problem was: "when India is under consideration (they had) always to reckon with the caste question but the following races which supply men to the engineering trades are likely to be available without serious religious and social difficulties."[15] These included Parsees, Muslims and Goans who were deemed to be "good fitters and turners" and of which there were at the time about "5,000 to 6,000" employed in railway workshops and dockyards in British

---

[§] "What is certain is that the *Rendeiro* are descended from the Bhandaris," Pereira A. B, *Ethnography of Goa, Daman and Diu*, as translated by Couto M A, Penguin, India, 2008, p 56.

[¶] There were the Muslim tailors also, who were called *Darzi* and most of the Muslim *Darzi* came either from Gujarat or Maharashtra and settled down in Goa. *People of India: Goa*, K S Singh, Delhi: Anthropological Survey of India, 1993, Volume XX1, xxv.

India.

Christianity freed the Goan from ritual, rigidity and the cyclical wheel of inevitability. It broke the stranglehold of the communal. Community would continue to be important to him but, at a very critical level, he understood the elevation of the individual above that of the collective and this understanding placed him in a favourable position. The freedom led him to barter his services as he saw fit and enhanced his market-value.

The simmering discontent of social and economic disparity coupled with political emasculation would fan a quiet rebellion in the hearts of young Goan men. While the upper-class Goan languished unfulfilled, professionally, politically and personally, the labouring class Goan sought a way out of his social and economic predicament. The disquiet and discontent might have fermented into social unrest but for the fact that, at the core, the Goan is passive and peace-loving. Instead, release from the frustration came from unexpected quarters.

* * *

In 1856, the Calcutta and Burman Steam Navigation, Ltd., was established in British India, later to become the British India Steam Navigation Company (BI). Some fifteen years later, its chairman, William Mackinnon, the Scottish ship-owner and businessman who built up substantial commercial interests in India and East Africa, launched a recruitment drive in Goa, with the slogan, "Join the BI and see the world, have a secure job for life."[16] Goans were no strangers to the sea. Fishing and river trade on the Konkan coast was a way of life. In fact, it sustained a way of life and made resettlement from the hilly interiors of Goa to the coastal plains possible. Indigenous fishing trawlers were often seen idling in the waters between Goa and Bombay. But it is with the establishment of the British India shipping and Britain's expanding trade route that acted as a powerful propeller to the Goan's career at sea.

The labouring class Goan born in the late 1800s would in increasing numbers work onboard British India ships plying from Calcutta and Bombay, taking them to Africa, Europe and as far as North America. Those that had previously been employed as bakers or cooks now found more lucrative employment onboard ships.

In Goa, these seamen are called *tarvotti*, which comes from the Sanskrit-Konkani word *taranti* or *tarun* meaning boat. Most *tarvottis*

3. A QUIET REBELLION

were recruited from Bombay where a *kudd* system was set in operation to facilitate entry into this occupation. *Kudds* or clubs as they became known had village affiliations and provided accommodation to men from that particular village while they were in Bombay. The Santa Anna Club, possibly the oldest, was formed in 1850 by three or four men from Saligão, the village in Bardez.

Although life in *kudds* has been glamorised and embroidered with nostalgia by later writers, others remember them as being quite dismal and squalid. Dark rooms lined with single cots and boxes with an overall foul smell pervading the air, the result of too many men residing in tight quarters. A recruiting agent was attached to these clubs who would advance money to the young, able-bodied men arriving mostly from the villages of Ambelim, Velim, Chinchinim, Cuncolim and Assolná. In a way, this advance, bonded them into contract from which it was difficult to extricate themselves.[17] It would be reimbursed to the agent from their wages when they finally managed to secure employment.

Were they exploited by these recruitment agents? Possibly to some extent. Goan butlers were put in charge of store provisions and recruitment of saloon boys. A lot of power came to rest in the hands of butlers, almost "monarchal" in nature, perpetuating recruitment within families or the extended family, the village.[18]

When the opinionated English explorer Richard Burton and and his companion Captain Hanning Speke set out on their East Africa expedition in 1856, Burton hired two Goans, Valentine and Caetano, from Bombay, as servants.[19] They must have been fairly young because Burton refers to them as lads.

The expedition set off from Bombay on December 3, 1856, arriving in Zanzibar. The boys would have missed Christmas celebrations with their families but the rather impressive promised salary of Rs 20 per month might have temporarily assuaged any angst they felt. It is unlikely they knew exactly what they were signing up for, but a look at Burton's face which bore the permanent mark of a javelin that had speared right through it on his previous adventures in Africa, might have been an indication. As the two Goans trekked deeper into the dense, frightening jungle, nothing in their previous pockets of experience, could have prepared them for the severity of Africa; where red ants could send a man screaming into madness, their path lay littered with dead corpses of men who had died on the way, the unbear-

GOAN CHAPLAINCY (U.K.)

St Thomas of Canterbury School
(K U) Ursyline Surrey, (U.K)
Commonside East, Mitcham,
Ph 020 8665 2176

R. No 712

Received with thanks from _____

_____ the sum of Pounds _____ £14

_____ towards Donation

By cash/cheque No _____

Advertisements/Subscriptions/Masses

Date 02-04-11

£14

E-mail: ‑ goans.uk@ntlworld.com Contact: (Library Staff Ms) Gloria Almeida / Mrs Goan Chaplain (U.K)

GOAN CHAPLIANCY (U.K)

St. Thomas of Canterbury School
Commonside East, Mitcham, Surrey (U.K)
Ph.: 020 86652176

R. No. 717
Ac 3765

Date : 08-03-11

Received with thanks from Mrs Maria Dias

sum of Pounds Twenty One Only

by cash/cheque No. 001037   towards : Donation

Advertisements/Subscriptions/Masses 2010

£ 21=00

Sd/- Goan Chaplian (U.K)

E-mail : goanchapliancy@googlemail.com

able heat, the frequent ambushes and the constant fevers which played havoc with their bodies.

Valentine often lay prostrate for days on end with fever and near blindness, longing for his beloved Goa. In Caetano's case, the fever eventually spread like a fire to his brain, causing him to have epileptic seizures. He became more and more scatter-brained and disoriented, crying in anguished Konkani *ang duk'ta*, body ache. Valentine, despite the raging fevers and lack of physical stamina to match the Africans on the team, proved himself invaluable to Burton. He was never far from his side, often delighting in taking charge and giving orders to the working team, having learnt in little time enough Kiswahili to manage small affairs and, to read the chronometer and thermometer.

His bravado may have at times put him and his team in danger. Upon arriving in a place called Wafanya, a brawl breaks out while Burton is asleep. A drunken local indiscriminately wields blows into a crowd. Valentino, fearing for his life, takes Burton's "Colt" revolver and shoots into the crowd, maiming a canoe-man who eventually dies. It takes all of Burton's persuasive powers and a negotiated settlement of the equivalent £100 in blood money, to spare Valentine's life and avert general mayhem.

Caetano, as described by Burton, was an incredibly fearless Goan man, who thinks nothing of throwing himself in the middle of a rowdy crowd or walking alone through the jungle in the pitch-black of night. On one occasion when Burton drops his gun into crocodile-infested waters, he dives straight into 12 feet of water, in a bid to recover it. But his manliness was possessed of a dual nature and he could be just as gentle and tender when tending to the sick in his party.‖

Zanzibar, from where Burton set out for the interiors of Africa, already had a minuscule population of about 50 to 100 Goans, operating general stores, soda-water factories and "grog-shops" selling contraband brew from neighbouring German colonies.[20] Possibly part of this was a floating population of sailors.

A more strenuous route took the Goan sailor to North America. C. D. Castelino, working onboard the *S.S. Croydon* as a cook, landed in San Francisco, California in 1911.[21] By the 1920s, Goans had become

---

‖ See Burton R F, *The Lake Regions of Central Africa*, New York: Harper & Brother, 1860.

3. A QUIET REBELLION

veteran seamen, having docked in far-flung ports and experienced the dangers and uncertainty of a life at sea.

Domingos de Souza and Pedro Goenxende arrived at the Port of Havana, Cuba, in June of 1927, setting sail two months earlier from Calcutta onboard the *S.S. Matoppo*.[22] Domingo was perhaps the more senior seafarer, for while his wage was £5.12 per month, Pedro earned just £2.12 per month. Wages were tied to the type of service and more importantly to length of service. Unfortunately, both men were jailed in Havana for some debatable infraction and discharged from their employment onboard the ship. They were stranded in Havana with their earthly belongings of a sea-chest and a tin-box between them, abandoned by their ship-master, uncannily reminiscent of Alexander Selkirk who in 1704 was abandoned on a Pacific Island with nothing more than his sea-chest by his ship master for picking a quarrel with him. Selkirk, of course, was later immortalised by Daniel Defoe in his book, *Robinson Crusoe*. Eventually, the *tarvottis* were repatriated to Goa, their so-called debts deducted from wages that were owed to them.

However precarious life was with the sea as its unfaithful mistress, it was a danger tinged with excitement and possibility. The Goan had inadvertently become an intrepid explorer in his own right. His expeditions, unlike those of European explorers, were not funded by the government but rather by necessity and his own gumption. He followed explorers into the depths of African jungles, setting up camp in dangerous territory, witness to bloody murder and mayhem, coursing the high seas at the mercy of pirate attacks and gun battles. It became apparent to the thus land-bound, agrarian Goan that it was possible to travel long distances and return enriched by the experience.

Men were no longer manacled to the existence they were born into, rather the sense of fatalism which accompanies agrarian societies subject to nature's temperaments was dissipating, infused by the confidence of the sea-explorer. Their stories were of heroic feats and exotic destinations, of strange sightings at sea, of superhuman strength and of unheard riches. Doubtless much of these stories were embellished giving rise to a popular song *"Hem Tarvotteanchem aikonk ghoddnam"*, loosely translated to mean, one cannot take seriously the tales carried by *tarvottis*. Nonetheless, these explorations ignited in the Goan village soul, a spirit of adventure. A whole class of Goans previously struggling on the lower economic and social rungs of society found the means to improve their financial lot in life, an outlet to prove themselves worthy and garner respect. They excelled at a job in which respect was hard earned and they reaffirmed their worth to the community by creating a brand name for Goans.

A 1937 report compiled by the British Royal Navy gives us an insight into just how valuable Goans had become as seamen:

> It has long been recognised that the Goanese as a race are particularly well adapted to these trades... and are generally accepted as being more efficient than other Indian races. A further advantage is that, being Christians, no religious difficulties arise in regard to handling food and wine.[23]

A typical examination for stewards, tested knowledge of catering, carving meat, keeping accounts, laying a table, caring for cabins, first aid and English. Their duties corresponded with those referred to as "above stairs" employees of Victorian England, like the butler, valet and housekeeper of high-ranking establishments.

The *tarvotti*, even if unlettered had to be intelligent, presentable and dependent on his social skills. On one occasion, the British Navy tried to replace the Goans with Ceylonese, but had to abandon this notion because of the "untrustworthiness" of the Ceylonese. Senior British Officers had grown accustomed to traveling with their personal Goan butlers, who knew both the native language as well as a smattering of English. The reputation of the Goan *tarvotti* was stellar.**

* * *

In the late 1800s, the relationship which had begun between the British and the Goan onboard ships, in the households of Poona, the

---

**A 1808 report of the Viceroy, Count of Sarzedas states: "The differences of castes among Hindus is a terrible obstacle to agricultural development; The Brahmins, bound by their false principles, do not engage in trade of any type except as agents and attorneys of causes and in nothing more; the Chardos as men of war, the Sudras as seamen." (Pereira A. B, *Ethnography of Goa, Daman, Diu*, translated by Couto M A, Penguin India, 2008, p 58). The seamen referred here were possibly the Kharvi fishermen and boatmen. By 1856, most of the seamen recruited by the British India ships were of Chardo stock, former soldiers who had been demobilised and left impoverished after the Portuguese India army disbanded. (Correia Assis, Goa: *Through the Mists of History*, Maureen Publishers 2006, p 282) The sea constantly reshaped opportunities and changed the social dynamics of Goa.

3. A QUIET REBELLION

railway workshops and Indian Civil Services expanded to the British Empire in East Africa.

There is a common perception that it was Goa's educated middle-class that migrated to East Africa. Anecdotal evidence tells us it was tailors, carpenters and cooks who first travelled to East Africa in search of work. The fact that there was a Saint Francis Xavier Goan Tailors' Society formed in Mombasa as early as 1905, bears this out. There is amongst Catholic Goans a certain amount of prestige associated with the very act of emigrating itself, an escape from the doldrums of the village into a wider canvas of life. Having emigrated, no other Goan would garner as much respect as the East African Goan, endearingly called *Afrik'kar*.

The second tier of out-migration to Africa was the literate class, not necessarily well educated but certainly with at least six to seven years of schooling, who applied for jobs as clerks in the administration of the railways being built from the interiors of Uganda to Mombasa, a port in Kenya, to facilitate transportation of cargoes. The railway initially at least proved to be quite worthless to the British. The colonization of Kenya became necessary, in part, to make the railway financially viable. As Kenya, Uganda and Tanganyika – now Tanzania – came under British control, Goans thronged the British Civil Services. A 1921 census[24] put the number of Goans in Kenya at 2,000 and the results of a 1931 census[25] puts the count in Tanganyika at 1,722.

The early decades of the 20th century saw an exponential increase in a wave of migration out of Goa and into Africa. By 1900, a Goan cook could hope to earn between £2 and £3 per month, commanding twice the rate of his African counterpart,[26] and by 1920 Goan clerks were earning between £17 to £30 per month.[27]

Work was steady and remuneration adequate to send remittances to the family left behind in Goa. Indeed, by 1921 Goan clerks had taken over the Secretariat, railways, P.W.D, post and telegraph offices in Tanganyika to a extent where British public opinion inquired as to why so many Portuguese nationals were required;[28] but such was their fondness for Goans across East Africa that it became the norm for district administration and remote outposts to be managed by one British officer and assisted by a Goan clerk.[29] The District Officer while on tour, would leave the running of the office in the hands of the Goan clerk. This position of responsibility which Goans occupied as

District Clerks or bank clerks and cashiers, at times entailed looking after substantial amounts of money, giving rise to the saying the "keys of all the safes in Africa are in the hands of the Goans."

* * *

Oil had been discovered in the southwest of Iran and was being drilled in commercial quantities by the Anglo-Persian Oil Company (APOC), forerunner to the much better known British Petroleum. This discovery led to another trajectory of Goan migration beginning in the 1920s. At first it was almost a trickle, hardly warranting the kind of attention bestowed onto the *Afrik'kar* . Eventually of course, it would become the epicenter of the migratory Goan worker.

By 1930, there were 658 Goans, including wives and children, mostly employed by the oil industry concentrated in Khuzestan, on the southwest of Iran.[30] Khuzestan was little more than a mud-walled town lying on the cross-border between Iran and Iraq. Its vast, desolate plains were intermittently interrupted by drilling oil-rigs emerging from the bowels of the earth. Some of the Goans employed worked in a senior capacity while most served as clerks. There were also about 50 odd Goans employed as domestics or tradesmen. As was often the case, there was a fondness for Goan cooks. Iran set up a cookery school in order to train its own people and compete.

Iran was not a British colony but entangled in an intricate relationship with the British, which all but rendered Iranians impotent in their own country. In the absence of a Portuguese presence, the British Consul assumed responsibility for Goans and extended them the courtesy of being British Protected subjects. They would use British Consular courts and services for settlement of minor disputes, passport renewal, obtaining "No Objection Certificates" and assistance with repatriation.

When in 1937, this arrangement came under scrutiny by the Iranians, the British upheld their right to continue in the tradition. H. J Seymour, Government Minister, in a letter to Anthony Eden, then Foreign Secretary to the British government and later to become Prime Minister of Britain, wrote: "I shall be reluctant to see a tradition of some antiquity broken, particularly as it is in our interests to protect Goanese as far as possible, since the greater number are employed by the Anglo-Iranian Oil Company or by Indian British subjects. There in no sufficient reason for abandoning a practice which though possibly anomalous appears to meet the needs both of the Portuguese Indians

3. A QUIET REBELLION

who have a tradition of faithful and useful service to British interests and of their mainly British employers."[31]

By the mid-century, Goa had become so dependent on emigration, her trade deficit was being made good by shipping and remittances from emigrants.

4 The war years

> My mother Ivy D'Souza was in a three-storey building in central Rangoon tutoring her pupils, when the bombs rained down. She ran down the steps, which were strewn with corpses, and onto the road. She ran and ran till a Burmese rickshaw runner called out "*la ba sayama*" (come teacher). – Isabel Vas, No Christmas Toys, in *Songs of the Survivors*.

IN MAY 1942, Japanese troops cut across Burma and stormed into Mandalay, turning this former abode of Burmese kings into a military camp.

In the same month, on a blistering hot summer day, a pig lay rotting on the streets of Altinho.[1] Dr. Froilano de Mello, President of Câmara Municipal das Ilhas, was perhaps short-staffed and unable to find someone to clear the carcass even as thick flies swarmed around it and its stench spread. Finally, after it had lain there for a good few days, he had the carcass removed by two sweepers but not before its unfortunate bloated body had blown up and spewed its innards onto

4. THE WAR YEARS

the street. The occasional drone of a monoplane heard in the still of day reminded everyone of the deprivations of war.

Lieutenant Claude Bremner watched the scene unfold from the window of his consular office perched on the slopes of Altinho, a short distance from the palace of the Archbishop and the house of the German Consul.[2] Bremner had been posted as British India's Consul to Goa, and was accompanied by his wife, Alice Bremner. Although Portugal remained neutral throughout World War II, there was always a nagging doubt that because of their neutrality they may allow Goa to be used as a docking bay for German or Japanese ships. Bremner's main priority was the gathering of intelligence which consisted of little more than gossip snatched from the *bazaars* and the dissemination of pro-British propaganda.

Claude and Alice Bremner detested this posting, carrying within them an almost Burtonesque disdain for the dogs barking in the vicinity, the heat, the native Goan and what they perceived to be an emasculated and thoroughly inefficient Portuguese Government. Their recounting of time spent in Goa frequently reads like the society pages of newspapers; stories about dances, dinner conversations with the Portuguese administration and the shenanigans of local personalities. These reports are consumed by large doses of verbal vitriol but at times quite out of character, sympathetic to the plight of the Goan. Shorn of their personal biases, they provide a first-hand account of Goa during the war years.

The state of Goa's municipal services was of much less concern than the water shortages;[3] the dry, parched earth, starting from Bardez and spreading fast to other parts of Goa. The town of Panjim with its usually bustling markets overlooking the quietude of the Mandovi River, bore the look of desertion. People had fled to the villages to escape the thick, stifling pre-monsoon humidity and scour what little water they could from wells running dry. The colonial Portuguese government tried rationing water to two gallons per head, which by mid-May was further reduced to one gallon. Water from the wells of Betim on the other side of the Mandovi was brought into Panjim on canoes and paid for at exorbitant rates. In the Salcete town of Margão, a quart of a clay pot could cost as much as three annas.

Earlier, in January 1942, the 62-year-old Archbishop José da Costa Nunes.[4] Patriarch of the Indies, had arrived from Timor to take his place at the Patriarchal Palace, resting atop Panjim's Altinho. A tall man with twinkling blue eyes, he had been at Manila Harbour when it was bombed by the Japanese and could recount the horror in great detail. He was well in time for the Exposition of the body of Saint Francis Xavier, scheduled from May 6 to 13, later extended to May 17.

Preparations were on, to meet the needs of the faithful intending to make the pilgrimage, although their numbers were expected to be far less that year on account of the water shortages and the war. Archbishop Nunes would play an important role in the religio-political affairs of the Indian sub-continent, earning him the *Grão Cruz da Ordem do Império* from Portugal.

Perhaps Goans in all their pious faith were anticipating a miracle from their patron saint, Francis Xavier, encased in the Basilica of Bom Jesus. Besides the water shortage, typhoid and influenza were also ravaging like wild fire, through Salcete and the villages neighbouring Panjim. It was a time to pray for miracles, at a time when miracles were unlikely, for there was little to be expected by way of relief, medical or otherwise. Goa sustained itself by importing grain, meat, vegetables and other essential commodities from Belgaum, Poona and sometimes as far as the Sindh region, now in Pakistan. With the war raging, British India diverted its resources to the war effort. It placed an export embargo, the most stringent of which was on rice, a staple of the Goan diet.

The effects of the embargo gutted Goa, causing acute food shortages. The Portuguese Governor-General, José Ricardo Pereira Cabral[5] responded by initiating strict rationing of food, kerosene and petrol and instituting severe penalties for hoarding.

Cabral was a curious man; somewhat tall with a sallow complexion, carrying the sort of moustache typical of the era and said to enjoy a gregarious sense of humour. He had given up a senior Governorship in Lourenço Marques, now Maputo of Mozambique, where he was stationed for twelve years, and instead settled comfortably into the less commanding dominion of Goa with his large bustling family.

For seven years from 1938, while Goans suffered dire deprivations and his much younger wife, Sara Medeiro e Alburquerque, busied herself with arranging fetes and dances, Cabral held Goa in his iron grip. He was responsible in 1941 for dismantling Goa's only independent newspaper, *O Ultramar*.[6]

In one instance, a wealthy Goan land-owner complained to Cabral

4. THE WAR YEARS

about the harassment he had received at the hands of a Portuguese clerk at the post-office. Cabral told him to seek redress before the Director of Postal Services. Heeding his advice, the land-owner did so, only to find himself being taken to the civil court and ordered to pay damages to the clerk for defamation of character. Bremner saw this entire episode as a frame-up to protect the prestige of the government department and Portuguese clerk.

But Cabral perhaps carried within him an earnest desire to rid Goa of the malaise and malignancy of corruption which ailed the government administration. An unhealthy nexus of greed was emerging between government officials and contractors. One contractor favoured for roadworks allegedly pocketed the one rupee allotted to each daily-wage labourer brought in from Belgaum, manipulating them into subsisting on food alone.[7] Cabral had effectively put paid to much inefficiency within the administration since his arrival, but his zeal for reform might have been countered by the general apathy.

An almost immediate effect of rationing petrol, was a reduction in the bus service. One of the disrupted routes was the Belgaum to Panjim service, which brought in food supplies. Rice became almost unobtainable. Long queues snaked around rice-shops and people took to eating millet instead. Even though supplies of sugar had been bulked-up by imports from Mozambique, they whittled to an extent where it was rationed at 1 lbs per family, under police permit and surveillance.

Goans prayed quietly for an early monsoon.

It was to this reality, that the Goan Diaspora would return briefly, fatigued and defeated, fleeing from the war-weary frontiers of British India. On February 15 of 1942, Bremner wrote:

> Goan evacuees from Rangoon continue to arrive. They state that they had to quit at short notice, leaving most of their possessions behind, in order to catch the first India-bound steamer [8]

and by March of 1942:

> The influx of Goan refugees from enemy occupied territories and British India continues unabated. Many of them, who have not seen Goa before in their lives. [9]

Burma had been home to a small but closely knit Goan community, lured and nurtured by the British Raj. After Britain annexed

Burma in 1886, it was initially and most foolishly governed as part of British India, making little allowance for the Burmese as a distinct race but thus allowing unmitigated migration of Indians into Burma. Indian traders, specially from the south, travelled to Burma to open up shops, engage in the rubber trade and more infamously as moneylenders. Britain had also undertaken some infrastructural construction in Burma, the more noteworthy of these projects being the railway. Work was plentiful. Goans worked as clerks in government offices, as teachers in schools, musicians in the more up-market clubs and as tailors and bakers. The war would permanently disrupt the lives of these people caught in the cross-fire. By May of 1942, nearly 300,000 refugees poured into India, having sailed from Rangoon and the port of Akyab.[10]

In Africa, the war marked a radical departure in the mindset of the Goan and brought to the fore questions about their own nationality. They were Portuguese nationals but, away from any sustained Lusitanian control, totally dependent on the British Empire for their employment and according to the British with a "good record for loyalty" to the Colony in Kenya. Was nationality determined by anything other than geography, government and circumstance? How was loyalty defined in an equation where they had interchanged one colonial government for another? Certainly choices had to be made in the interests of self-preservation.

In a secret meeting held at the Goan Institute Mombasa, a group of Goans decided that it would be in their interests to opt for British citizenship.[11] There were suspicions that Portugal may not be altogether unsympathetic to Spain's fascist inclinations and in the event of an Axis victory, it would seriously jeopardise their position, most of whom were civil servants in the British government.

In June of 1939, the Government House in Nairobi received a spate of forty-four applications, within a span of six weeks, for British citizenship, of which forty-three were civil servants. This set a precedent in the Diaspora. Until then, Goans had faithfully returned to Goa upon retirement; but now the umbilical cord was being loosened. The realisation, perhaps momentarily unsettling, had dawned on the East African Goans that their future was tied in with Britain rather than Portugal or even Goa. They were siblings separated from the family, bound by history and culture but certainly not by any immediate point of reference.

4. THE WAR YEARS

As hostilities mounted, Africa itself became a proxy for European alliances. In Kenya, Kilindini Harbour at Mombasa Port, took center-stage from where Britain's East African offensive was launched against Italian-occupied African territories. John Pinto's schooling in Mombasa was rudely interrupted when his family was forced to evacuate for fear of enemy attacks.[12] The ship bound for Britain, carrying John's exam papers, was attacked and sunk. Luckily, there were carbon copies of the papers kept.

It was the tumultuous, treacherous sea that finally swallowed the greatest number of Goan causalities during World War II. One tragic incident was the passenger ship *S.S. Tilawa* torpedoed by the Japanese. Onboard was the Goan family Maciel[13], who perished in the cold waters of the Indian Ocean. Mathias Joseph Assis Maciel with his wife Effigina, two infant girls and a three month old boy, had been on long leave from Kenya, spending time with Mathias' mother, Maria Francisca. Their ancestral house being in Salvador do Mundo, a village in Bardez, ironically meaning Saviour of the World. Mathias' first wife had passed away in childbirth, some years before and his three older sons, Joseph, Mervyn and Wilfred, were sent to Belgaum to continue with their studies at the St. Paul's High School. It was customary for the Goan-African Diaspora to send their children to schools in Poona, Belgaum and Bombay, urban areas outside the Goa borders.

Mathias Maciel and his family set sail on November 20, 1942 on the 10,000 ton *S.S. Tilawa*, carrying onboard 732 passengers, 222 crew and four gunners and plying from Bombay to Mombasa. Three days into their journey, as the ship was midway between Somalia and India, a loud explosion rocked the boat at the dead of night. Panic gripped the passengers as they feared the worst. Amidst the ensuing mayhem and scramble for life-boats, 252 passengers and 28 crew were lost.[14] The three boys in school would become the only remaining survivors of the Maciel family and Wilfred at least would carry life-long emotional scars from the tragedy.

The war raged on and entire villages in Goa silently donned the black of mourning. Their brave young men lost to the merciless sea. Goan seamen, working on British Royal Naval ships carrying ammunition and troops, succumbed in the prime of their lives. The *S.S. Gogra*, torpedoed and sunk west off the coast of Oporto, Portugal on April 2, 1943 had at least 10 Goans onboard.[15] Avertano Fernandes of Chinchinim, was the ship's cook and might have been in the galley preparing dinner when it was struck by a U-boat, at seven in the evening. He was just 33 years old at the time, leaving behind his young wife, Santan Dinnetina.[16]

Augustino Fernandes, aged 47 and husband to Pauline Denis, died onboard the *S.S. Rohna*, in possibly one of the most damning naval casualty endured by Allied troops during the war.[17] Augustino was employed as general help on the *Rohna*, which set sail on November 25, 1943, from Algeria as part of a convoy. Barely a day at sea and it was struck by a German Luftwaffe air raid resulting in over 1,000 casualties.

With soaring food prices and their own lives under constant threat, *tarvottis* requested for the war-bonus given to their European counterparts.[18] The British Royal Navy repeatedly denied them this bonus, citing various ambiguous reasons such as not being able to assess the economic impact of the war on Goa; but the price they paid in terms of endangered lives had to be acknowledged. Only in 1943 did an allowance of half a rupee per day come into effect, pegged as a "special bonus to compensate for changed conditions."[19]

Back in Goa, conditions were stretched to the limit, faced with the austerities of war. Those that poured back to Goa from various parts of the British Empire had been uprooted under less than favourable circumstances. They had fled with what could fit into a trunk to be carried onboard a steamer bound for India. The less fortunate left with just enough to survive a trek through Burma's jungles. Their arrival in Goa, with a fistful of British India Rupees, all wanting to exchange them for the Portuguese Rupia, put an immediate strain on the sole local bank, Banco Nacional Ultramarino. Even before the war, there had been an acute shortage of the Portuguese Rupia, but the British India Rupee, accepted as legal tender in Goa, generally made up for the short-fall. The Portuguese government's abrupt refusal to accept the Rupee during the war drove Goans into the arms of foreign exchange black-marketeers, who hoarded the Rupia and charged exorbitant commissions upon exchange. On August 24, 1942, a sizable crowd gathered outside the Secretariat, and implored the Governor to accept payment of taxes in the British India currency.[20] The plea was rejected and instead shop-keepers were strictly instructed not to accept anything but the Portuguese Rupia.

Scarcity gnawed at the population, so dire people started dying of starvation. A family in Pondá, being unable to go on, was rumoured to

4. THE WAR YEARS

have committed suicide.[21] The government's response was to crack its authoritarian whip and tighten its control even further. The Governor instituted draconian penalties for profiteering. A shop-keeper caught hoarding rice was fined Rs 45 per sack besides having his entire stock confiscated. A trader was fined Rs 600 for selling two cans of kerosene at Rs 5 each when the prevailing rate was Rs 4.20. Unfortunately, he did not have Rs 600 to pay as a fine, and as a consequence his shop was appropriated.[22]

A sparsely populated Goa on the Konkan coast with rampant water and food shortages, the ever-present threat of typhoid, small-pox and influenza and the shortages war wrought unto them was bound to disillusion those Goans returning from more populous and thriving cities. They were taken aback with the lack of running water, proper sanitation and electricity. One Goan refugee from Burma described it as a shock to the system, having to collect firewood for cooking and draw water from the well to wash dishes. Another Goan, whose letter was intercepted by the British Censor office in Belgaum, wrote to a relative, "we might be on a desert island here in Goa, no water, no petrol, no food except at exorbitant prices and disease everywhere. From childhood we had always been told that our motherland was a Paradise."[23]

Their expectations of Goa were blighted by reality; a brittle angst borne of their sudden displacement. Within a few years, most of them would leave Goa once again, taking with them rather sad memories of their time there.

5 The red book

What I see and know of the conditions of things in Goa, is hardly edifying. – Mahatma Gandhi's correspondence to the Governor-General of Goa, August 2, 1946.

At dawn today, about 6000 people, many of them bare-footed, walked in pilgrimage to the Church of the Good Jesus in Old Goa to pray to St. Francis Xavier to intercede for them and save Goa. The monsoon was blowing strongly and the rain came down in sheets, but nobody along the six-mile route seemed to be aware of it. – Goans for the right to self-determination. *The Times*, special correspondent, August 14, 1954.

I'VE KNOWN ANTHONY Fernandes, for a good many years, ever since he was a gangly young man and I, a child. He and his wife are close friends of my parents. When the talk turned to the Liberation of Goa, he related an interesting anecdote going back to the eve of Goa's Liberation.

It was a nippy winter's night and something was keeping Father Pinto, the Principal of Guardian Angel High School in Sanvordem, from his Advent preparations. On December 17, 1961, he had stayed

5. THE RED BOOK

up the night listening to the scratchy-sounding radio. In the morning, after Holy Mass, he assembled his boarders into the hall and announced the Liberation of Goa.

Anthony Fernandes watched wide-eyed as Father Pinto lowered the Portuguese flag and tore it to pieces. He then raised the Indian flag and prodded his students to join him in singing the Indian national anthem. The students of Guardian Angel were unfamiliar with the anthem; indeed, they were unfamiliar with what it meant to be liberated and unsure as to what it entailed. Goans had cheered as Indian troops with shiny helmets and long rifles marched into Goa, holding out the promise of change. But a quiet of uncertainty descended that December casting a pall of silence on Christmas and New Year festivities.

In the years following World War II, Goa experienced a mild prosperity buoyed by an optimistic post-War boom and a healthy export of iron-ore. India's independence and the socialist policies that followed also abetted in making Goa, still a Portuguese colony, a thriving port and trading center. This façade however hid more serious problems within Goa, mainly lack of employment opportunities for the labouring class and infrastructure to sustain any long-term development.

The Portuguese education system which should have addressed social and economic inequities, tacitly reinforced them. While the Portuguese had taken the initiative to provide *Primeiro Grau*, primary level education, a 1950 census still put the level of illiteracy at a high 78%.[1]

Number of people who can read and write	138,012
Illiterate	499,579

These figures may have been exaggerated, as those who were literate in Marathi were considered illiterate and those that could read in Konkani likewise escaped the radar. My grandfather, Joaquim Santan Cardoz, for instance, could read and write Konkani. He was a reader of the Konkani newspaper *Sot*, Truth, but literacy amongst his generation was rare in the villages. He became an unofficial cupid, a letter-writing scribe for women whose husbands were on board ships or in Africa, and who were in need of someone with a pen to pour their thoughts.

In the main, Catholic Goans enjoyed a higher incidence of literacy as more than likely the larger villages had a parochial school attached to the Church.[2] The problems with attending school were myriad; lack of adequate transportation was a disincentive. Some remember walking to school barefoot. Household chores, harvest times and taking care of siblings invariably took priority over schooling.

There were other pervasive elements, elitism and racism amongst them. Stories abound of *bhatkar* families asking for favours when it came to awarding marks to their progeny. Goans students were sneeringly called "*canecos*" by *mestiço* instructors, a Portuguese word which had colloquially come to mean of a lesser race or just stupid. Such stories may suffer from embellishment, but there was the feeling that education was wasted on the poor, lice-infested children of the labouring class who sooner or later would drop out and return to the paddy-fields.

For those who completed their *Primeiro Grau* by sheer dint of industry and perseverance, proceeding to the *Segundo Grau*, secondary level education, was an even bigger challenge. Under the Portuguese education system then, the Lyceum (Portuguese: Liceu), or National Lyceum (Portuguese: Liceu Nacional), was a high school that prepared students to enter universities or more general education. There were but three Liceu, one in Margão and Mapuçá, both known as the municipal Liceu. Besides this, there was the prestigious, *Nacional Liceu Afonso de Albuquerque* in Panjim.[3]

If one lived away from these principal townships, it was almost impossible to maintain a steady attendance.

The establishment of the University of Bombay in 1857 in British India would have a significant impact on Goa, more so in terms of emigration. Just 29 years later, the *College-Liceu diocesain de Saint-Joseph* was established at Arpora.[4] Among the English-medium schools that sprung up was the College-Liceu du Sacre-Coeur de Jesus in Parra, founded in 1911. Both were affiliated to the Bombay University.

The post-war years saw a mushrooming of schools affiliated to Bombay University, although one still had to go to Poona or Bombay to answer the board exam. The standard of these schools left much to be desired but they did allow for a previously disenfranchised section of society to avail of an education in English. More importantly, they produced an English-speaking Goan, whose skills were marketable in the Diaspora. Portuguese Catholicism had ignited aspirations of social and economic equality amongst the Catholics in Goa and the proliferation of English as a language empowered it.

5. THE RED BOOK

There were four commercial schools preparing students in bookkeeping, typing and stenography. The *Escola Normal* was a preparatory school for teachers and almost exclusively the domain of upper-caste Catholic women. The combination of an English-medium education and technical training in office skills produced a cadre of white-collar clerks much in excess of those let through the nepotism-ridden gates of the Portuguese administration.

Economically, Portuguese colonial governance had become a bitter pill of indifference and inefficiency. By 1960, the eight anna "*taxa do Fundo económico*" levied on the transportation of iron ore, had accumulated to one crore rupee, but hardly any significant amount was used for road repairs. Instead, road connectivity in rural areas was non-existent and in a dismal state on the main routes.[5]

Elsewhere, agriculture had been neglected with over 50% of Goa's produce being imported, stored by the *Junta de Comércio Externo* in four large purpose-built brick warehouses near the village of Cortalim. Even these in 1961 lay bare.[6] The lack of an electric power station made large-scale industry impossible. A hydro-electric station to be located near Dudh Sagar, the water-falls on Goa's boundary, had been mooted but the complexity of water-sharing arrangements with Mysore had led to its abandonment.[7]

The verdant south of Goa, hugging the Zuari river with its lush mango, guava, coconut and cashew trees was disconnected from the north. White-painted ferries plied the winding Zuari river transporting early morning travellers, but the required infrastructure of a bridge was absent. Even the capital town of Panjim was disconnected from the neighbouring market town of Mapuçá. A boat service operated on the Mandovi river between Panjim and Betim. There was but one respectable-sized tourist hotel, The Mandovi, rising majestically on the banks of the river that bore its name, a lone modern building somewhat ill at ease with the rest of mid-century Panjim. A weak European colonial power had managed to thoroughly neglect Goa's infrastructure. A palpable injustice when at one time revenue from Goa made up the bulk of what the Queen of Portugal received as an allowance.[8]

A minor consolation for the business community, during the Portuguese era, was a liberal foreign import policy. Goan domestic markets were flush with imported goods. Shops lined the pavement surrounding the municipal gardens in Panjim and Margão.

Bento Miguel Fernandes & Filhos sold imported wines, clothing and luggage accessories, on João da Crasto Road in Panjim, the equivalent of a modern-day department store. Caxinata Damodora Naique Ltd., were the sole agents for State Express cigarettes, of Ardath Tobacco Co., London and John Chagas Pereira were the distributors for Scripto fountain pens, Polaroid sunglasses, Continental German tyres and Worth French toiletries. Maganlal Monji Canji had shops in Panjim, Mapuçá as well as Margão, selling Swiss watches, Italian straw hats and porcelain dinner sets, all much sought after by traders in India who languished under strict import restrictions shortly following Indian independence.[9] This peculiar and advantageous status enjoyed by Goa in an otherwise restrictive Indian sub-continent had given rise to much smuggling between India and Goa, abetted by a proverbial Portuguese blind eye, thus buffering extensively the black holes of the Goan economy.

The mainstay of Goa's export, after the war, was iron-ore, an industry which in later years would come to be profoundly despised. In the 1950s, intense mining had lifted Goa out of its airless economic doldrums and ensured at least for a privileged few, a comfortable life.

At the dawn of the 1960s, Vishwasrao D. Chowgule, the patriarch of Chowgule & Co. Ltd, was a content man, having begun his career as a tally clerk at Mormugão port but established by then as the head of the Chowgules' mining empire exporting mainly to Germany and Japan. The Chowgules had upgraded their handling plant with machinery provided by the Japanese, in return for three million tons of iron-ore to be supplied over a period of four years to Nippon Kokan Kabushiki Kaisha, Yawata Iron and Steel Co. Ltd and Fuji Iron & Steel Co. Ltd.* They were bursting with plans, amongst which included a textile factory, and were in negotiation with a German company to purchase a pelletization plant which transformed fine iron ore into hard pellets.[10] Perhaps it was an enthusiasm that would be somewhat dampened by the downpour of restrictions which followed Goa's Liberation.

In 1961, the first sign of Liberation was the conferring of Indian citizenship on subjects who were previously Portuguese nationals. Simultaneously five crores worth of Escudo, which had been Goa's currency since 1958, was withdrawn from the Bank National Ultramarino, and an equivalent amount of Indian currency put in

---

*This barter of machinery for iron-ore would become famously known as the Chowgule formula in India.

5. THE RED BOOK

circulation.[11]

Goan loyalty was immediately put to the test. Dr Redualdo da Costa, President of *Junta de Comércio Externo*, had to sign an oath of allegiance to the President of India. Meanwhile, a deputationist,[†] in the guise of a Deputy Chief Controller of Imports and Exports, took up office at the Secretariat building in Panjim and would now exert influence over all import-export policy decisions. Overnight Dr. Redualdo da Costa's status had subtly altered with the changing of the guard. He would confess to T. E. Martin, a visiting British Assistant Trade Commissioner, that he was told what he ought to do by the deputationist and that the new policies were as baffling to him as to everyone else.[12]

Redualdo is remembered as a soft-spoken man, a tad self-deprecating but with an incisive mind. A man who had wielded much power from within the Portuguese administration. Alfred Tavares, a Goan journalist now resident in Stockholm, Sweden, was a neighbour of Redualdo and, in correspondence with me, speaks of him as a close friend and mentor. He was educated at the seminary as so many sons of Chardos and Brahmins were wont to do, not necessarily as a precursor to a life serving the Church but more for the strong administrative training one could receive in the institution. It was the equivalent of a latter-day business college where life-long contacts were made which served the young Goan men well once they left Rachol and began the tremulous climb up in their own careers in the administrative cadre of the Portuguese government. Whatever limitations race and politics may have wrought upon them, they did permeate the corridors of power in Colonial Goa. To be suddenly rendered impotent by Liberation came as a shock, as if the oft propagated prophecy of being disadvantaged in a Goa which was part of the Indian Union, was finally coming true.

Regardless of Nehru's promise to allow for a smooth transition and respect the uniqueness of Goa, bureaucrats would keep Goa entangled in the cobwebs of the Quota-and-License Raj for the next twenty years. At the onset, they insisted iron-ore be pegged at prices prevailing in India. This made low-grade ore expensive and coupled with a slide in world market prices for ore, Goa's economy slumped.

To stifle it even further by June 1962, the directives of the Indian

---

[†]The officers on loan from the Central government were called "deputationists". *Gazetteer of the Union Territory of Goa, Daman and Diu*, Part 1. Goa, p 457.

import trade policies, known as the "Red Book"[13] restricted imports to five percent of the volume for the period 1958-1961. Long schedules listed items which were banned altogether from being imported.[14] It included coffee, silk, tobacco, crockery, sugar, tea, biscuits, canned fruits, dental pastes, razors, gramophones, ink, leather, crockery, sewing machines, motor-cycles and radios. Indian consumer goods replaced foreign goods in the market, which, given the inflationary tendency of the Indian rupee, were not just considerably more expensive but of poorer quality.

The days of treating a cough with a French medicine, driving a German Volkswagen car or buying a Reckitt & Colman shoe polish were long gone even for those few who could afford to do so. The very face of Goa itself had changed from being an open, accommodating, accessible port to much like the rest of India in the 1960s, closed, shut off from the world in a layer of socialist suspicion and austerity. From then on, the Goan would have one fundamental question plague him throughout the century and into the new millennium, the question of his own, unique identity.

* * *

Author Maria Aurora Couto, in her widely acclaimed book *Goa: A Daughter's Story*, gives an intimate account of the days and years immediately following Liberation, when her husband Alban Couto took his place as a deputationist to steer Goa's course. Surely the air was rent with excitement, dreams of a new future and the hope of a better life. There were men of merit such as Dr M. S. Thacker, member of the Planning Commission, Dr G. D. Parikh, Rector of the University of Bombay, and G. C Banerjee, Principal of Elphinstone College, Bombay, who descended on Goa, eager to chart a new course.[15] Maps were drawn, funds allocated, aspirations gently gathered and given wings. Goa needed an army of men like Alban Couto, the Davids who would have taken on the Goliaths of corruption which ultimately reigned supreme.

Some 768 deputationists took office in Goa by 1963. A publication by the Department of Information and Tourism, Goa Government, 1964, justifies this as being necessitated as: "in the absence of officers conversant with development work, it was found necessary to bring officers on deputation from the Central government or the neighbouring states."[16]

To what extent these officers could appreciate the nuances of Goan culture or had any motivation to bring to fruition Goa's potential as a sea-port is a matter of subjective opinion. They relied heavily on directives emanating from claustrophobic, bureaucratic offices. Perhaps their own hands were tied in a fledgling democracy where the role of the Center was relatively young and undefined, where interpretation of rules and regulations often meant regional sensibilities were sacrificed and where notions of an instant homogenization of India prevailed.

For the salaried middle-class in Goa, the situation took a turn for the worse. The salaries of government employees had been well insulated prior to Liberation, buffered as they were by foreign exchange earned through the mining industry and mercantile trade. Prior to Liberation, a government clerk in Portuguese Goa earned Rs 250 per month. A clerk in India earned Rs 100-150.[17] Immediately after Liberation, pay-scales were made consistent with the rest of India. There was an immediate reduction in the standard of living. The hopes of the Goan were crushed. ‡ While unemployment previously stood at 4.6 per cent, six years after Liberation it shot to 10.1 percent.[18] The final straw which showed a complete lack of understanding of both the Goan economy and its culture, was when Morarji Desai, as Minister of Finance in 1967, threatened a prohibition on alcohol.[19]

Trade had always been a Hindu domain and taxes accruing from commerce financed the salaries of the government machinery. Besides traders, there was a layer of educated, professional Hindu doctors, lawyers, tax-collectors that were well anchored in Goan society. Upon Liberation, this power-base mobilised itself both politically and administratively to take their rightful, representative place in governance.

The Managing Committee of the Goa Chamber of Commerce in 1962, for instance, comprised largely of Hindu Goans.[20] José António Gouveia was its President, Prabhakar Shiwa Pai Angle was the Secretary and Vernekar the Treasurer. Other members were Madev Sinai Talaulikar, Bhagwant K. Naik, S. J. Thaly and Shirvoikar, coming from prominent business families, some educated at the *Liceu Na-*

---

‡Saksena, though making a case for post-Liberation economic policies, notes in *Goa: Into the Mainstream*: "The impact of integration of Goa with the Indian Union on the economic front uptil this time has belied the hopes of the Goans. They have been suffering from reduced income. Their standard of living has declined due to higher living costs." Saksena R. N, *Goa: Into the Mainstream*, Abhinav Publications, 2003, p 80.

cional Afonso de Albuquerque in Portuguese and later at the University of Bombay.

The Catholic Goan elite with the benefit of a good education who had thronged the clerical corridors of the municipality or the bank retained their place, in part aided by nepotism.

In Goa, one can still trace family lineage by surnames. There is an insider-outsider status created based solely on clanship. The one stranded without a web of connections and unable to mobilise a place for himself was the labouring class Goan, decidedly from the south. Agriculture was a non-profitable venture. He had lost his inclination and competitive edge in trade. He was prone to small, nuclear families. Extended families were mired in litigation most of it pertaining to property settlements. This made running family-owned businesses non-viable.

More often than not, he sought daily-wage labour or a salaried income as his source of sustenance. Given the lack of large-scale industry in the south, this practically impoverished him. He found himself lining up in queues outside tiny, seedy shops availing of rations and quotas. Unscrupulous shop-keepers grew fat on profits siphoned off the malignant black-market; sackful of pulses and grain hidden away in dark rooms, creating an artificial scarcity of mammoth proportions.

Babus, bureaucrats, the appointed guards against corruption, skimmed off on bribes. Corruption seeped into every artery of governance, clouded and protected by an opaque silence. The transition from an inequitable free market to a stifling socialist economy was but disappointing. A Goa freed from the shackles of colonialism presented a reality as bleak as the past they had bid farewell.

What were a great number of people, who might not have attended fine colleges but still sang the *mando* and played the *rebec* by virtue of music training in parochial schools, to do? However impoverished they were, they still owned a suit to be worn for a feast or a wedding and listened to Sunday sermons sitting in the magnificent white-washed opulence of Baroque architecture. They were a people who had become literate through cross-cultural socialization; who had tasted aspiration but had no recourse to its realisation.

What were they to do but travel in search of possibility. It was this section of Goan Catholics, largely from Salcete, that made their way to the Arabian Gulf, post-Liberation, heralding the second strong wave of out-migration. According to the *Goa Migration Survey*, 2008, some

5. THE RED BOOK

66% of the households surveyed in the south were emigrant households as opposed to 34% in the north.[21]

Just a few years after Liberation, Anthony Fernandes would leave Goa. Disenchanted with the "deputationists" assigned by the Central government, the lethargy of the local politicians and the slow pace of development, he boarded a ship bound for Dubai in 1968. Fourteen days after landing in Dubai he had a job. In 1974, he married Maria Olinda Pereira from Colváddo, Varca and they have three children. He has spent his adult life in the Goan Diaspora.

Part II

The Arabian Gulf

6 An illicit past

It is with the Portuguese, to whom nothing but Goa on the West Coast remains today of all those far-flung possessions, that begins the history of the Persian Gulf in relation to modern Europe and the dominant factor in that history is at every stage, sea-power. – The Persian Gulf, story of sea-power. *The Times*, May 1, 1928.

WHAT WAS FORMERLY known as the Persian Gulf is now called the Arabian Gulf, if one wants to be politically correct. This well-known stream of the most azure blue water creates a basin of states with Iran to the northeast, Iraq and Kuwait to the northwest, Saudi Arabia, Qatar and Bahrain to the southwest and United Arab Emirates and Oman to the southeast. The southern peninsular is arid and hot to the point of being airless in the summer, making vegetation without artificial irrigation almost impossible, save for a few hardy date palm trees. The winters are mild and pleasant. The soil is a pristine white of either undulating dune or *sabkha matti*, salt-flats.

With the sea a constant companion, traditionally, the Gulf Arabs have been fishermen, sea-farers and pearl-divers. Their earlier settle-

6. AN ILLICIT PAST

ment of huts dotted the shore-line; humble dwellings of palm fronds, which adequately ventilated the interiors to keep its occupants of humans and goats alive. Islam arrived by the 7th century, and, if folklore is to be believed, the Prophet Muhammad himself is said to have sent envoys to invite the region to turn to Islam. The truth may have been bloodier, although given the simplicity of nomadic *badū*, desert life one cannot imagine a great deal of negotiation having been needed.

The *abaya* Arab, referring to the long white robe worn in the Southern Gulf region, is very aware that his history is unique and different from that of the Mediterranean Arab. He is tall, with a fine Romanesque nose which lends him a regal bearing akin to the falcons he is fond of training for hunt.

Given to slight arrogance and what to the casual observer may seem like a brusque bordering on rude manner, he nonetheless veers away from strict conservatism and instead embraces a more progressive viewpoint, a position made possible by his recent affluence and always finely balanced in the face of conservative opposition. The Gulf states are separated from Iran by just a few miles of water, and on a clear day one can see the islands of Iran from the tip of the southern peninsular. The Emirati is of Arab and Persian ancestry and much of their character and culture reflects this admixture. British explorer Wilfred Thesiger described them as "friendly and charming."[1]

Thesiger was one of the notable British explorers, rather late in the day in 1945, after Bertram Sidney Thomas in 1931 and the Arabist John Philby in 1932, to make incursions into the deep interiors of Arabia, known widely as *Rub' al Khali*, the Empty Quarter or just the Sands, both names evocative of the endless expanse of nothingness that they actually were in those days. Thesiger developed a deep fondness for the *badū*, their way of life and their uncorrupted, unpolluted clean space of habitat, writing in a letter to his mother in 1946: "it is curious how the desert satisfies me and gives me peace... for to most people it is just a howling wilderness."[2]

The official language is Arabic although it is so peppered with words borrowed from languages prevalent in the Indian sub-continent, Urdu being almost second language to the Gulf Arab, that it is easy to trace a long and amicable relationship between the two regions.

For centuries, the Arab had made his way to the west coast of India, for sacks of rice, in search of Muslim brides, sending his children for higher education, seeking specialist medical treatment and smuggling gold under cover of dates. Even before the arrival of the Portuguese, Goa had been an entry-point for the Arabs into the hinterlands of India, supplying them with horses. In any case, Goa's position became central when, upon its seizure, Portugal made Goa its headquarters and the main port from where their trade in Arabian horses would be carried out.[3] From then on, the Persian Gulf route was integral to trade from India into Persia, the Mediterranean and Africa and at its heart lay Goa.

By the 20th century, the Portuguese dominion of Goa in many ways was a renegade port and acted as a foil to British India. In 1925, following the Second Opium Conference, held in Geneva, Britain showed an outward resolve to curb the smuggling of what became known as "Indian hemp" from British India. The open distribution of opium in the form of spurious medicinal concoctions and its use as a recreational drug had wrecked havoc in the opium dens and parlours of upper-class British homes. In Goa, opium was openly distributed until 1927, despite attempts by the Church to curb its usage.[4]

Following the conference, the government monopolised and strictly regulated its export through its agency, the Indian Customs Service. Portugal and Britain had long been bitter competitors in the opium trade, both in the Far East and India. Twentieth-century moral quandaries about drug usage did not prevent Goa's continued use as a port to ship opium.

In June 1925, A. Carvalho from Goa, acquired a permit to buy *charas*, cannabis from Karachi, and ship it via Mormugão port to Mozambique.[5] Carvalho had his permit certified by the Portuguese Consul in India and, in anticipation, shipped a sizable amount of *charas* to Goa with the intent of setting sail to Africa. The British got wind of this plan, as Carvalho had hoped to route it through Djibouti in the Horn of Africa, raising the possibility of it being smuggled into Egypt. Carvalho's papers were eventually revoked. Carvalho's case was not particular in any way. Goa's sandy coastline cut into by numerous rivers and lit by moonlight for most part of the year made it an ideal landing site for small boats. Poor road connectivity made overland communication extremely difficult, disconnecting the coastal region from any surveillance and providing a convenient cloak for nefarious activities.[6]

Much of the smuggling that took place through Goa emanated from and was directed to the Arabian Gulf. By the early part of the

20th century, Kuwait and Bahrain were the main centers of activity.[7]

Wooden *dhows* set sail from Kuwait, plying along the shoreline and stopping in Dubai and Muscat for refuelling. This traditional Arab sailing vessel with one or more lateen sails is primarily used to carry heavy items along the coast of the Arabian Peninsula, Pakistan, India and East Africa. From the tip of Muscat, it is a smooth-sail of fifteen days by *dhow* to Goa. Arabian *dhows* carried dates, horses and pearls for which they were paid in gold coins. Gulf countries hoarded gold as surety and a fair amount of gold left Indian shores via Goa.[8] In exchange, they purchased cotton, European broad-cloth and timber.

Restrictions imposed in Goa and India on exports during World War II added a further impetus to smuggling. Despite the threat of severe repercussions, hoarding was rife in Goa. Claude Bremner, stationed in Goa as British Consul during the war, writes in a letter dated February 15, 1942: "anticipating Japan's entry into the War, these charming gentry (shopkeepers) have laid in enormous stocks of Japanese cloth which is stored to capacity in godowns, private residence and the back premises of shops."[9] "A plethora of Arab *dhows* and vessels... are now anchored in both Mormugão and Panjim. Their masters and crew are obviously the descendants of the 'Forty thieves.' Allied with shops from Bombay and farther afield, they are attempting to buy up all available stocks of toilet requisites, cloth, silk, drugs, charcoal, bamboos, etc. The Director of Customs, Nova Goa, is waging a one man war."[10]

With the Independence of India in 1947, and Goa still a Portuguese colony, it became even more attractive as a port with access to Indian markets. Smuggling greatly buffered the Goan economy. Following a socialist model of growth, India soon became a closed economy with a ban on the import of gold and consumer goods. Arabs found it profitable to buy foreign goods in Goa and smuggle them into India.

This was the stepping stone to what later legitimately made Dubai the world's third largest re-export center. The Arabs from the Gulf were not breaking any of their own laws. There are no restrictions in the Gulf against the import and export of gold. All that was required was a good safe harbour to dock away from the mainland of India and a willing pair of hands into which to exchange the gold. The responsibility of illegality fell to the buyer once it entered Indian shores.[11] The Portuguese were under no great obligation to stem the tide of smuggling and for the most part they abetted in this trade by acts of omission. Allegedly, a few Goan businesses and political families made their fortunes off the coast in smuggling.

Despite the surge in smuggling after 1947, it was ultimately India's misguided Gold Control Act of 1962 which laid the foundations for Gulf wealth. In January 1963, Finance Minister Morarji Desai, a strict Gandhian, made the possession of gold, other than ornaments, illegal.[12]

In an agricultural economy plagued with a high incidence of inflation, gold had been the one surety families and businessmen alike could bank on, a traditional talisman of security. The well-spring of underground demand gave rise to the notorious smuggling rings that persisted in Bombay during the 1960s and 1970s. The gagged Indian anger over the stridency of government infringement on free trade, boils over in the 1975 classic movie, *Deewar*, where Amitabh Bachchan gives a raw performance as the anti-hero. He has very little control over his own life, pushed into making regrettable choices and driven into life as a smuggler.

The Konkan coast became a strategic hub from where gold travelled to "safe-houses" in Bombay, with millionaire buyers already lined up. Once oil was discovered in Kuwait, Kuwaiti businessmen found other lucrative and less dangerous ventures to engage in and the center of the smuggling operations shifted to Dubai. The tide had changed. Where once gold had been smuggled out of India via the Gulf, it was now being smuggled into India.

According to British reports two prominent Emirati adventurers, Mohammed Al Gaz and Saif Al Ghurair initially, are believed to have started out as agents for Kuwaiti ships, which docked at Dubai on their way to India, assisting them with provisions and refuelling. Eventually, they invested in launches and began their own operations.[13] By 1960, smuggling of gold to India was earning Dubai a profit of £2 million pounds net[14] and by 1969, it had laid the foundation for an airport, several hotels and the expansion of the harbour.[15]

The other smuggling which took place off the Arabian coast was of illegal immigrants. Intercepting ships with human cargo kept British Political Agents busy in the region. Political agents in the Trucial States were appointed by the British government to look after their interests in the region and acted like local mayors. They were subordinated to a Political Resident, based in Bahrain, who was the *de facto* British "Governor" of the Gulf.

6. AN ILLICIT PAST

Britain had not claimed the Arabian states of Kuwait, Bahrain, Qatar, Emirates and Oman as crown colonies but had instead added them to her legion as protectorates under the aegis of a Truce Treaty signed in 1835. The Arabian coast, more popularly known as the Pirate Coast, was notorious for pirates attacking British ships plying in the region. It was also an unsettled area where minor sheikhs, all vying for power, were in constant battle with each other. By virtue of the treaty, Britain guaranteed internal security in return for relief from piracy. Britain effected control through the agency of the local sheikhs, emirs and sultans. With the opening of the Suez Canal, Britain found it to her advantage to control the entire block of land from East Africa to the Middle East and then onto India to ensure her trade routes.

In February 1964, the British patrol ship *H.M.S. Flockton* intercepted a Pakistani trawler, *Al Fatah*, carrying 505 passengers, all of whom were illegal immigrants and near starvation.[16] In April 1969, an Indian *dhow*, *Fatih Salama*, arrived in Dubai from Basra carrying 71 Arabs, mostly Egyptian and Palestinian, none of whom had visas. They were refused entry and returned to their country of origin.[17] Quite a few Goans also made their way to the Gulf as stow-aways on these "launches", Indian wooden sail boats. Our Goan cook, the portly Michael, had boarded a ship in Bombay with the assistance of someone in the know. As the Dubai coast approached, he jumped ship and swam to shore, before the immigration officers could come onboard to inspect visas. It was a perilous adventure for these men, sometimes running the risk of no food on board and braving unexpected currents at sea as they swam to shore. Our stories don't record Goans losing lives in such ventures, perhaps there weren't any causalities, but then perhaps there were stories of shame swept under the carpet.

Illegal immigration had long plagued the Arabian countries but much of it from the Indian subcontinent was considered "relatively innocuous".[18] The local population had deep personal relationships with these countries sealed by marrying Muslim women from Pakistan and India. More importantly, labour was needed in the sparsely populated desert countries.

An illegal immigrant from the sub-continent may have been repatriated but, if he was an able-bodied man, more likely he would be engaged by a local Arab or company and legalised in due course. As the fortunes of the Arabian Gulf grew, this liberal attitude would change and strict immigration controls would be put in place. In time, for a Goan, a visa to the Arabian Gulf would become the most precious commodity of all. The shared history of smuggling Swiss watches and gold bullion off the coast of Goa with the help of a moonlit night and a Konkan fisherman, long forgotten.

7 The dawn of a new era

IN 1958, TWO MEN – each in their own way – set in motion a series of events which would alter the course of life for several people. One would radically redefine the Arabian Gulf and the other would change the fortunes of his family. At the time though, they were relatively minor events that transpired without much occasion to take notice of either of them.

My maternal great-grandfather, Patricino Santimano, a *bhatkar*, landowner in the fishing village of Colvá in South Goa, had a philanthropic bone. The tall, imposing, dogmatically religious man was instrumental in rallying the villagers of Colvá to build the small St. Anthony's Chapel where it rests today, still administered in part by the Santimano family. He was also known to lend money to those in need of an urgent loan for a dowry, wedding or funeral expense. Some of these loans had to be written off or were repaid in reciprocal acts of kindness. Patricino had helped a neighbour's son with his education expenses and, in return for this kindness, a job for Patricino's grandson was arranged in Kuwait by the neighbour.

In January of 1958, my uncle Lenny Gomes, a gangly youth still

7. THE DAWN OF A NEW ERA

in his teens, sailed via Karachi to Kuwait onboard the *S.S. Dwarka*. What were the expectations of this young man as he left the security of his home and ventured into a land of Arabs, as he sailed away from the familiar and braced himself for the unknown? He had grown up in the cloistered *vaddo* of Murda, on a parcel of land his family owned by virtue of which the title of *bhatkar* had been conferred upon them, but the family was not affluent in the true sense of the word.

The land provided a livelihood, a sustenance but other than that there was no revenue to speak of nor the means to earn it after their father retired from Poona. Being the eldest son of three siblings, the heavy burden of responsibility shifted onto his young shoulders. There was a sister (my mother) to marry off and a brother who was academically brilliant but whose education needed funding. They were a respected family in the *vaddo*. A family of some learning and status inherited through the notions of caste, however misguided those were. This was the typical middle-class family of the 20th century Goan village; impoverished in every way but in name. The only thing they carried in their satchels was their family reputation.

As he neared the shores of Kuwait, a glimpse of crumbling mud-walled houses with flat, thatched roofs came into focus. Life in Kuwait was rudimentary even to a young boy from the villages of Goa. Men dressed in white *abayas*, their faces crumpled with too much exposure to the sun, prostrated their bodies five times a day in earnest supplication to Allah; their wives covered themselves in thick, black robes in defiance of the heat and children ran about with matted hair infused with grainy sand.

The summer heat was oppressive. Drinking water arrived in English biscuit tins carried by over-burdened donkeys; so browned by dirt that it had to be filtered through a white cloth at least three times before drinking. Lenny could count a handful of Goans congregated at the small Our Lady of Arabia Catholic Church.

In the same year, another man in the Arabian Gulf would be called upon to take charge of his destiny. On September 10, 1958, Lieutenant Colonel D. G. McCaully, senior medical officer of the Trucial States, declared dead Sheikh Said, the seventy-six year old Ruler of Dubai.[1] The sweltering heat of the desert requires the body to be disposed off the same day. Funeral arrangements were made immediately.

The resident political agent gave an account of the day: Outside Shaikh Said's house crowds of white-clothed people waited silently, sitting where they could in the shade of the walls, for it was one of those hot clammy September days for which the Gulf is so justly infamous. There were a few rough wooden benches in the shade, and the more important citizens were sitting on these.[2] Visitors streamed into the house to offer their condolences with the customary greeting of "may God give you consolation."

There was a hush of death surrounding the house. In the desert, the death of a ruler is considered a personal loss. "Then a woman set up a high-pitched wail from inside, and a number of men in white carried out the rough wooden bier, covered with red checked cloth. The feet of the swathed body could be seen from behind. Everybody set off on foot to follow."[3] Among the straggly group of men that formed the procession, winding its way through Dubai's muddy streets, was the Regent Ruler; the tall, *abaya*-clad, Sheikh Rashid bin Said Al Maktoum. He was immediately noticeable by a sort of presence which comes with breeding and knowing the burden of his people would one day rest on his shoulders.

A few days later, Sheikh Rashid sent a letter to the British Political Agent in Dubai, saying: "Now that my father's days have ended, I have officially assumed government of the State".[4] With this simple pronouncement, he became Ruler. It was protocol for the Political Resident of the Gulf to legitimise this act and, in the case of Sheikh Rashid, there was no question of British dissent on the matter.[5]

Rashid was in his late forties and had been tending to the affairs of the small Emirate for quite some time. He had a charismatic streak, an inborn sense of leadership, a profound understanding of what his people needed and exactly how he would use every situation to the maximum advantage of the Gulf region. J. L. Bullard, Political Agent to Dubai, described him as "the merchant prince with the happy knack of picking the right horses, briskly disposing of business with a wave of his little pipe in one hand and a light match in the other, reading my thoughts far in advance and barking out his instant decisions."[6]

In May of 1966, David A. Roberts, the then Political Agent assigned to Dubai, sat at his desk wondering how to impress upon the Foreign Office in London the importance of Sheikh Rashid's forthcoming visit to London. If Roberts is to be believed, Sheikh Rashid had "no work to do"[7] and was hence planning on spending a few days in London.

Among Roberts' concern was who would meet the Sheikh on ar-

7. THE DAWN OF A NEW ERA

rival, and perhaps spend a day or two, taking him on a sight-seeing tour of the countryside. Finally, Roberts writes: "If this is not aiming altogether too high, I wonder whether he could be included in some occasion when Royalty was present so that he might be presented, if only for a hand-shake."[8] The absurdity and irony of Roberts' letter to J.H. Moore of the Foreign Office in London, trying to wrangle a royal handshake, can only be appreciated in hindsight.

On February 25, 1979, the Queen herself would pay a state visit to Dubai. It had become the epicenter of the Arabian Gulf, its importance as a shipping and financial entrepôt between Asia and Europe could not be over-stated and its place in the global spotlight confidently assured.

In the 1960s though, Roberts' concern that the Sheikh might be overlooked were well founded. If Britain mined India and Africa extensively for their resources, the Arabian Protectorates were considered "Britain's burden in Arabia."[9] Before the discovery of oil, there was no revenue to speak of from the Arabian Peninsular. Britain pumped aid into this feudal region euphemistically referring to it as "gifts," just to ensure that chaos did not reign as it so often did with the precarious nature of sheikhdoms. Dubai was only peripherally known to the world and of marginal interest to it. Nevertheless, it did have a certain verve as a trading port with a thriving population of 50-60,000.[10]

There was an inkling that oil in commercial quantities maybe found offshore, but a formal announcement to this effect would only be made in 1967, at the instigation of Mehdi Al Tajir, who would twist British Petroleum's arm slightly into making the announcement.[11] Continental and BP had been granted concessions to carry out exploration in the region. Mehdi, a Bahraini, as Director of Petroleum, was in fact one of the Sheikh's closest advisors and deeply distrusted by the British.

Despite the collapse of the British empire in India, Africa and elsewhere, Britain was nonetheless still engaged in the Gulf region, albeit in a redefined relationship of mutual benefit. It must be said the British carried within them a Victorian zeal for reform and this desire, more often than not, coincided with their other ambition of profiting along the way. Sir Archie Lamb, who was Political Agent in Abu Dhabi, 1965-68, told interviewer Malcolm McBain, that as far as protecting British business interests went, particularly oil, they didn't let anyone else in, not even the Americans. In his opinion: "In Kuwait, Bahrain, Qatar, Trucial States and Oman, we (the British) represented everyone. In fact we represented Her Majesty's Government, who was everybody."[12]

British Petroleum had the lion's share of the oil consortium. Costains, a UK based construction company, won the contract for Dubai harbour and Halcrow, a UK consultancy with a background in maritime, port and railway projects, were appointed consultants. Cable and Wireless committed themselves to expanding Dubai's communication infrastructure, while the British Bank of the Middle East held the Sheikh's bank account and would bank-roll many of the major projects in the early years. Roberts summarised the British position: "For good or ill, we have a predominant stake in the economic future of Dubai. We shall have to be vigilant to protect our interests and to ensure that we do not fall short on our side."[13] Thus consolidating a friendship which would last long after Britain pulled out of Dubai.

Meanwhile, Lenny Gomes began his life in Kuwait with Abdulrahman Al-Bahar, a Kuwaiti businessman who himself would come to head a virtual business empire in the Gulf region. But to begin with, those were humble days and Lenny developed a personal relationship with Al-Bahar. He spent the next forty odd years working for him, describing him as a "noble and gracious man to work for."

A few years later Lenny was posted to Dubai from Kuwait. By now, he had assumed a position of influence within the company. Eventually my entire family, and quite a few young men from our village of Nuvem too, made their way to the Gulf assisted by my uncle. He and Sheikh Rashid met briefly in 1967 and posed for a photograph together.

Both men heralded in a new dawn; one for his country, the other for his family. The success, the glamour, the gleaming towers of glass and steel would all come much later. In the beginning there was nothing but sand, crusty British officers who governed the God-forsaken corner of desert, a gaggle of sheikhs and a few hardy souls from the sub-continent who made a living plying boats or selling fruit. It was this world, that my uncle, my father and other adventurous, young Goan men like them encountered when they landed there in the mid-twentieth century.

8 Early arrivals in the Emirates

> It appears that the Goanese are a roving people, prepared to go to any part of the world for well paid employment. They will remain away from Goa for indefinite periods until they have accumulated sufficient money to enable them to settle down in idleness in Goa in their old age. — Captain J. G. Crace, Commanding Officer, *H.M.S Emerald*, Recruitment Report of the British Royal Navy, 1937

DUBAI WAS LITTLE more than an unyielding, arid stretch of sparsely populated land, with a smattering of wind-towers rising unceremoniously alongside its waterways to attest to the presence of civilization. Political Agent, A. M. Craig in one of his letters described Dubai in the sixties:

> The atmosphere is on the one hand imperial India. The guard at the compound gate hoists the flag at sunrise, and all day long it looks down upon the *dhows* and ferryboats in Dubai creek. Below the wind-towers, the bazaars are crowded with Sindis and Baluchis, Bengalis and Pathans, *dhobi-wallas, babus* and *chokidars*.[1]

8. Early Arrivals in the Emirates

In the mid-1960s, when the council of Dubai Municipality passed a resolution regarding business trade licenses, the following jobs had a tax attached to them payable by the employer:[2]

- Brokers

- Traveling salesmen and goldsmiths

- Cinemas, tailors, contractors

- Printers, ice-factories, soft-drink factories and concrete factories

- Masons, carpenters, ironsmiths, decorators

- Water-carriers (vehicle-owning), bakers, launderers

- Barbers, radio and electricity repairers

- Sellers of meat, vegetables, fruits, tanners, watch-repairers

- Porters with hand-carts and *abra* boatmen. (The abra is a traditional boat made of wood, used to transport people across the Dubai Creek.)

- Itinerant newspaper vendors, *coolies*, fish-sellers, water-sellers and soft drink-sellers

- Shoe-cleaners, letter-writers and milk-sellers

It poignantly denotes the extent of the Arabian promise, at the time; prized working opportunities if you happened to be a water-carrier, boatman or fruit seller but hardly the sort of land that beckoned with the promise of much else. The bulk of the labour came from the Indian subcontinent. Tall, bronzed Pathans and Baluchis worked in construction and as cab drivers, fruit and vegetable vendors, butchers and stevedores. Gujaratis and Sindhis were goldsmiths and traders. A few, like the Jashanmals and Choithrams, would go on to become retail giants. Lungi-clad Keralites had the barber shops, the laundries and the small, over-crowded general stores, selling 7 O'Clock razor blades and Patra perfume. Keralites, quite numerous at this time, came from the Muslim dominated Malabar coast and were called "Malabaris" by everyone.

There is a possibility that the suffix *bar* is borrowed or corrupted from the Persian-Arabic word *barr*, meaning land or wide open space. It signifies a longstanding trading relationship between the Gulf and the Malabar coast. Unfortunately, the word Malabari became a sort of pejorative as the years wore on, more so on the lips of their fellow Indian counterparts. Their indiscernible language, an almost obsequious manner, the ability to live in cramped quarters and work for paltry sums of money, made them a valued but somewhat curious community in the Gulf. An unhealthy ethnic rivalry exists between Goans and Keralites in the Gulf.

A sizable portion of Dubai's population was Iranian. An amicable relationship persisted between Indians and Iranians, owing in large part to the fact that Iranians could speak or at the very least understand Urdu or Hindi, again mirroring the close trading relationship of antiquity.

The banking sector was expanding in the Gulf. Commercial and industrial projects had to be financed. The British Bank in the Middle East first established itself in Dubai in 1946 and by the 1960s was well entrenched, steadily expanding its branches to Sharjah, Abu Dhabi and Ras Al Khaimah. A group of merchants with the help of Grindlays Bank and the National Bank of Kuwait established the first local bank in 1963, then known as the National Bank of Dubai.[3]

Labourers were paid cash as wages, since there were no deductions for taxes or provident funds. At month's end, accountants could be seen leaving banks with suitcases full of money to be disbursed as wages. More popular than banks, even amongst Goans, were the *hawala* (also known as *hundi*) traders operating between the Gulf and the Indian sub-continent. The word *hawala* is derived from Arabic meaning a bill of exchange, or an earlier form of cheque. Its existence in the region predates modern banking and was the natural choice for many Asian itinerant workers, uncomfortable with the clinical relationships of modern banking but frequently in need of remitting money home. They would pay the *hawala* trader in the Gulf and have an equivalent amount in rupees paid to their family in the home country. Perhaps a few of these were legitimate businesses, but by the 20th century the vast majority were unscrupulous, "black" *hawalas* laundering money from smuggling and tax-evasion in India. By then it became an underground activity.

Life took on a certain cadence, bordering on the prosaic and set-

8. EARLY ARRIVALS IN THE EMIRATES

tling into a routine. My mother, who had arrived in Dubai along with her brother and me, to join my father who had arrived the previous year, worked full-time and spent most evenings waiting for my father to return from work. Her only companions were our Goan cook Michael and me. The house was quiet, eerily quiet with nothing but the mindless swishing of the wind in an empty expanse of desert land. She hated the wind. It searched the hollows of the house, sounding like an anguished child crying in pain. It scared her. Had they really left the warmth of their large families back in Goa for this barren sense of loneliness? They didn't have the luxury of dwelling on such subtleties. They had a family to raise and themselves to sustain. In the evenings, the saltiness of the sea enveloped the small ramshackled settlement of mud-walled houses and palm-frond huts. In the gullies that criss-crossed into this maze of homes and humans was always the faint smell of urine and goat droppings. There were a few Goan families with young children. They quickly bonded, meeting often after work, unannounced, for a drink of Scotch whiskey or Heineken beer, enjoying the hearty camaraderie that comes with the company of fellow Goans. The *bazaar* with its raw pungent smell emanating for miles, skinned goats hanging from loops, vendors animatedly shouting above the din did brisk business in imported meat, vegetables, fruits and local fish, although the fish had a peculiar petrol taste. There was little by way of entertainment, other than house-parties and the one open-roofed cinema house, filled to the rafters with Pathani and Keralite men. One could as well watch the movie from the back of a truck as seated in the hall.

Possedonio Tovar and Manuel (Manu) Pereira were early arrivals in Dubai. Manu's son, Romulus Pereira, went on to distinguish himself in the United States as an inventor in the information technology sector and as a business icon. Such success would come later.

Then, there was not much to look forward to other than trudging to work in the torrid heat of an Arabian mid-afternoon sun after a four hour siesta break. The tall, patrician looking Posse is the son of Diogo and Umbelina from Chinchinim. He had been working in Bombay for the State Bank of India for some time when he heard of vacancies with the British Bank in Dubai. He was interviewed and selected. He arrived in 1957, his memories as clear as if they were in motion on a celluloid screen. There were no roads. Cars did not have license plates. Hurricane lanterns hung from poles as street lamps. Water arrived on donkey-back. There was no electricity. Luckily, the British Bank had provided them with company quarters and its generator supplied electricity. Possedon thinks, there might have been about 15 Goans in Dubai at the time. Possedon eventually moved into a building near the Dubai Creek and, in 1966, he married the porcelain-skinned, Maria do Carmo Proença, sister of the renowned Margão pediatrician, Doctor Aleixo Proença. Maria soon joined Possedon and became one of Dubai's much loved Goan hostesses.

By the late 1960s, the congregation of mosques, minarets and a few multi-storied buildings around the Creek spread outwards. The labyrinthine alleyways of the *souk*, the marketplace, with shops selling cloves, cinnamon, dried rose petals, dates, figs, plums and exotic nuts brimming from jute sacks and brought in from India and Africa, grew in trade. Stores selling Japanese textiles, Afghani carpets and gold mushroomed on the banks of the Creek. Indian businessmen were flourishing in the Gulf. Jashanmal's had a presence since 1919, when Rao Sahib Jashanmal opened his first store in Basra, Iraq. In 1956, Jashanmal opened a general store in Dubai.[4] Al Nasr Stores, Hasani Supermarket, Arts and Gems and Allieds were some of the earliest retailers in Dubai.

The Trucial States were painfully deficient in medical facilities. The British had done what they could without having to incur huge costs to themselves, which included financing a 20-room hospital. The Kuwait State Office was peripherally overseeing both education and health in the Emirates. There were a few clinics and serviceable hospitals, of which the Al-Maktoum was one.

João Carlos Fillepe de Mello was a young man when he sailed on the *S.S. Dwarka* to Dubai. His initial intention was to use the Gulf as a stepping stone to the west, but he spent his life dedicated to the medical services in the Arabian Peninsular. He is the son of Domingos de Mello and Anna Candida Fernandes from Candolim, a village in North Goa. He studied at the prestigious *Escola Médica-Cirurgica de Goa*, completing his training in 1966 and working for Goa Medical College for two years thereafter. A memory that sticks with him of his time at the *Escola*, was walking all the way from Panjim to Candolim on the day Goa was Liberated. Crowds had gathered in Panjim, anxiously inquiring about the situation. When he boarded the Mandovi ferry, he was told to leave the city in all haste because of possible bombing. The traffic at the ferry was only outward bound. No one

8. Early Arrivals in the Emirates

was allowed back into the city.

In 1968, he landed in Dubai. He joined a private practice in the Northerly Emirate of Ras Al Khaimah, about 90 km towards the interior from Dubai, tending to the needs of the *badū* and the expatriate sub-continental population. He soon became personal doctor to the ruling family, Al Saqr of Ras Al Khaimah, and has subsequently treated five generations of the Al Saqr family.

Dr Carlos de Mello reminisced with me about life in a simpler time. Hospital facilities were set up in small prefab houses. Mobile hospitals set up in truck-like ambulances toured the desert tending to the needs of nomadic people. Major surgeries and complicated cases were referred to Bombay. Most of the medical doctors were from India, Pakistan, Egypt and Palestine. There wasn't a single tarred road in the expanse of white sand, especially in the northerly Emirates. In Sharjah, there was one building, the Sheeba Hotel. If they travelled during the night there was nothing but darkness. Not a single light around. One of the routes to Ras Al Khaimah was alongside the beach. If they took this road, they sometimes had to wait for the hightide to recede before they could continue onwards. Water shortages and electricity cuts were frequent. In the summer they would douse themselves with cold water every hour to beat the heat.

Another group of Goans came from Africa fleeing the Indophobia of Idi Ami or made redundant by Africanization policies in Kenya and Tanzania. Cyril Fernandes, Alex Pires, Henry Fernandes, Manuel Furtado and Jerome Lobo were amongst the first to arrive. They were a vibrant lot who spoke of bungalows and clubs, of safaris and Swahili, drank copious amounts of whiskey and sang *Malaika* late into the night. It was only when I grew up that I realised *Malaika* wasn't a song about Goa, but an outpouring of their love for Africa. The Kenyan song, meaning angel in Swahili and Arabic, echoed the social struggles felt by native Africans at the time. Whether any East African Goan ever shed a tear for the social unrest, poverty and turmoil of indigenous Africans is difficult to say. Their Africa belonged to Colonial Britain. These were always immaculately dressed with pressed shirts and smart trousers. They spoke English with all the affectations of having spent a life-time in a British colony. East African Goans quickly garnered the creamy layer of banking and administrative jobs, having held clerical positions in the service of Her Majesty's Empire in Africa.

The mélange of Goans who came from India and those that came from post-colonial British Africa proved to be a formidable combination. The local population of Arabs as well the manual labour that filtered in from the sub-continent were painfully lacking in English proficiency and administrative skills.[5] They were much required competencies by the burgeoning commercial interests, many of them managed by the British. It was here that Goans distinguished themselves, being adept both in English and office work. They were employed as clerks and officers in banks, as secretaries, accountants, salesmen, nurses and teachers in English-speaking schools. Their seemingly Western aura proved to be an immense advantage. Gray MacKenzie, with a flat-roofed office at the mouth of the Creek, was particularly fond of employing Goans. They were a typical British company with a top-tier of English management and a second tier of Asian workers.

In May of 1969, Mehdi Al Tajir, the Director of Petroleum, announced at a conference in London, that Dubai would be producing 50-60,000 barrels of oil by the end of the year and that the projected initial revenue from oil was £12 million.[6] Oil wealth was the final lever that catapulted Dubai's growth and development into the stratosphere. In 1971, the British pulled out of the region. Bahrain, Qatar, Abu Dhabi, Dubai and the Northern Emirates became independent Emirates. J. L. Bullard, Political Agent, wrote in a letter: "We do not owe them more than a decent exit from the world stage but I think we do owe even the least of them that much".[7] Unlike Africa, the end of the British Empire in the Gulf did not mean the repatriation of Asians or instant Arabization. Their meagre population as well as the absence of technical know-how meant that Asians would continue to be employed in large numbers.

For Goans, the old order of colonialism, casteism and lack of opportunity was at last demolished. In its place, they achieved in great measure, a more egalitarian society, comforted by material well being and with tremendous possibilities for their children. This was a generation which had grown up without electricity, slept on dung-floors, walked bare-foot to school, helped their parents to harvest paddy-fields after the rains and pick watermelons in the off-season. Yet within a few years, their lives would be entirely transformed and unrecognisable.

9 The *M.V. Dara*

On April 8, 1961, while anchored off the coast of Dubai, a bomb explosion onboard the *M.V. Dara* resulted in the greatest number of casualties since the Titanic. Onboard the ship were a number of Goans returning home from Kuwait, Bahrain and Dubai and a Goan crew of stewards, cooks and technical assistants. Long before the word "terrorist" became commonplace in our vocabulary, Goans became unwittingly involved in an act of terrorism in the Gulf region.

An investigation carried out by the British Political Residency in the Gulf region and British Army Intelligence Service pointed to Omani rebels, a group, *"Ittihad al Wataniyah"* opposed to the Sultan of Oman, as responsible for the explosion. Disparate tribes from the interiors of Oman had chosen a tribal leader, mustering an uprising with the tacit support of Saudi Arabia and Egypt, hoping to oust the rather despotic Sultan of Oman, who nevertheless had the support of the British. The following account recreates the events of that day, based on newspaper accounts, the investigation report[1], detailed statements given by survivors to New Scotland Yard and conversations with the fam-

9. THE *M.V. Dara*

ily of Joe Fernandes[2] who was onboard the ship.

IN THE ARABIAN desert the day breaks suddenly with the voice of a muezzin imploring the faithful to "hasten to prayer." Twenty-five year old Muscati, Abdul Rahim, rolled up his prayer-mat and wiped away the few beads of perspiration persisting on his forehead. He looked away from Mecca and thought of his homeland, Oman. He had been forced to live in Saudi Arabia for the past few years. His heart ached with longing to see the walled city of Muscat, tenderly cradled between the sea and the mountains. Whatever else was in doubt, his love for God, country and family was beyond dispute. He picked up a soft paper-cloth wrapped package and tucked it under his arm. He shut the thick wooden door behind him. The stench of urine filled his nostrils as he made his way through a snaking alley-way to the Creek.

The Creek unfurled like a watery tongue cutting a swathe through a nondescript town. Wooden *dhows,* aged by sea-salt and overburdened with canvas-wrapped cargoes, lined the waterway. Abras crisscrossed ferrying passengers. A few cream coloured gulls circled the sky, swooping down every now and then into the water. At midmorning, Captain Elson of the *M.V. Dara* dropped anchor a short distance from the Creek. He stood on the bridge surveying the six other ships docked in the vicinity. He was running behind schedule and the weather did little to lift his spirits.

Elsewhere, Joseph Michael Fernandes reluctantly got out of bed. It was Friday, the Arabian weekend. He would have liked to spend his time at home but that afternoon he was scheduled to go onboard the ship *M.V. Dara*. The sky outside was heavy with the threat of rain. The white fan above provided feeble relief from the humidity. Not that Joe was a stranger to the extremities of weather in the Gulf region. His father, from Mapuçá a northerly town in Goa, had migrated to Iran in the early 1900s. He was born in Iran and grew up there alongside his eight siblings, returning to India at ten to avail of a more robust education than what was available in the Gulf. In 1956, he arrived in Dubai, a young man of eighteen, looking to make his own fortune. He had been working for some time in the passage department at Gray Mackenzie, assisting with passenger embarkation.

Joe and his office-boy arrived at the Creek. He had been warned not to go out to sea but he persevered. He boarded a wooden launch, a boat scurrying to the *Dara*, and took a seat next to bearded immigration officials and grim-faced passengers. Hawkers, with their *lungis* furiously flapping in the wind, crawled into the boat hoping to sell trinkets to the women onboard the *Dara*. It took a few minutes to reach the *Dara*. A rope ladder flung along the side of the ship took him and the passengers onboard. The immigration officer standing on the gangway, glanced at his identification pass and waved him through.

Bags lay strewn in a haphazard heap just outside the second-class cabins. Passengers and hawkers were milling about the deck. A shadow moved quickly. He removed the packet he was carrying and slid it behind one of the bags; a small device with a timer. By late afternoon, blustery winds and ice-cold rain hardened into shards of hail lashing the ship. Joe would normally have left by then, but Captain Elson had hurriedly put out to sea to escape the wrath of the weather. He intended to return when it had abated. Joe along with some hawkers and immigration officials was trapped onboard. Tumultuous waves rocked the ship making him sea-sick. He decided to take a walk along the deck. He returned to the first class lounge, picked up a book and spent his time reading. Still unable to calm his nerves, he went to his assigned cabin and took a bath. At four-thirty in the morning, Joe heard the explosion.

It sounded like a twelve-pounder gun going off, with a metallic edge to it; as if someone had banged shut a huge metallic door.[3] The screech of the fire alarm cut into the howling of the wind. A blanket of darkness enveloped the ship as the lights went out. Captain Elson ran to the chart-room, to see if he could get the emergency lights going. Peter Jordan, the chief officer, pushed through the throng of people crowding the alleyway. All along the decks, screams and prayers rose in tandem with fear. There was a huge hole in the upper-deck; a volcano, belching fire and spreading it like a virus to the rest of the ship. People were scrambling, carrying children, hurtling towards any open space they could find. Some had jumped overboard and were struggling to stay afloat in the water. A father watched helplessly as his two children drown.

"Sir, there is a fire in the bar, there is a hole in the deck with flames coming through it and it looks like as if there is a big fire in the engine room," Chief Officer Jordan reported to the Captain.

"See if you can get the CO_2 going on it and batten it down."

"It's hopeless."

"Advise all ships in the vicinity we are on fire and will need them to stand by. Send an S.O.S and get the boats away."

9. THE *M.V. Dara*

Joe ran back to the upper deck. He awakened Abu, the senior immigration officer and Chetani, a passage clerk. They wormed their way through the crowds to the second-class lounge. Joe found himself a life-jacket. He handed one to Abu.

"No," Abu edged away terrified at the thought of jumping into the sea.

He ran towards the boat-deck with Joe following closely behind. The hissing of the wind was rising in crescendo with the wailing of passengers. They stared at a bottomless dark pool of water lit up by fires all around.

"We have to jump, Mr Abu,"

"I can't. I don't have a life-jacket. I don't know how to swim."

"Take mine."

Joe removed his life-jacket and fastened it on Abu. Then he dived into the black pool of water plunging to the bottom. He pulled himself back up in time to watch Abu jump flat into the water. Abu never came back up.

Joe Fernandes was rescued by a life-boat. By nightfall the sea had swallowed 236 souls. D. Lobo, S. Dias, J. Rodrigues, P. P Fernandes, I. Fernandes, Salvador Pilero, D. Almeida, Aurelius Cardozo, M. R. Fernandes, P. Correia, J. Colaço, C. Almeida, C. Fernandes, Frederick Lobo, Anthony Gomes and Alfred Gomes were some of the Goans onboard the ill-fated ship.

Although Abdul Rahim was strongly suspected of planting the bomb or assisting the person who actually planted the bomb, he was never charged. The British, though wielding power in the Gulf region, did not necessarily antagonise local sensibilities. After being questioned, he was released, whereupon he disappeared into the mass of Arabia, aided by those sympathetic to the Omani rebellion opposing the Sultan of Oman.

Joe Fernandes was rescued by the ship "British Energy." He continued to work for Gray Mackenzie in Dubai till 1986 and passed away in 2005. He is survived by his wife Pamela Fernandes and their two daughters, who live in Dubai.

10 Of faith and learning

A FEW MEANDERING minutes drive from the *Mãe dos Pobres* Church, Nuvem, in the nearby *vaddo* of Kirbat, is another religious center founded by Biglu (name changed) now deceased. Claiming to have found a miraculous image of Jesus when working the mines, Biglu donned the mantle of a desert prophet and took to prophesy and healing. Biglu's center for many years was a gravitational force for *Shasti* Goans. They found his fusion of western religion and the more shamanistic elements of Goa's own indigenous spirituality, to be spell-binding.

Biglu asked for repentance, not the sedate kind required at the small window of a confessional box, but rather the visceral kind which needed physical sacrifice, self-mutilation and food and water deprivations, all in the name of cleansing away sin. In return, Biglu could divine the future, mostly by looking into a basin of clear water, and advise about it. It was not out of the ordinary for a visit to church to be followed by a visit to Biglu.

Goan Catholics are converts drawing from several layers of indigenous faiths. The community has embraced Catholicism but it has

10. OF FAITH AND LEARNING

been a syncretic embrace retaining sediments of the past. One of the more powerful threads that tugs at Goans is the enigma of the *Mhar*. Luis de Assis Correia in *Goa: Through the Mists of History*, contends that sometime in 3000 B.C, a Kol tribe from the Chota Nagpur region moved to Goa. The Chota or Chhota Nagpur Plateau is in eastern India, and covers much of what today is the Jharkhand State as well as adjacent parts of Orissa, West Bengal, Bihar and Chhattisgarh. The total area of the Chota Nagpur Plateau is approximately 65,000 sq.km. They were, in the *Mundari* language, known as *Marang* meaning, "of the elder," in later years to form part of the caste system in Goa and become known as *Mhar*, in Konkani, the plural being *Mharan*.[1]

Veteran journalist Valmiki Faleiro of Margão, who has been closely studying the various communities of Goa, acknowledged to me: "Mhars were the original settlers in the landmass of Goa, later subjugated by other Dravidian tribes. Their Gods were demonic, festivals eerie, involving slaughtering of cockerels, etc. Their powers of exorcism are acknowledged to the day. Even among those who converted to Christianity. Every Goan village used to have a Mharan vaddo."

The *Mhar* has always had a fascination for the converted Catholics, its influence strong despite centuries of Christian indoctrination. The Catholic, especially of Salcete, will often visit a *Mhar* when he is confused, overburdened by the world and unable to cope. In his shamanistic trances he finds solace. This was the triumph of Christianity propagated by colonial empires; that it did synthesise layers of existing spiritual beliefs to form a "truth" acceptable to indigenous populations. This concept runs through from Goa to Latin America, where indigenous native Ameri-Indian tribes have incorporated characteristics of former deities seamlessly into Christianity. It is not so much the eventual grudging tolerance of the Latin empires which culminated in this co-existence. Rather it is our inability as human beings to free fall from the past and embrace something entirely new and alien. Instead, we build on the past layering each new experience into another pleat to form a truth acceptable to us.

Converted Catholics can trace their Hindu roots back to a few generations and much emphasis has been laid on Goa's communal harmony based on a shared ethnicity. Journalist and TV anchor of a prominent Indian national channel, Rajdeep Sardesai, however deconstructs the so-called peaceful co-existence between the Hindus and

Catholics of Goa. In a speech delivered at the expat Goans conference, the Gomant Vishwa Sammelan held in Panjim in January 2005, he contended: "Let us be honest, there are two distinct communities – Goan Catholics and Hindus. They have lived for centuries through a process of what I would called 'civilised segregation' in the sense that there has been no open hostility between the communities, but there has been limited interaction at a personal level."[2] Sardesai's strident viewpoint however doesn't take into account the organic and composite nature of Goan society.

My parents grew up in a *vaddo*, thick with Catholic houses. In the Salcete taluka to the south of Goa, between Verna and Chinchinim, perhaps barring Margão, there are only pockets of Hindu dwellings. Within the vicinity of my parent's house there were four Hindu families, all living in rented premises, leased to them by Catholic landlords. One family ran a small *posro*, a general stores, while another ran the local rice-mill. It is a custom among Hindus that if a member of a family dies on an inauspicious day, they vacate the house for a period of six months or more. Following a tragic death in one family, they left the area permanently which meant just three families remained. They were in all respect an integral part of the functioning of the village. They enjoyed close ties with their Catholic neighbours, ties which went beyond just celebrating each others festivals and spun into intimate relationships of co-dependence.

At another level Sardessai's stance cannot, however, be easily dismissed. The Hindu-Catholic co-existence which understood that at the very core we were all Goans, still accommodated an unhealthy disdain for each other's religion. At the heart of human spirituality lies dichotomy, the constant evolution of the spiritual mind takes in new information and merges it with the older belief. Having synthesised a "new" ideological front, walls are put up immediately to act as barriers against all those who pollute the "new." Misconceptions about Hindus abound in Catholic households; that they are unclean, they don't bathe at night and they worship strange gods. Conversely Hindus are wary of being polluted by Christians. Historian Kosambi admits that his grandfather was so strict in his observances that he would take a ritual purification bath even after just talking to his Christian friends.[3]

It becomes evident in the Diaspora just how much religion is intricately woven into the identity of the Catholic Goan and why because of it there is a certain amount of self-imposed isolation. Redeemed only in the company of fellow Goan Catholics or other Christians from the sub-continent. The pageantry of purple robes, solemn processions, paintings of grieving saints, crosses of a humiliated Christ, the ritual of Mass, of sermons from the pulpit, of a morality based on Christian philosophy is so much a part of his psyche, that the Goan clings to it in an effort to find an external definition of himself. *A large part of life revolves around the physical structure of the church. Wherever in the world Goans are, they will find a church to adopt. In some cases they become major contributors in constructing a church. It becomes a community space. Here they can participate in familiar ceremonies, celebrate their feasts, meet fellow Goans and let their children play together. For young Goans it is an opportunity to meet suitable marriage partners. It is in the company of fellow Catholics, that they find resonance; their world-view upheld, reinforced and validated.

Dr Basílio Monteiro, Associate Professor at St. John's University, New York, with many years of experience in pastoral care in New York, emphasised in discussion with me, the importance of religion to first-generation immigrants. "Religion," he says, "plays an interesting role in the lives of people in general and in the lives of the Diaspora in particular. It depends on the religious convictions of the individual members. It cannot be generalised in one way or the other, but we can make some observations. In the initial phase of immigrant transition, religion plays a more dominant role. They find much comfort in religion because it provides a sort of social network, and of course trusting in the Divine is reassuring. Once the immigrant group is well settled, one can observe that for many members of the Diaspora, religion is more a socio-cultural exercise."

In Dubai, the central place of worship would be St. Mary's Catholic Church. In 1966, Sheikh Rashid, donated a stretch of land for the church to be built and Father Eusebius Daveri pioneered the project, at times literally building it with his bare hand.

The Peninsular Gulf states of Kuwait, Bahrain, Emirates and Oman take a more liberal view of religious co-existence than Saudi Arabia. Christian churches are allowed to flourish as long as there is no missionary work. The churches cannot display a Cross in its

---

*"On August 21, 1927 at the feast of Northfleet Church, Kent (England) 150 seamen participated in the procession. Europeans saw for the first time, to their amazement, 'Black' men participating in an English Catholic church procession." Correia Assis *Goa: Through the Mists of History from 10,000 BC – AD 1958*, Goa: Maureen Publishers, 2006, p. 285.

exterior façade, but other than that there are few restrictions. Open masses are often held with loud speakers and even processions within the confines of a courtyard are allowed.

Father Eusebius managed to turn a barren stretch of land in Dubai into a serene place of worship; an architecturally spartan church startlingly arising from the sun-dried salt-flats. Blue and yellow lovebirds fluttered in a huge aviary near the unplastered grey church while a lush garden aglow with red hibiscus graced the center of the courtyard. All day long one could hear the twitter of birds and the swishing of trees; signs of life in the midst of desert infertility. Goans were active parishioners organising prayer vigils, choirs, providing financial aid and devoting their time and energy to growing the parish.

Father Eusebius holds a special place in the heart of Goans in the Arabian Gulf. He was the unofficial patron saint of illegal immigrants from the Indian subcontinent, regardless of creed. Despite the risk of penalty, he sheltered illegal workers within the church grounds. In the morning, he set about finding them employment, knocking on company doors to see if anyone was looking to hire. He was an honorary Goan at heart. His contribution to the material and spiritual well-being of Goans in Dubai cannot be measured. He had a deep fondness for them. His entire staff, from the sacristan to the cook, consisted of Goans. One unusually charismatic Goan named Francis had managed to get onboard his staff and quickly convinced him that there were more from where he came.

In 1987, a dynamic Goan priest, Father Michael Victor Cardoz from Morjim, joined the Dubai vicarage. Morjim is a quaint fishing village in the Pernem taluka, lying on Goa's northerly border. The Chapora river winds through Morjim and it is more famously known for its Olive Ridley turtles. Father Michael, slightly dark, of medium height with a commanding voice and deep throaty laugh joined at a critical time when the church was about to expand. He admits that as a youth he had little inkling he would enter the priesthood. He worked for six years in Bombay and then took a job in Aramco, Saudi Arabia. It was here that he witnessed the injustice of religious intolerance. Worship in Saudi Arabia, especially for those from the Indian sub-continent was underground, organised clandestinely by Christian prayer groups. He met an American priest, known to everyone as "Uncle Bob", who encouraged him to become a Eucharistic minister. Later, he met the Italian Bishop and decided to respond to his late vocation. He studied at the Jesuit seminary, Pontifical Athena in Poona. His first posting was in Dubai. By the 1980s, the congregation had grown and plans to expand the existing church were afoot. Father Michael along with the senior parish priest Father Daniel took on this onerous task.

Closely tied in to a Goan's religious fervour is the emphasis on a robust education for his children. Both these needs are often met by the Catholic Church. The Trucial States, including Dubai, were not British colonies. What would naturally have unfolded by way of British schools being set up, never transpired. The education of the local population was left to the individual rulers.

Kuwait and Qatar periodically supported these efforts both in terms of financial aid and actual teachers. Britain had contributed towards two trade schools. The Indian community had an educational institution, Bharatiya Vidyalaya, established in 1957.[4] Later, it was to become the Indian High School. Its initial enrollment was of just eight students.

In 1963, a Flight Lieutenant Loughman taught children of British expatriates in the upstairs room of a rented villa.[5] Allegedly the Saudis tried to infiltrate the education market in Dubai, offering to set up a Saudi Office but on condition that the Kuwaiti Office be expelled. Sheikh Rashid refused.[6] For the most part, in the early 1960s, Dubai could boast no more than a motley bunch of schools, almost all of them in Arabic medium, causing much angst and separation for expatriate families.

The expatriate population was growing. The British felt the hour for an English medium school, whose aim was to "educate English-speaking children" had come.[7] The appropriately named Dubai English Speaking School came into being in 1967 at Oud al-Metha, a dry salt-flat land just past the Maktoum Bridge, set aside by Sheikh Rashid for schools and religious institutions. There, where nothing ever grew, the sheikh hoped knowledge and faith would blossom. Despite the school's egalitarian objective of admission "regardless of race, religion or colour" it became the school for White students.

Meanwhile the Italian, Father Eusebius, set about doing what Catholics do best all around the world, manage stellar educational institutions. He convinced the ruling family of the merits of a parochial school alongside the Catholic church. The St. Mary's Catholic High School, Dubai, was inaugurated in 1968, a flat-roof structure of about

15 odd rooms, some piled with asbestos for a roof, a thatched shed to offer relief from the relentless sun at break-time and a water-cooler which sprouted water from rust-crowned taps; not the sort of thing parents would accept today but certainly it was a start.

Run by Italian nuns, it had a disproportionately large number of Goan teachers who flaunted the clipped tones of Bombay's best convent schools. Initially it boasted a diversity of some 52 nationalities, predominant among them Indian, mostly Goan, Arab and British. There was a sprinkling of children from Dubai's royal family who arrived with their bodyguards. There was also a noticeable contingent of Anglo-Indian children. A hierarchy was established based loosely on looks and skin colour. The Europeans were at the high end of this pecking order, followed by the Anglo-Indians. Others trailed at the bottom or tried to establish phony quasi-European identities for themselves. My earliest understanding of race was formed within the four walls of a classroom.

It was slightly incongruous, perhaps, learning about Henry VIII and cheering on William the Conqueror in a Middle Eastern desert. Possibly it was a combination of racial hubris and lack of any initiative on the part of the management team which produced a syllabus completely devoid of local history, geography or culture. But unquestioningly, it was this solid liberal schooling and the opportunity to chew on it in the company of culturally diverse fellow students that lay the foundation for the next generation of expatriate Goan children.

Their parent's world-view had been shaped by a homogenised society, insulated from the world by a lack of access to information and hemmed in by the sort of parochial thought-processes prevalent in Goan villages of the 1940s and 1950s. Within a generation in the Gulf Diaspora, a new identity came into being, influenced profoundly by the liberal, the progressive and the modern. These second generation expatriate Goans would prove to be immensely skilled and capable in the labour markets of Canada and US, to where most of them emigrated and where they occupy white-collar, executive or professional positions. Three outstanding Goan teachers who dedicated their lives to the students of St. Mary's were Doreen Martins, Julie Menezes and Lorraine Fernandes, a gold medalist in history. Lorraine was most treasured by me for she inculcated in me a life-long curiosity of the past.

Like many of the teachers at the school, Doreen spent her early

10. OF FAITH AND LEARNING

years in the bustling metropolis of Bombay. She did her teachers' training at the renowned Sophia College. She joined St. Mary's school six years after its inauguration. When Doreen crossed the threshold of St. Mary's in 1974, she recalls being "rather naïve, with a million doubts" crossing her mind. She was one of the foundation stones of the school, seeing it grow from its small beginning to the institution that it is today. Having retired along with her husband Norman Martins some years ago and now residing in Benaulim, Goa, she told me: "The thought of having contributed towards the moral and scholastic development of so many children during my 29 years of service, and who are now in turn making their contribution to society, fills my heart with a great sense of satisfaction."

My formative years were the 1970s. The Vietnam War was raging, the Soweto uprisings were questioning the *status quo* in South Africa and Indira Gandhi had declared an Emergency in India, the country of my birth. V.S. Naipaul, a migrant of Indian ancestry, had just written *India: A Wounded Civilization*, about India's abject poverty, anachronistic systems which had failed her, the caste and clan of her land which had mired her in endless yesterdays and brought her to this moment in time where freedom lay suspended. I was too young to be aware of any of this nor did it unduly disrupt my parent's world inured by a sense of emigrant's complacency. Like Naipaul, their world was now divorced from the daily grind of India, viewed with a certain aloofness and cynicism.

As the Gulf region gained prominence, the Arabian vicarage and the school grew substantially. Father Eusebius faded into the oblivion of the Vatican's hierarchical nepotism. He was shunted from one parish to another within the Emirates and he died a somewhat broken man; but eulogised in the memory of those Goans who had washed onto the shores of Dubai in the 1960s.

11 Afrik'kar, Dubai'kar, Goem'kar

> We will tell the world we are Goans, tonight. – Leonor Rangel-Ribeiro, founder of ACDIL (The Academy for Community Development and International Living), writing in her diary, on winning the Opinion Poll (January 1967).

> Where the Konkans finally differ from other people is in regard to the Portuguese. While most dismiss the "Pork & Cheese" to the rank of the greasy Greeks, Konkans still think abnormally well of that long-diminished sailing superpower, which brought the rootstock of their culture to them in its little caravels. – US-based Mangalorean expat author Tony D'Souza in his novel *The Konkans*.

IN 1944, TRISTÃO de Bragança Cunha published his pamphlet, *Denationalization of Goans* wherein he questioned the indifference of Goans to colonial rule and attributed it largely to an elite section of society being indoctrinated by the Portuguese. T. B. Cunha is generally regarded as the "father of Goan nationalism," who saw Goa's future as best if linked to a post-colonial India.

11. AFRIK'KAR, DUBAI'KAR, GOEM'KAR

Around the time, Cunha's pamphlet would have been animatedly discussed behind closed doors in Goa, M. R. A. Baig took over from the acerbic Claude Bremner as British Consul to Portuguese India. Baig was an interesting choice. The Sandhurst educated man, a Hyderabadi from an influential Muslim family, was a close associate of Jinnah, a key figure in India's own Independence struggle, later to rise to the position of Chief of Protocol and Indian Ambassador to Iran.

Baig had a very different attitude to the situation in Goa from that of Bremner, and a richer understanding of its environment given his own race orientation. It made him a prudent choice by the British who clearly saw the end of Empire in the region. In 1946, two years after Baig took office, T. B. Cunha was arrested by the Portuguese for his involvement with the *satyagrahi* movement and subsequently dispatched to Portugal's infamous fortress of Peniche. The winds of discontent were blowing strongly across the Indian sub-continent.

On the day of India's independence in 1947, Baig unfurled the tri-coloured flag at the Indian Consulate in Goa amidst a burst of deafening fire-crackers. After spending a few years in Goa, Baig had his own opinions about Goans and their political inclinations. He took the phrase "denationalization" and interpreted it loosely to mean a general apathy amongst Goans. He assigned it to economics more than the indoctrination by the Portuguese. He expressed his candid views, in an intelligence summary, on February 1, 1947:

> Catholics are inclined to be 'priest-ridden' everywhere and, due to emigration, are much more so in Goa. Emigration completely robs the Catholics of potential leadership. The best boys leave Goa; the second best join local government service; the third join the Church. Only a few become lawyers, doctors or businessmen, with no leadership to speak of, the Church fills the vacuum. The above state of affairs also makes the demand for 'civil liberty' of little attraction. Civil liberty is attractive only to those who intend to take advantage of it. The urban Catholic has, over a period of years, been purely professional-minded and emigration-minded and is not the least political minded. Since his chief desire is either to get a job or leave Goa, he has little desire to speak or write about local affairs. It follows that the right of free speech etc. is of little value to him. Economics as much as the Portuguese have 'denationalized' the Goan.[1]

Was the Goan, collectively, an apolitical animal more involved with bread and butter issues rather than the finer nuances of civil liberties?

The Goan is an agriculturist given to sowing the land and waiting for it to yield results, a seafarer setting off on voyages that last for months on end or a baker firing a furnace and letting it take time to reach the right temperature for baking. He is used to long gestation periods which require calm and patience. At the core, he is a man of peace and passivity reflected in the word *sossegado* which loses all in translation. If emigration had subtly shaped the Goan's political consciousness, having escaped the economic stagnation, the Goan became markedly more apolitical in the Diaspora. Not for him the hostility of agitations or demonstrations. His main priority was getting on with the business of living. This he did not by making himself conspicuous in any loud manner or demanding his rights but by putting in long hours at work, hoping to be recognised in due course, being loyal to his workplace, ensuring a good education for his children and saving for retirement. His presence was marked by a quietude and general acceptance of circumstance.

In East Africa, despite colonialism, the British afforded the Goan a sliver of a socio-political voice. Regardless, his participation was minimal. In 1923, the Nairobi municipality recommended the council to be comprised of ten Europeans, four Indians, one Goan and one African.[2] The Indians argued for a more equitable distribution of seven Europeans, five Indians and one Goan. Kenya at this time had a large Indian population with considerable economic power and they genuinely held out the hope that they would have a wider share in the governance of the country. Indeed, Indians in East Africa were not entirely averse to notions of colonization itself. Just after World War I, the East African Indian National Congress, had passed a resolution calling for (German) West Africa to be colonised by Indians. It was generally thought by the Asian and African community that electoral representations offered by the British were manipulations and blatant attempts at a divide and rule policy. The separate representation for Goans in Nairobi's municipality was abolished in 1928, when it was decided that only British nationals could be allowed to contest and be an elected official. Goans at the time were largely Portuguese nationals.

Within the Goan community, Dr Antonines C. L. de Souza, who arrived in Kenya in 1915 had shown some political leadership. Dr de Souza was an arresting personality with a shock of salt and pepper hair and a stern voice which he modulated for emphasis and effect.

11. AFRIK'KAR, DUBAI'KAR, GOEM'KAR

The British had a representation for six Indian elected members on the Kenya Legislative Council. In 1934, A. C. L. de Souza became an elected member. He served just one term of four years. His dedication and vision were foremost towards the aspirations of the Goan community, having established the Goans Overseas Association earlier in 1927.

The British relationship with Goans was as ambivalent as it was evolutionary. They subjected them to all the prejudice they felt towards non-White populations. They never absolved Goans from the indignity of residential segregation, segregated public washrooms, the tacit prohibition against miscegenation or racial inequality on the work front. Yet they valued them tremendously, a relationship based on genuine mutual respect and trust. They were unfailingly described by British Colonial officers as the back-bone of the civil service, "people of high quality",[3] meticulous in their work and devotedly loyal.

Sir Noel Anthony Scawen Lytton, 4th Earl of Lytton, who served in the King's African Rifles in 1922-26, paid tribute to the Goan community: "They occupy in Africa the small places, the places of respect; a first class cook, a care-taker on whom you can absolutely rely on, a bank-cashier upon whom you can absolutely rely on... That is a mark of a not ambitious but rather humble status in life. Nevertheless one of complete integrity and respect. A very good community. They served Kenya very well."[4]

Their loyalty earned them a substantial amount of implied power. District officers depended on Goan clerks to teach them how to write a letter, address a grievance party and generally get on with business in remote outposts such as Kitui and Isiolo without making too many enemies. One could not procure a gun permit or open a business without the tacit help of a Goan clerk. The Goan had become a prominent member of Colonial Africa, but not through a process of legislative power rather through a partnership based on work and social contacts. The Goan survives by making himself socially amenable.

As the relationship grew, Goans inevitably became intermediaries between the British and the indigenous populations, perhaps even allies in a world where upholding racial hegemony required unequal partners. Ewart S. Grogan was typical of this era. A notable explorer, he became the first man to cross Africa from Cape Town to Cairo. Later he settled in Kenya, where he became the darling of White settlers who wished for Kenya to become another racially segregated South Africa. As a long standing member of Kenya's legislative assembly he seldom wasted an opportunity to lash out brutally at non-White populations, targeting particularly the Indian community. Ironically his vast sisal estates, in Taveta, which lies mid-way between Mombasa and Nairobi, were manned by three Goan families all part of the Sequeira family tree.[5] He trusted them implicitly, entrusting in their care everything from accounting to odd jobs. The families oversaw a sizable African workforce engaged on the estate. This was not an unusual position for Goans to occupy in Africa, that of overseers.

Goans enjoyed their status as a distinct nationality in East Africa. It was almost a relief not to be called "bloody Indians" or "coolies." For purposes of census records, tax and revenue collection and government correspondence, they were diligently accorded a separate notation. A distinction made based on them being Portuguese nationals and Catholics. A report compiled by Financial Commissioner, Lord Moyne, in 1932, referring to the inadequate school facilities available to Goans in Kenya, made the point that: "Indian schools are unsuitable for them (Goans) as they are of the Roman Catholic faith."[6] The Goan schools that were subsequently built were predominantly for the Goan community while Gujarati and Punjabi children attended the Indian schools. There was a yawning divide between the larger Indian community and Goans, particularly the Hindus. Gujaratis and Punjabis had formed an alliance while Goans were considered as "the others."

They were perceived as thoroughly "Westernized" in their comportment; the dances at the gymkhanas, women wearing dresses, men in cotton trousers and blazers, liberal mixing between the sexes and the use of English almost as a first language put them at odds with the more conservative Hindu society. Indian clubs were male dominated while women were an integral part of the Goan clubs. They were derogatorily called *"macchi khato rey"*, fish-eaters, and the more common stereotype of them as frivolous, alcohol-sodden spent-thrifts persisted. Indians remained wary of them, saw their loyalty as divided and their manner haughty and superior. This ethnically diversified society met in the *bazaars* and at work but the relationships never went further. They came together during sporting events where a certain amount of camaraderie existed but also fierce competition; the Gujaratis and Punjabis pitted against the Goans.

There were a few prominent Goan men like J. M. Nazareth, Pio Gama Pinto, Fitz Remédios Santana de Souza (Dr. F.R.S de Souza)

11. AFRIK'KAR, DUBAI'KAR, GOEM'KAR

and Eddie Pereira, who involved themselves in Kenya Indian politics, but they were the exception rather than the rule, more often than not earning the ire of the Goan community. Many of the Goans were employed as civil servants in the British Colonial government and discouraged from engaging in political activity. Not that this burdened them in any major way; they were content in life, not wanting to upset the delicate balance of things, in which they were not too unfavourably placed.

Decades later, Fitz Remédios Santana de Souza, the prominent Goan lawyer in Kenya, speaking at a function held at the International Center Goa, in April of 2009, contended that it was the British who first propagated the myth that Indians were crooks and thieves and Goans were honest and that unfortunately many Goans believed in it.[7] Whether the British intentionally created the divide that existed between the Indian and the Goan or merely acknowledged its existence is subject to opinion, but they certainly encouraged it both politically and socially. In Uganda, the Triangular cricket tournament pitted Europeans, Indians and Goans against each other.

The Goan Institute flyer, courtesy of Marilyn Gomes.

Portugal's tentacles too exerted themselves. Portugal was ever vigilant not to give the slightest credence to the notion that Goans and Indians were connected; not even in matters of diet. In August of 1948, the Portuguese Consul in Nairobi, on behalf of the members of East African Goan Cooperative Society, registered a complaint about the food rationing system. Allegedly, the British had failed to take into consideration the dietary requirements of Goans, whose diet was said to be "basically similar to that which White Portuguese nationals normally consume" and this oversight had caused "much hardship to Goans".[8] He requested the Society be authorised to import Portuguese and Portuguese Indian foodstuff for Goans. In actual fact, Goans shopped regularly for their spices, pulses and herbal medicines at Indian shops.

By 1950, the lines were firmly drawn in the sand. The GOA demanded the reinstatement of separate representation for Goans in Nairobi's municipal council. [9] (Goans had made similar demands in 1946 and 1947, but took it up more forcefully in 1950.) By this time, the British had witnessed the end of the Empire in India and were faced with the delicate question of the status of Goans in Kenya. Instead of acceding to this demand, they proposed Goans and Indians be merged in a common electoral roll. Goans refused, and the Portuguese Consul objected vociferously for under no circumstances was there to be the slightest indication that Goans and Indians constituted one nationality as "this would tend to increase demands for the annexation of Goa".[10] The British stalled for time, anticipating rightly that the matter would be resolved by the emerging situation in India. However, Colonial Officer P. Rogers was of the opinion: "I do not see that whatever happens about possible Indian annexation of Goa will really change the problem in East Africa, where by race and sentiment the Goans are a distinct group."[11]

Despite the sentiment expressed, ironically, P. Rogers was one of the colonial officers instrumental in denying Goans a separate representation. Goans did have separate representation on some local governing bodies in Uganda and Tanzania, but the Kenyan colonial government ultimately felt it was unwarranted in Kenya, given the small percentage of the Goan community in relation to the overall population. There was a complex dynamic operating on the plains of segregated British East Africa. Each faction was striving to hold onto a reality which best suited its needs. Catholic Goans had every intention of safeguarding the Western orientation of their identity. For one thing, it assured them of an easier transition in societies dominated by Europeans.

In the Diaspora, the Goan became more "denationalized" than ever.

* * *

In December of 1952, celebrated British author Evelyn Waugh of *Brideshead Revisited* holidayed in Goa with his six children. Waugh came from Gloucestershire in southwest England, an area not dissimilar to Goa in its untouched rural beauty. This was a time when foreign journalists were invited by Portugal to observe Goa and the unique

11. AFRIK'KAR, DUBAI'KAR, GOEM'KAR

identity of Goans, as part of the work of their propaganda machine. It could be entirely possible that he was "persuaded to visit Goa" or perhaps he genuinely wanted to attend the 1952 Saint Francis Xavier's Exposition. A few months later, he wrote a casual letter in *The Times* of London, making the comment: "It must be noted, that wherever Goans are found either in Africa or India, they form proud, independent and exclusive communities."[12]

First generation immigrants all over the world invariably form close communities. It is a safeguard against a world which seems alien, and which at times can threaten their very lives. What is unique about Goan communities around the world is that their dominant objective is almost always to meet and enjoy the spirit of community in a joyous and spontaneous expression of song and dance, of food and wine, celebrating birth and bereaving death.

There is a pulse, a central nerve to the communities, but it is a soft nerve; preservation for the Goan is not about leveraging his political rights but rather about ensuring survival through safe-guarding the cultural identity. The most obvious manifestation of this preservation is the Goan Association, which emerges everywhere and which in many ways compensates for the lack of political engagement; its chairman the voice of the community.

In the Gulf, the lack of civil rights and complete stifling of political rights meant there was little evolution of the Goan political consciousness either through a process of assimilation into the host country or the freedom to explore its own depth and dimension. The Gulf Goan would never assume citizenship of Gulf countries so there was no steady evolution of one's own identity. In time, being a Non-Resident Indian (NRI) itself would become an autonomous identity but that would belong more to second-generation Gulf expatriates rather than the first flow of immigrants. Goans who emigrated to the Gulf shortly post-Liberation or after the collapse of the British Empire in Africa, held on steadfastly to the identity they brought with them; that of being Goan above all else.

One prominent voice which emerged in Dubai was that of John Baptista Herculano Lobo. He was the son of Acácio Lobo and Isabel Carvalho from Pirazona, Moira, a village in the north of Goa. John came from a socially conscious family. His father, a sailor, had relentlessly taken on corruption and social reform in his time. John was a tall, sprightly lad, a middle sibling to two brothers and a sister.

Early on in life, he would be witness to family tragedy. One night, in September of 1960 prior to Liberation, a disgruntled mob gathered outside his house on account of a family dispute. As emotions intensified on both sides of the fray, the mob began pelting stones, at which point John's elder brother Wolfango and two cousins gave chase. The mob having gathered momentum furiously attacked Wolfango and his cousins with *coitos*, choppers. Wolfango was murdered on the *ximm*, the border of their property.

A few years later, John left his job at Mormugão port to seek employment in Bombay. He worked at the Bombay Gymkhana for five years during which time a bout of typhoid nearly killed him. Eventually, in 1968, he boarded a ship to Dubai. Initially he worked at Gray Mackenzie and later at McDermott, near the Clock Tower, as a radio-room operator. In 1974, he joined Dulsco and spearheaded the manpower supply division of the company. Dulsco began operations as stevedores to British India ships that would dock off the Trucial coast. Later they would have a much deeper impact on the local economy by supplying labour in bulk. One of their first major contracts was to supply clerks to the Dubai Petroleum Company. It was in this capacity that John, who rose to the position of general manager, was instrumental in providing jobs to Goans, a firm believer in Goan unity.

Whilst in Dubai, John met Hilda Mesquith. a Mangalorean, and they married in 1975. They had two sons and a daughter. John's expanding family meant an expanding circle of friends. To begin with, these friends gathered in John's villa to celebrate Christmas and New Year, lustily singing *Auld Lang Syne* and burning the Old Man at midnight. Steadily as the years went by, the circle expanded to some fifty to sixty families. The time had come to form some sort of association. John along with his brother Concie, the Crasto brothers Joe and Seby, and Francis Rodrigues formed the Friends Club, which banded the fledging community together. This was to be the genesis of the Goan Cultural Society of which John was president. There was also the Goan Sports Club, which occasionally organised football tournaments. John would lobby to bring all informal groups under the banner of the Goan Cultural Society, thus at last giving Goans a unified platform.

These early Goans in the Gulf would undergo a steady transformation within the context of their new environment. Most of them were young men and women in their twenties and thirties. Listening to the

11. AFRIK'KAR, DUBAI'KAR, GOEM'KAR

BBC news in the early hours of morning on radio was a ritual for the men. Everywhere, a post-war and post-colonial society was emerging, more confident and aware of its rights.

The Gulf Diaspora was rooted in more egalitarian times. For one thing, unlike Goans in Africa who had rigidly segregated along caste lines to the extent of having separate clubs to accommodate this division, Gulf Goans didn't import with them the excesses of the caste system. The number of Goans in the Gulf in the early years was nominal and this inculcated a sense of brotherhood. It would have been foolhardy to further factionalise the already paltry numbers along caste barriers. Caste was never openly mentioned and second generation expatriate children grew up quite oblivious of caste affiliations. Doubtless, its ghost inhabited some conservative corridors but it seldom peeped outside or constituted any sort of social hegemony. The demons of disparity driven by family name, connections and other semi-feudal privilege, dissipated in the Gulf. In their place, success was measured by merit and material well-being; by promotions at the job and the type of apartment one lived in or how well the children were doing at school. Freed from the biases of caste, Gulf Goans emerged with renewed vigour and confidence. Much of this solidarity was celebrated at the Astoria Hotel.

In the absence of a club house, the Astoria Hotel became the chosen venue for almost every Goan function held. There wasn't a Goan in the Emirates who hadn't parked his car at the Astoria sometime or other. Sumptuous buffets of sorpatel, pulao, cafreal, mayonnaise salad and bebinca sometimes brought in all the way from Goa, would adorn the white-linen draped tables of the Astoria. Trevor Fernandes, Basil D'Cunha, Max Braganza, Francis Rodrigues, Diogo Braganza, Lawrence Fernandes and Clement Misquita, among others, worked tirelessly to keep the Goan cultural identity alive in the Gulf. They arranged mando singing competitions, New Year's Eve dances and the well known inter-village Goan football tournament held during Ramadan, the Muslim month of fasting,

Ironically, despite Goans in the Gulf living in a cultural vacuum of sorts, or rather because of it, they clung to the culture they brought with them. *Tiatre*, the popular musical dramas in Konkani, had always been the voice of the working class Goan. The tiatrist's creativity gestated in the bowels of poverty. He understood the little man; the powerless, the disenfranchised, the widowed and the orphaned of

Goan villages. In the Gulf, *tiatre* gained respect as an artistic genre in its own right which best encapsulated the pathos and comedy of Goan life. A bond with the past, a raw expression of cultural identity to be preserved for the future.

Gulf Goans began to expend enormous amounts of money in sponsoring *tiatres* to the Gulf, which gave the industry a much needed emotional and financial fillip. In October 1986, M. Boyer, a *de facto* Goan cultural ambassador, briefly visited Dubai. Perhaps what made M. Boyer a legendary tiatrist was his uncanny understanding of the human heart. That it was fragile, vulnerable and lonely and that it needed expression and an appreciative audience to sustain itself. Nowhere was this more true than in the Gulf.

12 Disparate, unequal society

> Outside the office there still exists an uncomfortable similarity to those far-flung Colonial outposts of earlier days. – Richard Allen on Dubai, *The Times*, March 21, 1975.

WANGLES (NAME CHANGED) is a British pub operating at one of the oldest hotels in Dubai, and was in existence when barely a hotel chain was heard of in the region. The only traffic that needed accommodation was the airline stop-over staff. On one occasion, a group of British friends deciding to lunch there had a stunning sari-clad, Indian girl in their party. They were told in no uncertain terms, that while the rest of them could go in, the girl could not. Post-colonialism produced its own racial dynamics in the Gulf.

Wangles used to be the quintessential "Whites-only" pub, much like the membership clubs, mess-halls and hunters' lounges of White settlers of East Africa that spawned across the cities of Kampala and Nairobi in the early half of the last century. They deftly ensured segregation from the indigenous "coolie" or "coloured" population while initiating the expatriate White population into a cohesive unit, where business contacts and cultural bonds could be strengthened and nour-

12. DISPARATE, UNEQUAL SOCIETY

ished. On the face of it the idea seemed innocuous enough, if one could get past its racist implications; but given the rich contacts one made on these occasions and the business that got conducted in such casual surroundings, it served to further disadvantage those who stood on the wrong side of the pigmentation fence.

There might have been a profusion of these clubs springing up in Dubai but for the fact that their hosts were Asian Arabs. The post-Empire Briton himself was a paradox, caught between an old world of White *nabobs* and *sahibs*, in which he had for so long occupied a favourable position almost as a birth-right and a new world in which liberal ideas about class and race equality were sweeping across the continents. Emerging from an imperial coçoon where it was common place to use words like "nigger" or "coolie", it became, at least on the face of it, quite vulgar to show racial prejudice.

How did this dichotomy play out in a region which was no longer under British control but still predominantly under its influence?

In the early days, the Gulf was not the destination for young, university-educated, British expatriates. Rather, it was the destination for those having served a life-time in some paternalistic British organization, were being given a foreign posting of insignificance in their twilight years or for some retired CEO lured by the Arabs to act in an advisory capacity. Many of the expatriates had grown up or at least had a brief encounter with East Africa and they carried this colonial hangover to the Gulf. The other Briton who made his way to the Gulf was the adventurer, the ne're-do-well from a working class background, who might have heard about the place from an aunt and was willing to endure its hot suns, as the alternative in Britain for someone without a strong academic education was far worse. The working class Briton brought with him the stereotypes he had back in England of the "factory-worker Indian" and the "Paki-shopkeeper."

That the mid-century Gulf was still an outpost of colonial mindsets, sensibilities and segregation is without doubt, albeit tempered cosmetically by a façade of egalitarian notions. The retinue of workers emerging from the Indian sub-continent had their own issues; a passive, subservient mindset endorsed by years of colonialism. Some had played clerical second-fiddle to the British either in India or Africa.

One British report tittled, *Progress of Arabisation*, 1966, candidly reports: "Some expatriate managers take on more Indians than Arabs because they are more efficient at clerical work and more ready to accept that orders come from above."[1] It was not hard to fall back into a relationship which seemed comfortable with the European at the helm of affairs and worker-bees from Asia taking orders. In the main, it was unheard of that a White would be reporting to an Asian, and if by some quirk of fate such a situation did arise, it was remedied by creating a spurious consultative post, which quickly reversed the pecking order. The trading house of Al-Futtaim, the largest non-government trading company in Dubai, had an almost all-White management followed by a tier of Indians or Pakistanis. An old joke at Emirates Airlines is that it is an acronym for "European Management, Indian-run, All Total Expatriates."

The British for the most part disguised their disdain for the Arab, the African and the Asian under a thin veneer of liberal-minded sophistication. One frequently heard sniggers and racist remarks such as "Ahmed bin out-to-lunch", "big, lazy Africans" and "darkies" muttered in the guise of a joke but stinging nonetheless. An oft heard refrain was, "What can you expect in this part of the world?" Looking back it seems almost impossible that such attitudes and actions could persist in the late 20th century, actions which would have been punishable by law in their own countries. Yet nothing happened in the Gulf. It was all par for the course. I even laughed along with them. It is only in retrospect that I wince and anguish over its blatancy and injustice.

Other forms of discrimination prevailed. The more obvious was job-advertisements with the requisite, "Only UK/US-educated need apply," appearing on the crisp, white pages of leading newspapers, to be interpreted as only Whites need apply. I remember clearly sitting in the air-conditioned offices of a recruiting agency, having all the qualifications for a particular job and the recruiter candidly telling me that the employer wanted only a White. There was no legislation at all to address racism. But the most insidious form remained that of discriminatory wages. Asians could be hired for sometimes as little as one-fourth of their European counterparts for the same job description. This persisted across the board from highly technical and skilled jobs to secretarial or administrative. One absurd logic extended for the disparity was the exchange-rate differential, which put the Asian at an advantage with remittances to his home country and disadvantaged the European.

Although there was no residential segregation based on race of

12. DISPARATE, UNEQUAL SOCIETY

the type that had prevailed in colonial Africa, economics in the Gulf ensured a segregated existence nonetheless. In Dubai, the Europeans lived in the high-rent area of Jumeirah, the beach-front graced by luxurious villas. The Arabs owned their own properties, in traditional Arab settlements of Al Muteena and Hamriyah. The rest of the population rented where they could afford to rent. Areas like Naif Road were predominantly working class, rented by single men sharing accommodation with other men. The colonies of Al Shaab and Karama were the neighbourhoods of the middle to working class families.

The dynamics of relationships are rarely straightforward nor should they be depictions of the extreme; the villainous pitted against the virtuous, the protagonist against the antagonist. Rather, relationships are interpreted in their nuances and balanced by the delicate play of light and shade. No matter how stinging British racism was, they were also agents of change in the Gulf region.

They took seriously the premise set by Rudyard Kipling of the "White man's burden", to change the social fabric of those perceived to be insufficiently progressive. Whether there was any merit in these notions spurred on by the very idea that the British had the monopoly on civilization is subject to opinion. But it cannot be denied they engineered fundamental and necessary changes within the Gulf. The British were instrumental in abolishing slave ownership, just as they had done in Africa. By 1960, all slaves could seek manumission from British Political Agents stationed in the region.

The Gulf was conspicuously lacking in any sort of labour law pertaining to the welfare and rights of labour. The British urged the sheikhs to put in place at least a skeletal framework of labour law. In a memo dated September 7, 1961, P. C. D. Archer of the British Embassy in Beirut wrote: "In the Trucial States of course, the outlook is even less promising. There is probably a current need for a simple Workmen's Compensation... and there might well be a need fairly soon for some kind of industrial safety and health legislation."[2] Sheikh Zaid, the ruler of Abu Dhabi, drafted two rudimentary pages, and sent it to the British for perusal. This would eventually become the blue-print for the UAE Labour Law, which remains very much the same as that draft of 1961.[3]

The British also brought with them a sense of fair play about what constituted good work practices: severance pay, gratuity, grievance procedures and service contracts. The collaborating evidence that the

British did in fact herald progressive work practices comes from the scores of applicants who queued up to join Gray McKenzie, British Petroleum, Halcrow, Cable and Wireless and the British Bank of the Middle East. The British laid the foundation for what would become modern Gulf states.

Prejudice flowed freely from other quarters and by no means did commonality of colour ensure solidarity. Arabs had long enjoyed close links with the Indian sub-continent. Indian businesses were essential to flourishing trade in the region. Arabic royalty were known to take Muslim Indian or Pakistani wives. Arab youth travelled to India for higher education. However, the years of oil wealth transformed Arab cities into gleaming towers of modernity. Juxtaposed against this stood the woeful, manual labourers from the sub-continent. They were poor, uneducated, shabbily dressed, many suffering from tuberculosis, accustomed to nothing but the moors of simplicity, transported by a dubious visa agent and a magic aircraft into a haven of chrome and glass, with promises of untold riches. As with most immigrants, it was the labouring class who was the most disadvantaged and suffered the wrath of anger from the local population.

Thursdays and Fridays became *bataka* raid days at Naif Road or at cinema houses playing Hindi movies, where a large number of working class Asians would congregate. *Bataka* is the labour card issued to workers which legitimizes their presence in the country. Anyone not carrying it on their person was rounded up and hauled off in a van to jail. Arresting officers were known to used their *ghutra*, the thick black cord which anchors the white head-dress, as a makeshift whip on those being rounded-up.

The most heartbreaking racial slurs were those spun from benign words and used to disparage an entire community. The word *malhind* simply means "from India" but within a generation of Gulf wealth it became a pejorative. (In the clutch of Hindi-Urdu-Persian-Arabic languages, the word "*mal*" is used either as a prefix or suffix to signify "originating from", amongst its other meanings.) I learnt fairly young that my skin colour and nationality were an indictment on my character as neighbourhood children called me "*malhind*" and ran into their prejudice-contaminated homes.

Not that prejudice wasn't manufactured behind Goan closed doors. Arabs were called *buddū*, from the Hindi word meaning an imbecile, uncouth and illiterate. The word is common to Urdu and in Arabic, the

12. DISPARATE, UNEQUAL SOCIETY

phonetically similar *badū,* means of the desert. The *Badū* tribesmen of unkempt hair, rotted teeth from date consumption and infected eyes from fly droppings would always arouse curiosity when they travelled to the city for medical attention or other such dire necessity. Very often they announced themselves with the phrase, "*ana meskeen, una badū*" meaning "I'm poor, I'm from the desert." No doubt, the word *badu* travelled circuitously to become a pejorative.

A curious form of maltreatment was the "plantation" style running of businesses which resulted in Indians effectively disadvantaging their own. * It was not uncommon among the small-time Arab traders to hire an Indian accountant who oversaw the finance, administration and personnel of the office. This accountant, mostly from South India, would have far reaching control over the professional lives of at least 20-30 other Asians. He usually meted out the most stringent interpretation of labour law, cut corners with wages and ensured that promotions were scarce. The Indian style of management insisted on unconditional servility from their employees.

By and large though, Indians did not wield any social or political power in the Gulf to be pervasive with racism; racism without power is rendered defunct. That this cauldron of Arab, European and Asian ethnicities worked together with very little outward displays of racial tension, and achieved what they did in the short span of twenty years is perhaps a test-case for how benevolent dictatorships can sometimes produce the greatest good for the greatest number of people.

---

*Southern states in America employing slave labour on their cotton plantations would promote slaves to the position of overseers, knowing they would extract the maximum advantage.

13 The Gulfkar

THE 1970S BEGAN with an acute housing shortage, spiraling rents and double digit inflation; a period of economic "stagflation" following on the heels of the first oil boom. By this time, the Goan in the Gulf had come of age. He was firmly entrenched. Even though his status was that of guest-worker, this impermanence did not bother him. To him, the Gulf was a long-term commitment, just as Bombay and Africa had been to his forebearers.

Oil had transformed the ruling Arabian royalty from obscure sheikhdoms into families of immense importance in a world-economy driven by oil consumption. The sheikhdoms, however forgiving one is inclined to be towards this sort of governance, were dictatorships albeit benevolent. The oil-wealth accrued to the royal families. In the initial stages, in keeping with the teachings of Islam, it was doled out as gifts to needy citizens. But if stability was to be maintained, discontent dissipated and the local population kept at bay from the clutches of strident imams, then the wealth had to be successfully redistributed. One of the more effective ideas the sheikhs hit upon was to lease land, extend guarantees and offer interest-free loans to locals who wanted to

13. THE GULFKAR

build private houses or commercial buildings. The *abaya*-clad *arbab* had come into his own. *Arbab* in Arabic means leader; a term generally reserved for the elite of their society. It came to be loosely used for businessmen. The seed for prosperity among those not connected with the oil industry came from real estate. This triggered off a building boom which should have addressed the Emirates' perennial housing shortage. Instead, the incoming influx of people as well as unscrupulous landlords who, in the absence of rent-control preferred to leave their space vacant rather than lease at a lower rate, only made the situation worse.

Unable to manage rents and the rising cost of living, many Goans took in "paying guests" or moved in with other families which made the phrase "sharing accommodation" part of the Gulf vocabulary. Some men repatriated their wives and children and stayed on as "bachelors". Despite the fiscal crunch, the economy was buoyant driven by its oil wells drilling furiously for black gold.

People poured in to build the towers of glass and concrete that rose like mythical giants from the belly of the earth. In order to counter the influx of people into the Gulf region, except for those that were necessary for building its bare bones, the Arabs devised what seemed like a full-proof solution. Sponsorship of the family was tied in to the earning capacity of the head of the household. Anyone earning less than the specified amount, which varied arbitrarily every few years, was denied the right to bring in his family. What should have been a right, now became a luxury. A society traditionally known for its skewed demographics of a high ratio of women to men, on account of desert strife, was experiencing the reverse. This phenomena persists. In 2006, according to the Dubai Statistics Center, of its 1.24 million population 73% were males and only 27% were women.[1]

What seemed like the ideal solution was at a tremendous social cost paid for largely by guest-workers. At the mouth of Naif Road in Dubai sits an old Portuguese watch-tower marking the passage of time. Every Friday, a near-exodus of men converge on Naif road, filling up its gullies with the heat, sweat and grime that exemplifies the underbelly of the Arabian Gulf. The pain of separation from their families writ large on their faces. A separation that affects not only their own emotional well-being but of the children who grow up without fathers. In Goa, a generation has grown up in the custody of single parents, aging grandparents or worse still in boarding schools.

Sheikh Rashid's visionary leadership and social conscience would come to the fore once again. In a daring move which infuriated local landlords, he undertook an ambitious project to become Dubai's most prominent landlord. He began construction on Al Shaab, a rent-controlled housing colony that enabled workers to live in reasonably priced accommodation. Many Goans moved into Al Shaab; the pressure of rent abated if only for a while.

The skyline of Dubai was changing. Not a glacial change but one which galloped into the modern world. The wind towers and minarets rubbed shoulders with glass towers gleaming in their newness. The old derelict buildings which had huddled lamely around the creek were torn down and in their place a magnificent, miracle city was created within a span of twenty years. Offices with plush, thick, rich carpeting; temperatures controlled by the marvels of central air-conditioning; dark, mahogany desks for CEOs; flashy Mercedes Benz for the prosperous, the humbler Datsun for the middle-class; men and women sporting the latest fashions from Gucci and Chanel; silks and polyester from Japan and China; lush lawns and purple periwinkled gardens now became part of the landscape.

The intensity of Arab ambition was dwarfed only by its magnitude. Behind the façade of this Utopian city was the well-oiled machinery of a large, heaving, work-force who laboured under some of the world's most stringent laws and regulations. It was engineered and re-engineered to derive maximum benefit to employers, earning the Gulf the unflattering label of running "work camps".

One law which comes in for particular flak in the region, and which reduces the employee to the status of bonded labour, is the "six-month" ban. It restricts the free movement of labour within the market. Labour is contracted and then sponsored into the country by a company. Thereafter, the employee is bound to work for that company until such time as he wishes to return home. High level managerial positions are exempt and so it is basically aimed at the lower and mid-level employee. Should the employer terminate the worker or should the latter wish to leave the firm, he will be stamped with a "six-month ban" and his re-entry prohibited for a period of six months. In particularly contentious cases this can be extended upto a year at the discretion of the employer.

* * *

13. The Gulfkar

I met Sanjeev in 1988. He was a handsome, barrel-chested Keralite man who worked as an office-boy in the small-time construction company where I was employed as a secretary. He had paid a not insignificant amount of money to an agent to secure this job in the Gulf, which promised to be the answer to his financial woes in Kerala. Sanjeev shared bed-space with a hundred other odd construction workers at a work-camp.

I have rarely come across another human being with a more accommodating disposition than Sanjeev. He had a passion for Hindi songs which he would sing melodiously while dusting the office. He said they were from old black-and-white movie classics. My knowledge of Hindi has always been deficient but we cobbled together conversations and enjoyed the sort of non-competitive camaraderie shared by lower-rung employees.

Unfortunately for Sanjeev, the Jordanian half-wit that we worked for had taken a great dislike to him. He lost no opportunity to belittle him or needle him at the slightest pretext. One quiet, otherwise ordinary morning there was a sudden kerfuffle over spilt coffee on the Jordanian's desk. Not being able to endure anymore affronts to his self-respect, Sanjeev exchanged some terse words. That was enough for him to be fired on the spot. Sanjeev pleaded with the indignity of a child, but to no avail. When all entreaties had been exhausted and with the cumulus clouds of a six-month ban gathering above his head, he did the only thing he could. He fled. He was reported and registered as an absconder with the Ministry of Labour.

I was barely into my twenties and fresh out of college. Having grown up in Dubai, I was all too familiar with such stories but had never actually witnessed one. I was eager to believe that Sanjeev somehow deserved the treatment meted out to him, that he had brought it upon himself, but I couldn't. I knew a gross violation of the most basic human rights had just occurred. That it was unfair for a livelihood to depend on the whims and fancies of another individual. But worst of all, I knew that the Gulf had spawned a multitude of cowering cowards like me who were emotionally castrated enough to never voice a protest or stand in solidarity against injustice. I never heard from Sanjeev again. Rumour had it that he was hiding out at a friend's place. A fugitive over spilt coffee. The only way back for Sanjeev, without doing any jail-time, would be as a stow-away on a cargo ship.

No matter how affluent the lives of Goans in the Gulf would ultimately become, they, like all its guest-workers, would always have the Damocles' sword of the six-month ban hanging over their heads. Their tenuous dreams resting on a single arbitrary decision.

Despite what seemed like unimaginable injustices, we stayed; Goans, Keralites, Sindhis, Pathans, Sri Lankans, Filipinos, Lebanese, Egyptians, Sudanese, Ethiopians and the British. What else was there for us back home beside poverty? Here, we lived comfortable lives. By the 1980s, we had an endless supply of water and electricity. The roads were clean, crime was minimal, alcohol was affordable, even pork was available. We didn't see slums, old people, people with limbs missing or stray dogs. The flies which used to play havoc were now gone, killed with insecticides. Everything ugly, impure and old was washed away from sight. All that remained was the city; picture-postcard perfect. All the basic needs of first-generation immigrants were being met.

Censorship of newspapers, Sharia law, deportations, lack of civil liberties, lack of citizenship or a social security net were things that did not affect our everyday existence. Human beings are almost always concerned with the immediacy of their survival rather than the eloquence of principles. Ours was not a world based on Maslow's hierarchy of needs. We were not in pursuit of self-actualization. If our self-esteem took a beating, it didn't really belong to us anyway. It was bought and paid for by the cheque at the end of the month. Our only concern was surviving irascible bosses, the next recession and lay-offs. The job was paramount. Everything else was secondary.

The Goan *pobre fidalgo* died.

* * *

At what point did the *Gulfkar* become a *Gulfie* in Goa? More importantly why did the *Gulfkar* become a *Gulfie*? "*Kar*" is a Konkani verb stem attached as a suffix to a noun to denote the act of doing something. *Ponjekar* lives in Panjim while *possorkar* runs a general-store. The words *bhatkar, mundkar* and *Afrik'kar* are all coined in this vein. The word *Gulfkar* never actually came into being. What emerged was *Gulfie* which would become part of the Goan lexicon. *

---

*Early emigrants to the Gulf travelled to Basra, Kuwait and Bahrain. *Basurkar*, *Kuwaitkar*, and *Bahrainkar* were commonly used to mean someone who worked in the Middle East.

13. THE GULFKAR

The general prosperity in the Gulf amongst the local Arabs meant they could afford domestic help to assist in their households. With the currency advantage of the Gulf Dinar or Dirham against the rupee, it was easy to engage domestics from India. The wages paid were a pittance to the Arabs but a fortune to Indians faced with acute lack of employment opportunities. Goans from the unskilled and semi-skilled sector made their way to the Gulf as maids, houseboys, drivers, office-boys, waiters and room-boys. Just as the *tarvotti* had at one time been hailed as a worthy role-model to aspire to and then subsequently diminished by ridicule, Goan society turned on the *Gulfkar* drawing a cheap caricature of him as someone who dressed loudly, wore too much gold, spent conspicuously but remained uneducated and uncouth. He would be called a *Gulfie*, which contains a certain amount of disdain and ridicule. The word bears a resemblance to "hippy" and "shippy," both in varying degrees eliciting ridicule amongst Goans.

In every society there is an inherent bias against its labouring class. Why did this bias persist in Goa even after that very labouring class had managed to substantially raise its standard of living? Post-war European economies transformed large sections of their working class into the bell of the middle class curve. In Britain a generation after the war, children of coal-miners, char-ladies, handy-men, gardeners and factory workers, the low-income, working class of their society entered film, arts, music and on the whole were virtually swallowed up by the creation of white-collar jobs. Four lads from the tough neighbourhoods of Liverpool became musical legends known as The Beatles. Affluence had changed not just the economic scenario but the social dynamics of this society. Why then did a similar transformation not take place in Goan society when Gulf remittances, tourism, a building boom and iron ore exports made Goa a state with one of the highest per capita incomes in India? Why wasn't respect part of the new equation for those sections of society that came from little but achieved much? Writer and poet Armando Menezes echoes this sentiment in his essay, On Titles of Nobility:

> There would be a few families of this kind who, strangely, were known as *girest*, even after wealth had mushroomed around them to the extent that each of the 'common' newly-rich could buy their property ten times over... the traditional landowners, who had now fallen into poverty and were taking loans from the enterprising, newly rich,

> ... (they) continued to call their debtors *girest* and paid them the old respect.[2]

We retained the little preordained compartments allotted to us. Positions we were bound to by an invisible decree. They remained unshakable even in the light of a different economic reality.

A myriad reasons dove-tailed to stagnate our society. We didn't have the sort of robust institutions needed to create change. We didn't have an artery of primary schools to strengthen the very process of change, an efficient polity to effect it or a solid judiciary and police force to protect it. Did we even have a widespread intelligentsia to propose it? Goan Catholic society has been divided for so long; the Konkani versus the Portuguese or English speaking population; the fair, high-cheeked pitted against the dark, snub-nosed; landed gentry against tenanted labour; those considered "*descent* and *delicade*", cultured and those considered "*volkoti*", uncultured.

The walls of Goan society did not come crumbling down. They were acrimoniously cobbled together with centuries of rivalry and fear of miscegenation with those considered genetically inferior. Our walls were more resistant, our moats of divide deeper than other societies. If anything our conflict was similar to a racial apartheid. It should perhaps have been tackled from this point of view. The returning *Gulfie* found himself on the outside looking in. His role remained essentially the same. A man born on the wrong side of the class divide, yet to encounter class equality. But change when it does occur is often imperceptible to the human eye.

The single most definitive factor that affected Goan affluence in the Gulf region was the free fall of the rupee. By 1985, the Rupee slid to 12.36 per dollar. Overnight Goans became rupee *lakh-pattis*, millionaires, enabling them to make sizable remittances back to Goa. India had begun taking notice of remittances from the Gulf. To ensure these continued and against the reality of a foreign exchange crunch, the Income Tax Act of 1961 and Foreign Exchange Regulation Act (FERA, 1973) provided a definition of the term Non-Resident Indian. A new identity now came into being, that of NRI.

This affluence reverberated back in Goa. The village of Nuvem once the abode of *mundkars* was now raisoned with beautiful villas in place of crumbling, dilapidated, mud-walled houses. The aspirations which had lain dormant in the hearts of parents and grandparents became a reality, as the sons of the soil returned and bought the properties their *mundkari* ancestors had lived on. Building a home was making a statement.

The human heart more often than not affects the most fundamental changes in society. Love and marriage in defiance of caste barriers, made possible by sudden affluence, were important levers causing cracks in that impenetrable wall of caste hegemony. NRI grooms became the rage. Men were likely to "marry-up" from their social standing. Parents learned to swallow their pride rather than insist on caste pretensions. For the women who married men in the Gulf, it was a chance to travel abroad and an almost immediate improvement in their living conditions. Armando Menezes writes in On Titles of Nobility:

> Fortunately for social progress, economics has played havoc with these class bastions. Soon the impoverished 'good family' was compelled to dispose of their daughters to the less 'good' families, and the prosperous commoner married into the decayed aristocracy.[3]

The Arabian Gulf, most often criticised for denying their women fundamental rights, ironically empowered Goan women. Maria (name changed) was a young widow from Nuvem when she made her way to Qatar. Her husband died leaving her with three young children to look after. She was lucky to have landed a job in a reasonably decent household of eight people and two adults.

Nonetheless, her days began at five in the morning and ended at ten in the night without a break. Neither were there days off to recuperate from the arduous work-load. She was one of the fortunate ones though to have escaped without any mental or sexual harassment. Domestic workers in the Gulf are not covered by labour laws. They are vulnerable to abuse. Maria isn't a victim. She is a woman of substance who held her family together in a crisis.

Economics has created more social and gender equality in Goan society, than religious ideology alone could ever bring about amongst Goan Catholics. Even though the *tarvotti* and *Gulfkar* are often ridiculed, they more than anyone else have been instrumental in scaling down the divisions of caste and class, and transforming Goa into a more equitable society.

***

If Goan society changed collectively, change also permeated at the individual level. In very trivial ways at times but triviality too is important to human beings. There is a desire in us to become at some level the very people that reject us. We hope to gain their acceptance by becoming more like them. Goans in the Gulf wanted to be like those Goans who resided in the grand houses with verandas that ran across the length of the house. We wanted to acquire the airs, the dress, the niceties which had eluded us for so long.

One such manifestation appeared in the form of Vasco. He was a gangly young man with rakish hair and an excellent piano teacher. Goan mothers decided that regardless of whether their moldable children were musically inclined or not, they had to be privately tutored by Vasco and earn themselves the distinction of being classically trained in music. Presumably this affectation was borrowed from the parlour rooms of upper-caste Goan families.

Francisco João da Costa writing at the turn of the 19th century, noted in his novel *Jacob e Dulce*, "the head of the family thinks of having a son-in-law and a piano at the same time."[4] It was imperative that a lady of a certain background be instructed in the piano, her marital worth greatly enhanced by her proficiency at it. For the Gulf Goan acquiring such niceties for their own children suddenly assumed a magnified importance. So Vasco graced sitting rooms listening to murdered renditions of *Blue Spanish Eyes* and *I Found My Love in Portofino*.

In the late 1980s, Chris Perry, his wife and sons moved to Yousuf Baker Road, barely a five minute walk from where we lived. They set up the Dubai Music School and it became fashionable to attend the school. My brother Gary joined this school which in the beginning comprised of three large rooms and a handful of students. My father knew Chris Perry, going back to his days in the *Kunbi Jackie* tiatre. Chris Perry then had assumed the stage name *Bab Pinto*. His sons Glen, Miles and Giles were more actively involved in running the school. My brother called them the long-haired musicians. They instilled in him a life-long passion for music. Chris Perry confined himself to teaching the wind instruments, although when it came time to prepare students for the London Trinity College piano exams, he tutored them personally. He had a penchant for safari suits, wearing them like the jazz legend that he was, with the top-two buttons open.

The Yousef Baker area by the late 1980s gave way to seedy "rent-

13. THE GULFKAR

by-day" motels. The quiet neighbourhood of small Keralite and Iranian shops selling groceries and knick-knacks became a haunt for Russian prostitutes and their johns. Dubai was changing once again. Its meteorite rise to success had created an underbelly of nefarious activities; of prostitution and underworld dons.

After fifteen years on Yousuf Baker Street, we moved to Al Muteena. An area my parents thought would be more salubrious. Chris Perry and his sons left as well and re-established their school in Bur Dubai, where it enjoys a stellar reputation. Chris Perry lived the life of a musician, feted in his prime and almost forgotten in his twilight years except by those loyal fans who loved him.

***

Sheikh Rashid died on October 7, 1990. The General Assembly and the Security Council in the United Nations observed a minute's silence to honour the man. The silence in our Goan hearts was much longer. It was the end of an era.

14 Saddam's war

ODDLY ENOUGH, IN THE summer of 1990, I was in Frankfurt on holiday when Saddam's tanks rolled into Kuwait, in what commonly became known as the First Gulf War.* Watching it on television with a German voice-over, it seemed surreal. The magnitude of what was happening struck home only when my plane landed in Dubai two weeks later. A lull had engulfed the city, suppressing its desire to scream in fear of what would happen next.

The war became personal when our dearest friends Tovar Dias and their youngest son were detained in Kuwait. Their Kuwait Airways flight from America on its way to Dubai, had landed for a routine refuelling and was awaiting take-off. In what must have seemed like a split-second, the Iraqi army took control of Kuwait airport. After three terror-filled weeks of bombs going off nearby they were released and told to make their own way home. They travelled to Amman, Jordan

---

*On August 2, 1990, the Iraqi dictator Saddam Hussein invaded the neighbouring state of Kuwait. A US-led coalition force was successful in repelling his forces. This operation was called "Desert Storm" and the short war that transpired is more commonly referred to as the First Gulf War.

14. SADDAM'S WAR

by road, amidst the fear of impending ambush. From there they flew to Dubai.

The eerie quiet that presided over Dubai in those months sometimes gave way to the comical. The German girl in our office came back with a gas-mark and evacuation plans from her embassy. The Indian embassy remained silent. We bought scotch-tape to seal our windows and bulked up on candles, rice and sugar. In the event of a catastrophe, presumably we were planning on a sugar-high. Amidst news of scud-missiles aimed at Saudi Arabia and Israel, we learnt to make jokes and live in a time of unending uncertainty.

Kuwait has possibly the largest and one of the older concentration of Goans in the Gulf region. Carmo is the son of Armando Veiga dos Santos and Luiza Bertalina Fernandes of Mercês, a small village on the outskirts of Panjim. After a brief stint in the Indian Navy, Carmo made his way to Kuwait in 1979. He joined Abdulrahman Al-Bahar as a tally-clerk under the stewardship of A. B. Fernandes and Joaquim Rodrigues. By 1987, Carmo was charting his own course by joining forces with a Kuwaiti businessman to establish the Al-Qatami Shipping and Trading Co. Carmo was living the Gulf dream until that fateful day when Saddam's troops walked into Kuwait. Carmo shared with me details of the unsettling events of that day.

It was a Thursday. His wife, two-month-old baby girl Christabelle and he were asleep. A friend of his knocked on the door at five in the morning. He went straight into Carmo's bedroom and said, "*Te bitor aile.*" They've come inside.

"*Konn?*" Who, Carmo asked him.

"Iraqi."

His first thoughts were for his two month old child. He rushed to the supermarket and grabbed most of the baby food and milk. Almost two trolleys. He was living on the fourth floor. On the way to his flat, he ran into the building watchman, Harras. He paid him the full month's rent, thinking he maybe evicted. His mind was in turmoil. He wasn't thinking properly. He had a family, a small child to think about.

Having his own car may have literally saved his life and that of other Goans. He made several trips from Kuwait to Basra, shuttling Goans to Baghdad airport. Iraqis were generally kind people, he tells me. It was their regime that was evil. Air India, Indian Airlines and the Indian Air Force air-lifted Indians from Baghdad airport. All the

Indians paid for their own transportation from Kuwait to Iraq. Goans evacuated in a hurry. They had no time to pack. Carmo didn't evacuate. He stayed back, trying to help as best he could. When the Indian Red Cross arrived, he assisted with the orderly distribution of rice, cereal and grains.

For those of us in Dubai, a little distanced from Kuwait, the uncertainty was intolerable. The possibility of tragedy is as terrifying as tragedy itself. In the early morning of January 17, 1991, my mother woke me up to the news that America had struck. There was a collective sigh of relief.

Overnight our city was bustling once again, this time with sailors and soldiers who used Dubai as a refuelling and R&R port. I was young and part of my job involved taking the troops on tours and safaris to the desert. Suddenly the macabre reality of war was replaced by our fickle desire to forget, to dance and to make merry. There were endless parties to entertain the marines and naval officers who strangely never spoke of the bombs, the fires, the wounded or the dead. They spoke of the green, green grass of Wyoming and the cattle-ranches of Texas. People are inclined to repress memory of such events or perhaps people dehumanise and sterilise the worst aspect of being human. Killing other human beings.

By February 17, it was over. I watched from the window of my office as scores of Kuwaiti refugees streamed into the streets waving American flags. I have never seen so many American flags in Arab hands. The Saudis and Emiratis were safe. We were all safe. The threat had passed away guided as if by the invisible hand of Divine justice. †

---

†Carmo currently lives in Kuwait with his wife and two daughters. He is an active community leader in Kuwait involved in resolving labour disputes, organising cultural events and financially assisting the Goan community. One of his many cases was that of a Goan maid from Verna forced into a sex racket. In 2004, he was elected president of the Goan Welfare Society, a Goan entity registered under the Societies Act of 1860. Carmo's major achievement was in assisting Goans to return to Kuwait after the invasion. He put out an advertisement in the *Herald*, the Goan newspaper published in Panjim, offering help to those who needed it. He has been awarded the Community Service Leadership Award for community service in the Gulf. The chief guest presiding during the ceremony was NRI Commissioner Eduardo Faleiro. When he organised World Goa Day, a record of 4000 Goans attended.

15 Homeless in Utopia

A MITA GEJJI, MY CLOSEST friend, drove me to the airport. The atmosphere in the car was swollen with the grief of my parting. The immigration officer at the airport, all of 20 perhaps, asked me why I was leaving Dubai. My Utopia of no slums, zero-crime rate and 362 days of sunshine.

I thought of the ship that had brought me to Dubai, the countless hot and humid summers I spent there, the mud houses crawling with lizards and cockroaches that had given way to spanking new apartments as prosperity flooded Dubai, the places I had worked at and the friends I couldn't take with me. I was leaving everything and everyone behind. Yet nothing in this country had ever truly belonged to me. Not a single piece of paper or title had adopted me as its own.

Behind me, Japanese tourists were impatiently shuffling their feet. From the full-length windows I could see flashing lights guiding airplanes into landing. I was holding up the flow of life in Dubai and in its wide scheme of things I was irrelevant. A transient passenger.

Myron Weiner in *International Migration and Development: Indians in the Persian Gulf,* writes:

15. Homeless in Utopia

> In the five small oil-producing states that line the Persian Gulf – Kuwait, Qatar, Bahrain, the United Arab Emirates and Oman – two-thirds of the labour force is imported. Nowhere in the world have societies experienced such massive labour shortages satisfied not through open migration but through the use of temporary imported workers.[1]

In 2004, an HSBC Bank report concluded that Dubai has an expatriate population in the region of 1.05 million. The status of these expatriates is always that of guest. Children born to guest-workers do not acquire citizenship. They have to find work and company sponsorship by the time they are eighteen.

One wonders how an entire region of the world has managed to create and foster an artificial society. They cannot partake of the welfare services, participate in the political systems, form trade unions, have any form of political representation nor in the course of time earn a right to citizenship. The Arabs did not set out to disenfranchise the guest-worker. This reality emerged against a backdrop of the political dynamics in the region.

The barren deserts of the Southern Gulf peninsular had, up until the dawn of the 20th century, been unable to sustain large populations. Their tribal societies were meagre and nomadic, scattered around marginally fertile areas or along the shore-line; fishing or holding their breath to dive for pearls.

The Gulf state of Kuwait was one of the older states which first attracted large populations after the discovery of oil. This was not just from the Indian sub-continent but also the Middle East Arabs of Egypt, Jordan and Palestine. At first, these Arabs enjoyed much the same privileges as native Gulf Arabs, but the two are ideologically different.

The Middle East Arab has been colonised by the Romans, the Turks, the British and the French. They have a long and glorious history of past civilizations, a strong tradition of writers, playwrights and poets dwelling on the conversions and transformations in their society, a fusion culture which integrates the influence of European colonialism within the larger framework of the Arabic culture. The Gulf Arab comes from a tribal society led and governed by turbaned sultans and sheikhs. While the glory of the past belonged to the Middle East Arab, the future was to be defined entirely by the wealth of the Gulf Arab.

Although on the face of it a facile pan-Arab consciousness is carved out to present to the world a united front, the two Arabs rarely have anything in common besides language and religion.

While the Gulf was coming of age, Britain was still active in the region. Middle Eastern Arabs were thought to be troublesome, widely influenced by communist ideas, anathema to Britain and America. The "domino theory" of communist world domination held much currency in the 1960s and created a near psychosis. British Political Agents spent considerable amount of their time keeping tabs on possible "communists" who might infiltrate the Gulf region. Teachers came in for close scrutiny as they had the opportunity to influence young minds.

In a letter dated April 14, 1969, the resident Political Agent from the Emirates writes to the Foreign Office in England, about Ibrahim Hafiz, a Jordanian who ran a school in the Northern Emirates: "Up to now Hafiz has been regarded as something of a joke, but I have asked those concerned to keep a closer eye on him. Whether he is a communist, I cannot yet say. Of course it is true that most of the teachers in the Trucial States are either Palestinians or Egyptians, and that by comparison with the Saudis they have strong left-wing tendencies. For the most part, however, I should say that this stopped far short of communism."[2]

Coupled with Britain's desire to keep a watchful eye on the "radicals" and the Gulf Arab's desire not to become embroiled in the extreme, radicalised politics of the Red Sea, the sheikhs took a strong stand. Palestinians were refugees of the Palestinian-Israel conflict. Mostly, they wanted nothing more in Kuwait than to earn a living but there were some factions who wanted to engage in a proxy war with Israel from their exile in Kuwait. Perhaps there were even some extreme factions who wanted to usurp political power in Kuwait itself. In 1966, Kuwait deported 40 "nationalist" Arabs, mostly Palestinian as "subversive elements after disclosures of anti-government activities at a secret session of the National Assembly" came to light.[3]

Such episodes left a bitter taste in the mouth of the Gulf Arabs. They were oil rich and their future was intricately woven with America and the West. Gulf economic interests depended on the West's technical know-how, their oil refineries and their capacity to consume the product in huge quantities. Gulf Arabs are traders and wily businessmen. Their survival for centuries has been dependent on trade.

15. HOMELESS IN UTOPIA

They couldn't alienate the West, as the Middle East Arab had done. They had no intention of jeopardising the security of the region with the threat of bombings, kidnappings and constant unrest. The Middle Eastern Arabs found themselves disenfranchised from any political leverage within the Gulf Arab states. With the doors firmly closed to the possibility of naturalising them and granting them citizenship, the question of granting anyone else citizenship became moot.

Still, the thorny question of ethical obligations to such a large work-force, especially from the Indian sub-continent, did rear its head now and then. Various possibilities were bandied about; long-term visas for those who had proven roots in the country was one. None of these ever came to fruition. Although Asian immigrants did not pose a political threat, their sheer numbers overwhelmed the Arabs.

Some estimates say the sub-continental worker outnumbers the native Arab, three to one. Asians are culturally inclined to support extended families, have a propensity for high birth rates and are in all manner entirely loyal to the country of their origin. There might have been a certain advantage in allowing them citizenship; the large remittances that made their way back to the sub-continent might have been curtailed. However, Gulf countries were not particularly in need of growing their own savings. They were flush with oil wealth. The minor advantage was off-set by the eventual disadvantage of having to deal with a society that would become increasingly non-Arab and non-Islamic.

A pattern of transiency set into the Gulf. It became a steady experiment on how to create a society tethered to impermanence. People of all racial hues work together or mill about in malls but foster their own communities for support and socialising. The lack of assimilation has not proved to be a hindrance to the main objective of Arab governments, that of achieving a highly efficient and productive workforce. Much of the incentive to overlook lack of civil rights comes from higher than market-rate wages free of tax deductions and a high standard of living in ultra modern cities offering first-class amenities. Issues of ownership of fixed assets, land lease and citizenship are entertained only in the context of trade and commerce.

What sort of a society is engendered in a place which is never home? A society tied neither to a past nor a future, where relationships are as transitory as the jobs held, reflection doesn't run deeper than what car to purchase, plans address only the immediate and no one can trace their family roots nor put down any? It's a society where one does not invest of oneself emotionally. There cannot be an emotional involvement in a relationship destined to come to an end.

The situation is hardest on second generation expatriate children, migratory birds of the desert. Goan children born in the Gulf states don't know of a home other than the Gulf and yet are homeless in the Gulf. They never become part of its society, cultural heritage, historical past nor its future. Most join the workforce when they come of age in the Gulf. Those who can afford it, make their way to America, Canada and New Zealand first as students and eventually settling there permanently. Very few actually return to Goa.

As I boarded the plane, I glanced back at Dubai. Memories rained in sheets on me; dunes crumpled like white linen sheets, orange sunsets melting into the Gulf waters, boatmen ferrying people in overcrowded *abras*, indiscernible tongues speaking in Farsi, Hindi, Arabic and English. I bowed my head to hide the tears. Would I ever be back? I didn't know. With a thud on my passport, the young immigration officer stamped me out of the country, my place of abode for 28 odd years. I was a stranger just passing through.

A multi-racial life for Jose Xavier Fernandes (second row, fourth from left), Composer Julian Costa Silva (fifth from right, white suit) and colleagues of the East African Railways and Harbours, Mombasa, Kenya, in the 1950s. The railway project initially brought many Goans to East Africa.

Mervyn Maciel with Rendille tribesmen of Marsabit, Kenya, 1949. Mervyn worked as District Clerk at Marsabit, an outpost of the British Colonial administration. Often, a Goan clerk would single-handedly man remote posts when the District Commissioner was away.

Manuel De Souza and family, Mombasa, 1949. A typical Goan family in Colonial East Africa. By then, there were 7,159 Goans in Kenya.

Send-off party by the Entebbe Goan Institute in 1951 in honour of Sebastian "PCSC" Nazareth (at the centre of the first row of adults, seated, wearing glasses and white suit). PCSC was President of the EGI for five terms. The Goan club, institution or gymkhana was the life-blood of the social life for East African Goans.

Goan journalist Wilfred Maciel (in tie) with Kenyan President Jomo Kenyatta. At right, Peter Zuzarte in 1930, who travelled to Africa from Guirim, Goa in 1897. He was the father of Kenya's second Vice-President Joseph Zuzarte Murumbi (1911-1990). Murumbi, of Goan-Maasai ancestry, was Vice President in 1966, and a close associate of Pio Gama Pinto. He is credited with having co-founded African Heritage, which became the largest Pan-African art gallery on the continent.

Wedding of Pio and Emma Gama Pinto, Nairobi, 1954. Pio would play a pivotal role in Kenya's history.

Below, Pio and Emma Gama Pinto at Kabarnet, Kenya. Pio was under Restriction Orders at the time, because of his support for the Mau Mau movement fighting for Kenya's independence, 1958.

Seraphino Antao, who won Kenya's first gold medals at a major championship, gets a guard of honour at the Dr Ribeiro Goan High School, Nairobi, 1962. Antao (in below pic too) won gold for Kenya at the 1962 Commonwealth Games. Interestingly, Kenya's first athletics champion was a sprinter, a marked contrast with the country's current middle and long-distance running fame. Between 1960 and 1964 Seraphino Antao was one of the world's greatest sprinters, as the Kenyan media recalls.

The *S. S. Dwarka* of the British India line was one of the main ships plying between India and the Arabian Gulf in the 1960s. The discovery of oil had led to a migration of Goans into the Gulf region.

Lenny Gomes seated to the left of Sheikh Rashid bin Saeed Al Maktoum of Dubai.

Lira Fernandes (at left) on Carnaby Street, London, 1967. Like many early East African Goans, Lira came to England as a student. By the 1950s, East Africa Goans had taken British Overseas Citizenship and would steadily make their way to the UK.

Young Goans in Swindon, UK, 2008.

Second-generation Goan expatriates return to Goa from Canada, Mozambique and the UK, as part of the KnowGoa Programme 2010 to learn about their cultural heritage.

Preserving Goan culture in the Diaspora. Young Goans dance in Swindon.

A roomful of prominent community members, at the home of InvestCorp Principal Betty Pires (centre, seated), 2010. Among those see are Rene Barreto (seated, left), Cliff Pereira (standing second from left, middle row), Tony Luis (last row, third from left), Fr Francisco Rosario (last row, fourth from left), guest of honour Fr Delio Mendonça of XCHR-Goa (last row, second from right), Candy Fernandes (second row, centre) and Ramola de Souza (standing first from right).

Benegal and Neville Pereira, with then Presidential candidate Barack Obama, later to become the first Black American President of the US, at a campaign stop in New Hampshire, 2008.

Part III

The New World

16 Ten thousand lakes

In January 2001, my husband Savio Carvalho and I landed in Newark, USA. To our untutored ears it sounded so much like New York, we thought we'd landed right in the middle of Manhattan, perhaps even at the foot of the Statue of Liberty. As it turned out, Newark is a city which lies about 15 kilometers away from Manhattan and the airport seemed isolated from humanity. Little did I know then, that America itself would prove to be an immense expanse of land isolated and insulated from everything I had previously known. It was midwinter. I had never seen snow in my life. My instinct was to grab some and lick it. It was the first of many new experiences.

My husband was assigned to an overseas project for a period of six months, which eventually stretched to seven years. America was the natural berth for my liberal ideas.

Here what had germinated by way of a British education in Dubai, grew into a veritable vineyard of liberal mindedness. Nothing in my previous pockets of experience could have prepared me for the land size and abundance of intellectual capital, that to me came to exemplify America.

16. TEN THOUSAND LAKES

In its sheer vastness, my Goa-centric identity dissipated like an Alka-Seltzer tablet in a glassful of cold water. No one was aware of India's regional identities, no one knew where Goa was, much less cared to find out. To them, I was Indian, period. My Goan identity became just a personal affair, like an old cameo locket worn around my neck, containing pictures of those dear to me but irrelevant to the world.

There would be days when I would cling to it, seek answers about its validity and mourn its lack of representation in America. Did my identity as a Goan exist only when it was reflected in someone else's awareness of it? Given this reality, I have had to extrapolate our Goan experiences and the transformative effect American has had on our society from that of the larger Indian community.

From Newark we took a short flight to Minnesota, a state dotted with numerous glacial lakes; the land of ten thousand lakes. Trees with snow-laden arms and Huckleberry Finn log cabins lined the road to our guest house. There was much to learn about in this New World, but on that day the sounds of the world were muffled by the snow. The sun was reflecting slivers of light onto its pristine whiteness. Strangely, I felt I had come home.

17 A land of immigrants

> We are Goans, we have spread the world over, we have built huts on the crests of waves. – Peter Nazareth, in *Rosie's Theme*.

WHILE YOUNG AND RESTLESS men in Goa were setting sail for European colonies in the wilderness of Africa, men in Europe found their own Eden. Thousands were leaving for the colonies that would later become the United States and Canada, landing in New York or Quebec and fanning out inlands.

The age of adulthood in European countries was quite young. In Ireland, a 12 year old boy was considered a male adult. Those who set sail on these journeys were men and women escaping the potato famine, the tyranny of religious persecution or the overbearing servitude expected of the peasant class. They were young, spirited men and women setting out to discover the world. All journeys are ultimately journeys of self-discovery.

Whatever their expectations might have been, the voyage itself would have muted them. A tradesman, travelling to America in 1835, wrote:

17. A LAND OF IMMIGRANTS

> Sea-sickness drives the poor people to their berths ... chests, boxes, tins and provisions, breaking loose and rolling to and fro. Perhaps the captain closes the main-hatch, and not infrequently 200 human beings are pent up in that miserable hole the "steerage." Who can describe the misery of being sea-sick? Unable to stand, famishing for a little water to drink, almost stifled with the intolerable stench, the piteous cries of women and children affrighted, the curses of men, the creaking of the hundred berths, the rattle of the tins (for everyone must find cooking and washing utensils), and the horrid noise on deck produced by the howling wind or the dashing angry wave, and no one near who is able and willing to bring even a drop of water.[1]

The "coffin ships" as they were called because one in every five passengers onboard died, were dirty and overcrowded. If one survived the cholera and food and water shortages, there was always an accidental fire to cut lives short.

Despite the arduous journey, thousands poured into the New Land as bakers, butchers, plumbers, printers, brick-layers, masons, carpenters, joiners, coach makers, tanners, dyers, engineers, gardeners, millers, miners, clerks, painters, paper makers, plasterers, farm labourers and all the other hapless men and women who couldn't eke out a living in Europe.[2]

With the birth of the transatlantic ocean liner, another community who frequently crossed the treacherous Atlantic was the Goan *tarvotti*. The favoured ports were New York and San Francisco. A crew of three Goan sailors arrived on the *S. S. Kentucky* in San Francisco on May 24, 1919. Onboard were R. Alvaris, as Second Cook, L. A. Dias, as Saloon Boy and D. A. Saldanha as Mess-Room Boy. Alvaris was fifty-six at the time, the youngest was Dias, just twenty-seven. They were all engaged in Calcutta.[3] *Tarvottis* started at sea as young boys and grew into old men, making the sea their life. Some of these Asian sailors, or *lascars* as they were generically called, would congregate in the port-towns where they docked. *The Reno Evening Gazette* (1934) said:

> In 1849 and 1850... at that time the bay (San Francisco) was full of ships without crews and they lay idly in the cove extended from Telegraph to Runcon Hill. By and by the sailors came back from the mines or *lascars* arrived

from Asia and were willing to sign on as crew for the ships. The little community became a bustling city.[4]*

There came to be a floating population of sailors in the port-town, while they waited for their return voyage home. The Bay Area of San Francisco still has a thriving Goan community, many from the East African Goan Diaspora. Its links to Goan maritime history maybe lost in the mist of time.

Some Goans who landed in the Americas did not return home, at least not immediately. Thirty-seven year old Silvester Fillipe de Souza landed in the French territory of Montreal in 1917. He spent some time in the lumber mill-town of Deseronto, Canada, which offered plenty of employment to casual workers without asking too many questions. In early 1918, at the tail-end of a Canadian winter when the ground was still a frozen waste-land, he tried to make his way to Bridgeport, Connecticut, United States. He was refused permission to enter. In all likelihood, men like Sylvester were amongst the first Goan immigrants in North America.[5]

The development of human societies is such that, having established a self-sustaining group, they tend to erect barriers which exclude others from entering their domain. Many of the Pilgrims from Europe that went to America did so with a messianic belief in finding a new Eden to await the second coming of Christ.

Political forces joined hands with the quasi-science of Eugenics and the breeding of races to create the perfect race, a notion extremely popular in the early half of the 20th century. Charles Davernport, a leading figure in Eugenics, was a close associate of Prescott F. Hall, founding member of the Immigration Restriction League, both being at one time members of the Committee on Eugenics. Prescott was blatant in his racist views and a relentless propagandist. When the slightly-built Davenport became Director of the Eugenics Record Office, Prescott enlisted his help to influence Congressional debate with evidence of racial superiority. President Woodrow Wilson for some time had kept at bay the hounds calling for restriction on entry, but

---

*"I think the term *lascars* is somewhat misleading for in-liners trading to the East nearly all carry *lascar* crews, meaning they are natives of India or other countries in the East. In the Press this term '*lascars*' has been used for all natives and this may do an injury to many good and brave men. The crews are as follows: first the sailormen or lascars; secondly, the firemen; and thirdly the saloon crew, these latter being nearly always Goanese." A letter to the editor, *The Times* of London, August 5, 1922.

in February of 1917 Congress humiliatingly nullified Wilson's veto, bringing into effect the Immigration Act of 1917. For obvious reasons it became more commonly known as the Asiatic Barred Zone Act. It barred the entry of Asians into America along with "idiots, imbeciles, feeble-minded persons, epileptics, insane persons... polygamists... anarchists"[6] for purposes of settlement.

The legislation became retroactively effective so that even those Indians who had acquired citizenship could have it rescinded as was the case of Reverend Theodore Fieldbrave.[7] Born in Lucknow, he came from a long line of religious ministers. As a young man, he emigrated to the United States to attend the Crozer Theological Seminary in Pennsylvania. After graduating in 1882, he began missionary work among Hindus in the San Francisco area. To facilitate his work, he applied for and was granted United States citizenship. By 1924, his citizenship was revoked as being null and void and he found himself without a country. The much touted "land of immigrants" had become the land of Whites only.

The problem of seamen slipping off their ship and disappearing into the vastness of America continued. Senator William Henry King, a Mormon from Utah, supported by the Seamen's Union, championed a Bill which would disallow ships to bring Asian seamen into American ports.[8] If found, they were to be deported immediately at the expense of the shipping line. The Mormons of America have a long history of racial discrimination particularly against dark skin, thinking it to be a curse and a mark of God. Whatever the political rhetoric, the reality was quite different. British ships continued to employ Asian seamen who regularly docked at American ports.

One daring *tarvotti* in search of a new life was Donny Guiao (name changed). Like many a Goan son, he had to shoulder the responsibility of five brothers and two sisters. He started his career at sea in his early twenties. For fourteen years, he toiled in the sweaty galley-kitchens, as a steward and as a maintenance man. In 1971, while on shore-leave, he decided not to go back to his ship, the *Orianne*. A friend of his had previously contacted an agent in New York. They made their way to the Bronx instead. The grey houses that line the weathered concrete pavements of the Bronx are home to America's Irish, Mexicans, Jamaicans, Puerto Ricans, Blacks, Indians and other first-generation immigrants that need work and a roof over their heads. One has to be extremely hardy to survive its tough streets. At the best of times, they are a Babel of competing languages and music and at the worst of times, an opportunity to exercise aggressive racial prejudice. In the Bronx, Donny was housed and fed by a fellow Goan.

Soon after, Donny made his way to the manufacturing town of Peekskill, which lies along the Hudson River in New York, bathed in the tranquility that pervades small-town America. Here he was assisted by Lourenço Ribeiro, good-naturedly called "the God-father of Goans" in Peekskill. Lourenço himself had been a seaman and managed to stay on in New York, in the 1960s, where he married a woman from Puerto Rico. Lourenço was the foreman at a production plant for making tags, labels and tickets. He arranged for Donny to start on the assembly line. It was back-breaking work; long hours for a minimum wage of $1.60 per hour, at times with no lunch breaks or rest periods if the machine was running. The threat of immigration checks was ever present. The last remnants of segregated wash-rooms and drinking fountains persisted, although racism in Peekskill was muted compared to the larger cities. For the most part, Donny was safe and content.

He left the factory job within a year and took up the position of chef at the St. Mary's convent. It was here that Donny would experience the tolerance and acceptance, that America in a way is known to afford its immigrants, even if illegal. The nuns put him in touch with an immigration lawyer and helped legalise his status. In 1977, he finally returned to Goa and got married.

The community in Peekskill has grown over the years. Now in its third generation of Goans, it comprises of fifty to sixty families. There is a Goan Association of Hudson Valley, initially started by Carlos Lopes as the Goan Club of Peekskill. Given the emphasis on a good, robust education by first-generation Goan immigrants, almost all the children are college educated and engaged in white-collar jobs. One of Donny's son is an engineer and his daughter specializes in the science of thermology, the medical science that derives diagnostic indications from highly detailed and sensitive infrared images of the human body. Donny has come a long way from the galleys of the *Orianne*.

It wasn't until the Immigration and Nationality Act of 1952, that race ceased to be a factor in determining eligibility for entry into the US and the ban on Asians was finally lifted. A minor concession had been made to Indians, and a quota of 100 Indians per year had been allowed since 1945.

18 The exiled intellectual

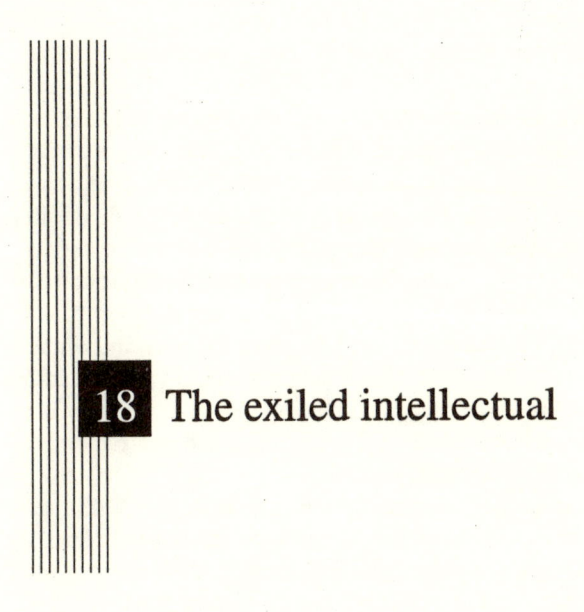

J. J. HILL HOUSE on Summit Hill at St. Paul, Minnesota, is renowned for a number of reasons not the least of which is it neighbours the house of F. Scott Fitzgerald of *Tender is the Night* fame. Walking the dimly lit and dank corridors of these imposing Victorian houses, I can understand how a young Fitzgerald would have created an imaginary world to escape the incarceration of a Minnesota winter.

All this reminds me of how strong the literary tradition is in Goa. The beautiful melodic narratives of Goan authors, tinged with melancholy, transport us to a time which would be lost to us forever were it not for these faithful and eloquent chroniclers.

The Minnesotan writes because for six months of the year he is imprisoned by winter's wrath. The Goan writes because he is blessed by nature's elegance throughout the year. But Goan authors are not just writers, they are lyricist, writing the songs of our tales. It is astonishing how a small state in India managed to produce so many writers spanning several languages, notably Konkani, Portuguese, English and Marathi. There is a wandering minstrel and poet in the Goan soul

18. THE EXILED INTELLECTUAL

and it stirs to life with pen and paper. He is the intellectual nerve of Goa.

There is a prevailing notion that it is the working and middle class who mainly emigrated in search of a better life. That the grand old families of Goa stayed back or at the very least returned from long terms of exile in Portugal. Yet it is hard to imagine the intelligentsia flourishing either under the strict censorship which prevailed during the Portuguese era or the stifling closed economic model that followed Liberation.

In 1890, writer Francisco João da Costa, mourned of "a land where there exists districts like mine with a hundred thousand inhabitants without either a library or municipal reading rooms."[1] The very infrastructure to support the intellectual spark of Goa had been neglected along with its other infrastructural needs.

Maria Aurora Couto†* poignantly writes in her *Goa: A Daughter's Story*, about this dolorous discontent which afflicted her father's generation, arguing that "some reflection is called for to account for a kind of disillusionment that did confront the Goan at the time. The hegemony that gave birth to the romantic illusion of my father's generation was being threatened."[2] Who can blame the sons of these grand families for wanting to escape to a more libertine and stimulating world? Even if it was just a train-ride away to British India, to the more heaving metropolis of Bombay, to breathe the clear, pure air of intellectualism, to bandy ideas with other heavyweights and to give in to the sheer joy that such a journey of self-discovery brings? By the early 20th century, doctors, lawyers and writers made their way to Bombay. Goa was never far away, always lurking in the shadow of their consciousness. Was she the wife or had she become a mistress?

Notable writer and poet Armando Menezes sheds light on this feeling of being away and yet permanently tethered to Goa. In a speech delivered on April 17, 1965, despite being a resident of Bombay and Hubli, he railed against Goa's proposed merger with Maharashtra, defending its distinct identity. "Loving our country," he said, "we have gone into exile; but though we soared, we did noṭ roam: our hearts like the skylark's, were ever in our little nests."[3] Armando was born

---

*"It seems to be that education for my father's generation enlarged the mind and developed the personality in ways that could not find fruition within the feudal and Colonial structures of a tiny geographical space", See Couto M A.,(2004) *Goa: A Daughter's Story*, New Delhi: Penguin India, Chp: La Grande Illusion, p 351, for an expansion on this theme of upper-class restlessness in Goa.

on the small island of São Matias, Divar, in 1902, within "sight of the river".[4] The river cut a swathe through his heart and ran wild through his veins but he never wanted to be confined by it. Of this he is explicit in his writing. He never wanted to spend his entire life on an island. He wanted the river to take him away to new horizons, where lay a more expansive point of view.

Armando spent a good part of his adult life in Bombay. He taught at two of its most prestigious colleges, St. Xavier's and Elphinstone. In that first wave of unbridled nationalism, India like a huge, benevolent mother goddess gratefully and lustfully consumed these sons of Goa and churned out Indian nationalists, something that would never be repeated in successive Goan generations with equal intensity. Armando was a fierce supporter of Nehru, dedicating a poem to him and frequently sporting a *khadi* Nehru jacket.

He wrote prolifically about Goa, prompting one critic to describe his poetry as that of an exile. He himself admits it might well be. In *The Emigrant*, 1933, he expresses the hope of attachment, either physical or metaphysical to the "Land of my fathers! May'st thou also be the land my children shall be proud to own."[5] This was the dichotomy of Armando's generation; even though Goa had failed to contain them, the hope existed that the future would somehow bring home their progeny. Was Armando's poetry confined to the rhythms of Goa? Was his poetry Goan? Or was he part of a more malleable cosmos; universal and timeless? Outside of Goa, the poet had become whole, larger, wider in his breath of vision and all encompassing and yet it seems he was intrinsically Goan. The Diaspora needed the Goan as much as the Goan needed the space.

Goa's literary talent which came of age as the colonial era snaked to an end, doubtless found little encouragement to pursue the artistic life, given the burden of their parent's surrogated dreams; of "settling down" with a good job, marriage and children. Nevertheless the mistral persevered. For young Goan men graduating in Bombay with more of an emphasis on liberal arts than science, there were three choices which beckoned and which they invariably embraced; academia, advertising or journalism.

One writer who began his career as a teacher is Victor Rangel-Ribeiro. He was born in 1925, when Goa was still a Portuguese colony. He grew up in Porvorim, today a fledgling suburb of Panjim more noted for its water deprivations in the summer months than

143

18. THE EXILED INTELLECTUAL

as an intellectual bastion. Victor began his scholastic life at the Mater Dei Institution in Saligão, and at the age of fourteen left for Bombay, moving to an ethnically diverse neighbourhood of Goans, Anglo-Indians, Bene-Israelities, Hindus, Muslims and Parsis. This diversity would have a profound impact on the writer, paradoxically teaching him lessons about racism and tolerance at the same time.

Later at St. Xavier's College, Bombay, he and eleven fellow-students formed a writing group called the ChesterBelloc Club, which published a typewritten fortnightly magazine. ChesterBelloc was perhaps a curious choice as a group-name; Hilaire Pierre Belloc and Gilbert Keith Chesterton were two prominent writers in 20th century England, their close friendship sealed by a shared devotion to Catholicism. It subsequently led to the term ChesterBelloc being coined. The Goan artiste himself is strongly influenced by Christianity. It seeps into strands of his artistic output. In any case, quite a few members of the group – John Correia Alfonso, Carmen de Souza, Gerson da Cunha and Violet Dias Lannoy – achieved wide acclaim and in no small part contributed richly to Goan literature in English.

The Bombay dream stultified for many Goans immediately following Independence. By 1950, Victor had established a career in writing and journalism, holding editorial positions at the *National Standard*, the *Times of India* and the *Illustrated Weekly of India*. Later, he changed direction and joined J. Walter Thompson Co., a mammoth advertising agency, breaking the racial barrier and rising to the post of Head of the Copy Department. Regardless, he still found himself less of an equal than he wanted to be. I'd met the indomitable Victor, at a GoaWriters' meeting in 2007. Unfortunately circumstances prevented us from getting to know each other in anything other than a cursory manner. Nonetheless, the miracles of modern technology enabled us to gain a somewhat better understanding of each other. In a private mail to me, he acknowledged he had had great success at J. Walter Thompson Co., and had been appointed Head of the Copy Department, a post previously reserved for Englishmen. With the appointment came the realization that Indians were still expected to work for less pay even after Independence. Though he won that fight, it left a bitter taste in his mouth. His sister in New York had gifted him and his wife a trip to the city, as a wedding present. His wife had been admitted to the Juilliard School of Music at Lincoln Center, New York. It seemed like a chance of a lifetime. He applied for a six month leave of absence and left.

The young Victor arrived in America with his wife Lea and eleven month old daughter in 1956. Victor had bid farewell to post-colonial India but what sort of country had he adopted? The ban on Asian immigrants had only been fully repealed in 1952. In 1956, there were but 314 Indians admitted into the United States.[6] Victor would have been one of this minuscule number. America of the 1950s was still a deeply segregated world rent asunder by racial tension.

Just nine months prior to Victor's landing, the Montgomery bus boycott had officially launched a boycott of public transport which insisted "coloureds" sit at the back of the bus. A Black man earned half of what his White counterpart did and the word "nigger" was commonplace. Nor was literary enterprise a thriving business. If the statistics compiled by the Department of Labour are any indication, just about five-hundred thousand people were then gainfully employed by the publishing and printing industry, including newspapers, across the country.[7] America, Victor says, treated him as it treats most immigrants – very well and very roughly. When he applied for jobs, he was told either that he was under-qualified and could not be offered anything or that he was over-qualified. He finally got a break writing on music for the *New York Times*, which meant a lot to him. He left the *Times* in 1959 to become a copy chief at a small advertising agency just off Fifth Avenue.

Still, it was New York, which at the time was undergoing a transformation. It was a beacon for artists, writers, poets and the political intelligentsia. They congregated in Greenwich Village, on the south side of Manhattan and in these bohemian buildings many a revolutionary idea in art and politics was born. It was the place another intellectual from Goa would flee to in 1967, the artist Francis Newton Souza. Born in 1924, in the village of Saligão, a few miles away from the city capital of Panjim, he moved to Bombay with his mother aged just four. He studied at the J. J. School of Art, where he was penalised for his predominantly leftwing views and expelled for his support to the Quit India movement. Shortly after India's Independence he left for London arriving there "almost penniless". In *The Times* of London review of a 1955 exhibition at Gallery One, he is described only as one of five "youngish" artists who participated alongside much more established ones, although he is recommended as the most interesting.[8] The review was blighted by the faint suggestion that his originality may not be that original. Seven years later, *The Times* was comparing his work to Picasso, and describing him as an artist "remarkable for harsh and thorny imagery, and able to use it to express feelings of anguished rage, he paints now with a sort of acid tenderness."[9] Was he, like Picasso, battling his tender personal demons which found expression onto canvas? Just five years later he left London for New York, leaving behind a family and a mistress.

I try to imagine Souza as a young boy perhaps visiting his native village Saligão. How could a frenzied mind like his have found any resonance or release in this village? And yet Souza took his inspiration from the landscape, the architecture, the pageantry and the pathos of Christianity, whether he encountered it in Goa or the Goan enclaves of Bombay. So many of Souza's paintings depict the emblematic Cross of Christ, jagged and sharp at times, dark, menacing, forbidding and bringing terror with it, as in the painting *Man with Monstrance*, 1953, or elsewhere in the distance, a more subtle, comforting presence of Christianity, receding but visible nonetheless as in *Landscape with Tree and Church*, 1954. I can imagine the shock Souza would have caused in India or Goa, with his nudes lying languorously or in torrid embrace with a partner, fully aware of their sexual power. Was it all a little intimidating for the society he was born into?

Like so many geniuses, he never found the full recognition he deserved in his lifetime. I was shocked to find a friend of mine, Yvette Coelho, return with a Souza sketch after a holiday in France. Souza's sketch had been in the custody of her uncle, Reginald Coelho, who lives in Chinon, France, and who had acquired the sketch from Souza's years in France, when Reginald worked for an art-dealer. Perhaps in his early years, Souza had little understanding of the monetary worth of his work, although like the true great artist he was, he lived outside of himself and had a clear understanding of his own artistic value to the world, declaring once: "Now that Picasso is dead, I am the greatest."

Writer Vivek Menezes, the grandson of Armando Menezes, made the artist's acquaintance in his later years in New York and enjoyed a close relationship with him. Vivek maintains in an article in the *Herald*, August 14, 2009: "He (Souza) remained a very proud Goan all through his life, even into multiple (partly self-inflicted) exiles in Paris, London and New York, Souza also remained bitter about the provincial hostilities he faced in colonial Goa when he first showed off his brilliant canvases in the forties."

"Who had ever heard of a professional painter in India," Souza had moaned bitterly in his autobiography, *Words and Lines*, 1959. "An 'artist' was a fellow who could draw designs for pillow-cases, cushions and petticoats for girls to embroider and paint your name and address on your trunk lest it be stolen on the Indian Railways," he wrote.

For so many of our intellectuals, exile was the only way to self-preservation given their incarceration by provincial limitations. They were in fact in exile long before they ever left. But memories of Goa lingered. Souza remembered old flames from Goa even to the end recalling them in conversations and he wrote letters to Goans in New York, including one to Victor Rangel-Ribeiro.

For Victor Rangel-Ribeiro, the vibrancy of the city took over; a welcoming berth for his artistic output. The paradox of America has always been its openness, its ability to embrace the new, the foreign, the modern, the rational, the liberal and the progressive while at the same time clinging desperately to the orthodox, the conservative, protecting the old order and putting up barriers to create a world of exclusion. It was this challenge that Victor would have to tackle head on and he did, bringing America his gifts of the Magi; his music, his writing and his intellect. Besides being a novelist, Victor is an accomplished musician, authoring books on music and serving at one time as Music Director of the Beethoven Society of New York. It was his very Indianess that America embraced. He says his knowledge of Asia made him relevant there and they were hungry to consume of it in large doses. America had borrowed this intellectual. Yet he never relinquished Goa. In 1999, his novel *Tivolem,* set in Goa, was published by Milkweed Editions and won the Milkweed National Fiction Prize (1998).

In an interview with Derek Alger, Victor describes how the characters of his novel, *Tivolem*, claustrophobically crowded into his mind struggling to break free. They haunted him with conversations at odd hours of the day.[10] There was the village thief, the *grande dame*, the priest, all distinctly Goan, weaving their stories in a fictional village of Goa. Yet, the characters had a universal appeal.

The Goan intellectual is bound to a cultural past and much like the wandering Jew is set free, strengthened and fortified by his years in the Diaspora. But can the first generation or even the second generation

18. THE EXILED INTELLECTUAL

Goan intellectual in the Diaspora ever think in a voice alien to his own? Can he for instance become an America first and foremost, entirely in his being or is he bound to a heritage from which he draws his sustenance? And because he draws his sustenance from a distance, does his voice weaken in this exercise? Does he lose the sense of urgency, the sense of objectivity and immediacy which Goa offers to those who stayed behind? Is he in a way an outsider both to his home as well as to his host?

In an essay titled, 'The self-exiled Goan novelist', which appeared in the *Ekvott* magazine, 2008, Victor reflects: "Does our sense of Goaness, our sense of having a Goan identity increase as the term of our exile goes from months to years to decades?"[11] Interestingly, Victor has echoed the same sentiments as Armando Menezes, this wrenching banishment of self-imposed exile. Is it just a writer's sense of drama or is it a real longing for the motherland that carves itself onto the soul and refuses to be erased? More importantly, would Goa's future have been any different, had these exiled intellectuals never ventured forth? Would Goa have nourished their needs or would they have starved from intellectual deprivation? Victor now spends much of his time between New York and Goa, mentoring budding writers, holding workshops and encouraging the pursuit of arts in Goa.

At the core of all good art is the desire to tell a story that speaks of a fundamental truth and gently nudges our inner moral compass towards compassion and empathy. It is the desire to redeem the disenfranchised and the disillusioned. A society bankrupt of its artistic heritage is a society bereft of imagination, values, foresight, morality and ultimately its soul. Goa at least will never be bankrupt for its artistic sons of the soil, whether in Goa or in the Diaspora, refuse to abandon her.

19 Heathendom, Christendom

IN 1657, THE PROPAGANDA Fide, a department of the Vatican entrusted with the onerous task of spreading Christianity and with the regulation of Catholic ecclesiastical affairs in non-Catholic countries, wrote that in Goa "confessions had to be undertaken by means of an interpreter and by showing penitents a list of sins."[1]

Given these impediments to successfully spreading Christianity in the east, it was imperative for the Portuguese Church to cultivate a native clergy. Professor Olivinho Gomes, in *The Religious Orders in Goa*, gives us a detailed account of how a college came into being with the precise purpose of preparing a clergy from the ranks of the indigenous population.[2] Two ambitious Franciscans, Miguel Vaz and Diogo de Borba, started the project of building a confraternity of the *Santa Fe*, Holy Faith, in 1541, on the "road of the Horse's trade," in the area now called Old Goa. The main purpose of this confraternity was to act as a sort of correctional facility, a remedial course for wayward neo-Christian converts, given to "heathen" lapses. The idea of attaching a seminary to the confraternity in order to prepare a native clergy soon took seed, and the College of St. Paul came into existence.

19. HEATHENDOM, CHRISTENDOM

André Vaz, the first Goan priest to emerge from this college was a *Chardo ganvkar*, from the nearby village of Karamboli (Carambolim). Unfortunately the assessment of the rest of the novitiates was not that favourable. It seems in their haste to create a native clergy, the Portuguese had been indiscriminate in the selection process. Most of the recruits were found to be unsuitable for a life devoted to spiritual matters.

From then on, entry was restricted to the upper-castes Goans. This decision was purely pragmatic. Brahmins were already well instructed in a life devoted to ritual and asceticism. More importantly they were the power-base of the Hindu society that the Portuguese inherited. However much conversion might have diminished their status, they still belonged to that section of society which commanded respect. It was simply easier for the Church to perpetuate this political and social power structure rather than create an entirely new one.

The success of the experiment astonished the Portuguese. When the Polish Apostolic delegate, Wladyslaw Michal Zaleski Boniface was sent by the Pope to India, he was to write in 1887 that: *"Dans l'Inde Porrtugaise, tout le clergé est indigene, et il n'est pas inférieur à celui de beacoup de dioceses de l'Europe"*[3] (in Portuguese India, all the clergy is native and in no way inferior to most of the diocese of Europe). By the 1900s, almost the entire clergy in Goa was of native extraction. The priesthood, with its firm emphasis on education, had managed to provide the upper-caste Goan man with an intellectual and spiritual outlet. In time, it became almost a matter of honour to have at least one son in the family devote his life to God. Today, one of Goa's significant export to the Diaspora is its clergy. European and American dioceses have come to depend on them to tend to their parishes.

Nicholas Soares arrived in America, as a young Goan priest, in June 1973. His parents, Thomé Angelo and Virginia Soares, had moved from Aldona, Goa to Valsad of Gujarat, sometime in the 1920s to work at the railway workshop. Valsad was a fledgling town which had gained prominence as the maintenance hub for the Western Railway, formerly the Baroda, Bombay and Central India (BBCI) Railway. Most of those who worked at the railway office or maintenance workshop were either Goans or Mangaloreans and a handful of Anglo-Indians. They formed a small thriving community of about 150 Christians. Determined to keep their faith alive they would congregate every Sunday at the St. Anthony's Church, also known as the White Church, on Dharampur Road, built during the British Raj, to specifically cater to the needs of the railway employees. Both Thomé and Virginia were devout Catholics. Virginia could recite the Sunday sermon *verbatim* upon returning from church. Nicholas arrived into the family fold in June of 1934. The early influence of a solid Christian upbringing was to shape his world-view.

He grew up in a bustling household of nine children. On the cusp of his adolescence, Virginia decided he should join his brothers at the Don Bosco's boarding in Gujarat. There, eagle-eyed Salesian fathers immediately spotted his potential and sent him, barely fourteen, to a seminary preparatory school, the Sacred Heart School at Tiruppattur, Tamil Nadu. Nicholas never looked backed. After he finished his novitiate, he did two years of philosophy, in Kotagiri, a hill-station in the Nilgiris district of South India, followed by a Masters degree in economics and another degree in political science both from the University of Madras. In 1961, he was sent to study theology in Shillong. By 1973, he had been administering to his flock in Bombay for seven years, when he requested permission with his diocese to pursue a doctoral programme at Fordham, the Jesuit university of New York.

America in the 1970s was markedly different from an India, emerging from Colonialism, crippled by socialism and handicapped by its refusal to give birth to modernity. America had already taken huge technological strides and Nicholas was confronted by a world quite alien to India. It was lonely in those initial months. He rarely came in contact with fellow Indian Christians. He kept himself busy with his writing; a series of books, *Better Living*, materialised and are still popular in India. The initial sense of isolation he felt was soon to abate as he made friends with an Irish couple. Providence played a part in providing Nicholas with yet another opportunity. While on his way to enroll at Fordham University, he was offered a ride by an unknown lady. The very next day she requested him to join the Holy Name of Jesus Parish as an assistant priest, in Rochelle, an affluent New York neighbourhood. During his first mass there, he found himself to be the only brown face amidst a sea of White parishioners. Undaunted, he delivered his sermon which included a short anecdote about the Italian conductor, Arturo Toscanini. After mass, a young man came up to him to thank him for including his uncle in the sermon. Nicholas Soares had made an impression on the well-educated

19. HEATHENDOM, CHRISTENDOM

congregation.

Nicholas' trajectory of success would be unstoppable. He became the first Indian priest to be incardinated by the Archdiocese of New York, at a time when only European priests were considered suitable for the diocese. He was put in charge of St. Clement and St. Michael, both churches in Statton Island. In 1990, he was appointed Monsignor.

Nicholas had moved from India, a country that is deeply committed to its religious beliefs to a country known more for its materialistic leanings. Despite the obvious differences, Nicholas has always found American Catholics to be as devout parishioners as their counterparts elsewhere in the world. He maintains: "No matter the technological advances, no matter the wealth, no matter how much we may give God the absent-treatment, life and death invariably takes their toll on everybody and draws us closer to God."

It is ironic perhaps that the European who sailed perilous seas in order to save the world from "heathendom", who sent out missionaries by the scores so that the heathen's blackened soul could be purged, salvaged and offered to Christ, is now having his pastoral needs met by descendants of those "heathens".

20 The independent Goan

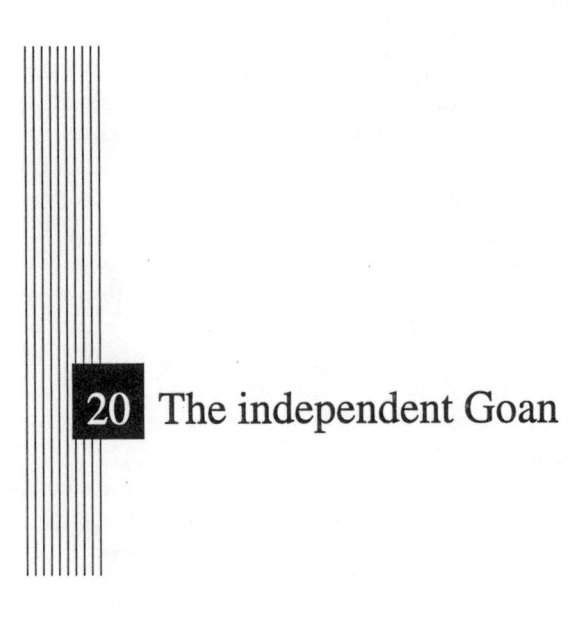

> Is it not high time that the leaders of the Goan community should cast away their years old timidity and declare in bold and unequivocal terms the legitimate aspirations of the Goans for equality in all walks of life in the country? – Eddie H. Pereira, letter to the editor, *Colonial Times*, Kisumu, Kenya, December, 12, 1945.

> Our children are Americans first and Goans second. Like so many ethnic minorities before us, the memories of the motherland will fade. Our children will vacation not in Mombasa or Goa, but in the Grand Canyons or Yosemite, criss-crossing the lands of America and in these vast plains they will be unable to see the misty slopes of the Western Ghats. – Benegal Pereira, New Hampshire, 2008.

AMERICA WAS CONCEIVED in the bosom of dissent; in the desire to flee orthodoxy, religious persecution and the overbearing weight of European monarchies stifling the very breath of freedom. Every newcomer to America must instinctively understand this national ethos which is woven into the very fabric of its politics and culture.

20. THE INDEPENDENT GOAN

Very few countries in the world have seamlessly synthesised their political ideologies into precise compartments. Despite the racial and cultural diversity, American politics is driven by just two parties; the Democrats and the Republicans. There is no third party. The Depression, the dust-bowl and Roosevelt made the Democrats the party of choice for the nation's minorities, the disadvantaged and the disenfranchised; which in the 1930s were primarily African-Americans, rural poor Whites and immigrant communities in large urban areas. Roosevelt was not particularly a man ahead of his time in matters of race relations but he was deeply aware of the indignity borne by African-Americans and the injustice mob violence wrought unto them. He frequently appealed to the Whiteman's sense of justice to navigate the compass of American morality.

Frustrated by the inaction and indifference of the nation's political establishment, Richard Hatcher, the first Black-American mayor of Indiana, expressed the hope of a third party, in a keynote address delivered at Gary, Indiana, on March 11, 1972:

> And when if they (Republicans and Democrats) leave us no choice – and if we form a third political movement, we shall take with us Chicanos, Puerto Ricans, Indians, Orientals, a wonderful kaleidoscope of colour.[1]

This hope never materialized, partly because a third front has as yet to prove sustainable in American democracy and largely because the aspirations of ethnic minorities do not overlap. What the Asian-American hopes for is not mirrored by the African-American, nor does the Latino necessarily seek the same redress as the African-American.

Benegal Pereira arrived in the United States in the 1980s. He grew up in Kenya, son of the nationalist freedom fighter Eddie Pereira. Eddie, was a Tivim*kar*, born in Mombasa, Kenya. He was a peer of J. M. Nazareth, and a member of the East African Goan National Association, a group of Goan young men, vocal in their demands for an independent Goa.

Eddie's fire-brand nationalist politics, his vehement opposition to the Portuguese regime in Goa and his perception of himself as an Indian rather than a Goan was ahead of its time and put him at odds with the Goan community in Kenya. He was profoundly affected by the inequities of colonial rule, the subordinated relationship it entailed, the disparity in income and the subjugation of individual freedom.

Benegal's early political views were greatly influenced by his father's politics. To Benegal, liberty meant "the freedom to reap what he may sow, enjoy the fruits of his own labour and pursue all possibilities open, no matter where in the social structure he was born." Unfortunately, the independence of African countries did not herald the dream of freedom for Asians. This time they found themselves at the receiving end of what some would say was racism by Africans while more benevolent commentators would call it misguided nationalism. They had exchanged one political master for another.

Benegal arrived in America at the tail-end of a recession which would remain President Carter's ill-fated legacy. What followed during President Reagan's era was a reaffirmation of novelist Horatio Alger's America; the possibility of being part of the "rags-to-riches" script. The "American Dream" was resuscitated.*

Asians are thoroughly convinced the "America Dream" is theirs to be had, if not for themselves then certainly for their children. To a very large extent, the American Dream has become a reality for many immigrants. In a 2004 American Community Survey by the US Census Bureau, the median income of an Indian family in America was found to be $69,000, about $20,000 more than what the average family in America earns.[2] This effectively makes them the wealthiest ethnic minority in America. They are likely to live in affluent neighbourhoods as well as be over-represented in the country's prestigious learning institutions. Benegal found Ronald Reagan's trickle-down economics to be an effective strategy and successful in re-invigorating the economy. Soon after taking up American citizenship in 1997, he registered as a Republican.

Indian-Americans are courted by both Republicans and Democrats during election time. Their higher incomes make them a target for fund-raising and their standing as a "model ethnic community" make them an attractive minority mascot on either side of the electoral aisle. The "Friends of India" caucus in the US Senate, formed in 2004, had as its first co-chair the then Democrat Senator Hillary Clinton as well as Republican Senator John Cornyn.

There is a steady evolution in the political consciousness of new immigrants. In the early stages where the links to the homeland are

---

*Horatio Alger was a 19th century novelist. He wrote adventure stories featuring young children from impoverished backgrounds who grow prosperous through hard work and determination.

barely severed, voting patterns are influenced by which party is seen as soft on immigration issues. Part of the family may still be back home waiting to be reunited. Identification with the homeland is strong at this point. For the Goan Diaspora in America, the concept of home is further fractured, having emigrated from Africa or the Arabian Gulf.

Benegal and I started sharing our views on the transformation of the Goan's political consciousness in America.[†] Benegal has often observed ambivalence to where community members refer to as home. For a great many Goans in America, he says, the perception of "home" is diffused. It is the African hinterlands of Kenya, Uganda or Tanzania. In these places, they came together in pocket communities. When they look back at the sub-cultures they created, they cannot duplicate that in America. There are too few Goans and they live too far apart. They do not populate urban tenements or create ethnic neighbourhoods where a language or traditions are shared. Yet they are drawn by a common bond of a vague memory of the motherland.

America, more than anywhere else in the Diaspora, is where the Goan loses his cultural, religio-ethnic identity and learns to embrace a wider one. There is nothing particular to distinguish him in the eyes of a fellow Chinese-American or Irish-American. He is forced to come to terms with being an American of Indian origin. For the first time in his Diasporic existence he does not live in the close-knit communities engendered in Africa, the comfort of sheer numbers in the Gulf region or even the organised cultural associations of England. Here he is confronted by dissipation, first geographical and secondly by an overwhelming mainstream culture which is at once facile and easily absorbed.

Though Goans rarely show the inclination to organise politically, in America, neither have they been able to recreate the strong social organizations which so mark Goan communities in the Diaspora. The sheer size of America makes its geographically impossible to garner strength in terms of numbers. There are *ad hoc* church gatherings and celebrations such as the St. Francis Xavier's feast. A few small

---

[†]Milton Esman provides a classic definition of the Diaspora consciousness: 'a minority ethnic group of migrant origin, which maintains sentimental or material links with its land of origin, either because of social exclusion, internal cohesion or other geo-political factors. It is never assimilated into the whole society but in time, develops a Diaspora's consciousness which carries out a collective sharing of space with others.' Esman M, *Diasporas and International Relations*, New York: Oxford University Press, 1996.

associations are formed by concentrations of Goans in bigger cities – the Goan Institute of San Francisco, the Goan Association of Florida and the Goan Association of New York. These are hardly significant to a Goan residing in Texas or Idaho. Their aim remains solely to meet and celebrate festive occasions.

Second generation immigrants remain ignorant and indifferent to Goa's rich literary or architectural heritage, its history and its current political problems. The emergence of virtual communities has to some extent re-ignited the spirit of community but as Benegal reflects, "It cannot replace the importance of face-to-face interactions of more traditional communities."

Interestingly, because Goans can no longer cling to a regional identity it has accelerated their assimilation into mainstream America. Goans are likely to be college-educated and employed in white-collar jobs. They have bought houses, put down roots and a few like Romulus Pereira (mentioned in the chapter *Early arrivals in the Emirates*) have gone on to become high profile businessmen. They see themselves as Americans first and Goans incidentally. They are acutely aware that the process of becoming American involves becoming conscious of the issues that affect them: health-care, education, foreign policy and national security. These issues configure their political affiliations.

Although there is no statistical evidence to validate the collective voting patterns of Goans as a community in America, we assume that they follow the pattern of the larger Indian-American electorate, which votes Democrat. The premise that Goans are hardened Democrats could be misleading. There is the more profound matter of whether Goans truly find resonance with the liberal values of the Democrat on issues such as gay rights and abortion or do they tend to be social conservatives at heart, bowing in to the power exerted by the Church. It is pertinent that two of America's most prominent political figures of Indian origin, Bobby Jindal, Governor of Louisiana, and Dinesh D'Souza, former policy advisor to President Ronald Reagan, are staunch Republicans. Dinesh is of Goan parentage and embraced the Conservative platform of American politics very early on.

Benegal's own allegiance has shifted over the years. Although he still retains a firm belief in Conservative values, he now sees the "hard-core right wing politics of fear, slogan-mongering, dogma and distortion of truth, as an attempt to preserve their place at the top."

20. THE INDEPENDENT GOAN

Benegal grew up in Western Kenya, a region that is also home to President Obama's father.

It is conceivable that he might even have crossed paths with Obama the Senior, given the small macrocosm of the region. In any event, Benegal did meet the younger Senator Obama from Illinois, the day after he announced his candidacy for the US Presidency on a campaign stop in Concord, New Hampshire. Benegal lives in New Hampshire with his wife Debbie. He is successfully employed in the pharmaceutical industry. He immediately felt a resonance with Obama's vision, which puts a "ceiling on privilege and a floor to poverty." His decision to support Obama in the 2008 election was a vote for change, the ushering in of a new era. He takes great pride in living in a country that has in place the "checks and balances" on its governance with a deep respect for the tenets of freedom enshrined in its constitution.

As the Goan in America evolves so will his political consciousness. At this stage being an Independent voter maybe the only legitimate and responsible position for Goans to take.

21 The student

IF AUTHOR TONY D'SOUZA was writing a book about my family, he would say my brother was the first born son of a Konkan. My father owed him a first-class education or at the very least one that would secure him a stable future. Like so many sons who came of age in the 1980s, my brother Levis Cardoso found himself on his way to America. The arms of the Goan Diaspora had extended wide and embraced him.

My brother was barely eighteen when the future course of his life arrived in the mail by way of a crisp letter saying he had been accepted at Brevard Community College, Florida. His only point of reference up until then had been Goa and Dubai. He had led the sort of sheltered life an adolescent boy leads in a Goan family; with his parents as dominant figures, limited interaction with the opposite sex, an emphasis on the Church and education being the path to success.

If there was fear and doubt clouding the boy's mind, we didn't see it. With all the naivety and optimism that resides in the hearts of young restless men, he boarded a plane into the unknown.

Much like him, many decades ago, our grandfather had left for

21. THE STUDENT

Africa and our father had left for Dubai. For our family, the Diaspora defined our existence. Through it all, from the plains of Kenya, to the cities of America, we were always Goans. What else could we be? What other identity could we cling to, in this life of impermanence?

Just as my brother was preparing to embark on a new life, the oldest President-elect was preparing to take his oath of office in America. Zero-degree temperatures held Washington in its grip during the second week of January, 1981. On the commencement day of inaugural festivities, Ronald Reagan and his wife Nancy listened to a military orchestra serenade them with "*A Great New Beginning*" at the Lincoln Memorial. Overcome by the solemnity of the moment Reagan remarked, "America's pretty wonderful."[1] It seemed an appropriate anthem for America, which was experiencing one of the worst recessions since the 1930s. It was also an appropriate anthem for my brother, standing on the threshold of his own adulthood. A few months later, Levis landed in America.

His initial feeling was one of disappointment. Where were all the high-rise buildings, the big cars, the men with tall cowboy hats, the cops chasing the bad guys? Endless hours of television had embedded a not uncommon stereotype of America in his mind. What greeted him instead was small town America in all its humility and geniality. Still, its newness was intoxicating. He had left the nest, the country he knew, everything that was familiar. His life beckoned. The first person to greet him was his University Advisor.

It was a predominantly White student college with isolated spots of foreign students bobbing their heads. Nonetheless his immediate peer group was the Foreign Students Association, comprising of Middle Eastern, South American and Far Eastern students. He was a long way from Goa, where he had spent his childhood cocooned in the warm folds of his grandmother's love, chasing pigs, running after buses and stealing mangoes. He was even a long way from Dubai; a society which had subtly indicated to him that Whites were superior and Asians subordinated. The friendly, laid-back Americans were a welcome change. His world was already changing. The relationships and *status quo* had been reinvented.

As a student he escaped much of the prejudice attached to first generation immigrants who make their way straight on to the American job market. F.O.B, or Fresh Off the Boat, is a frequently used disparaging acronym for new immigrants. Its etymology could refer to the original *Mayflower* that landed with the Pilgrims, the ships that brought in droves of European immigrants into Ellis Island, the boats that carried slaves to the Deep South or the tiny sails that routinely try to cross over from Cuba to Florida carrying onboard illegal aliens. Whatever its origins, it does wrenchingly bring home the fact that America is formed by waves and waves of immigrants that wash onto its shores and that each wave of immigrant is the subject of much bigotry until they conform to certain standards.

There is nothing America loves more than standardization and homogenization, particularly of dress and language. In fact so averse are Americans to people who can't speak English, they consider it an affront to their sense of nationalism. Even the use of Spanish, which is the second most widely spoken language in American, is hotly contested and resented. The dress code in America is blue-jeans and a T-shirt. Anyone wearing turbans, national costumes, displaying obvious signs of ethnic, religious or cultural affiliations, would come in for curious if not disapproving looks.

There were myriad adjustments to grapple with all at the same time but, in this free and libertine society, Levis had to make friends across the racial divide and the gender divide. It was a frightening and yet exciting moment for a young man who for the first time encounters life without the reins of his parents pulling him inwards.

Meanwhile, President Reagan declared 1983 a Banner Year for America. Whether it was Reagan's interest rates cutbacks and deficit spending policies or capitalism's natural cycle of bust and boom, by 1983, inflation had fallen to 3.2%, the dollar saw its highest rise in ten years and a growth rate of 4.5% was anticipated by the Commerce Department.[2] There were still men, women and children queuing up outside American soup-kitchens, some jobless, others had lost their homes and been forced to live in shelters or shabby hotels. A situation Edwin Meese, one of Reagan's senior aides, would explain away as: "Because the food is free and that's easier than paying for it."[3]

Reagan himself, would go on ABC's Good Morning America on January 31, 1984, and assure Americans that "The people who are sleeping on the grates, the homeless who are homeless, you might say, by choice." American optimism and belief in the capitalist way had been reaffirmed; this was the era of "greed is good" and can ultimately deliver you to redemption. Although Levis remained a Democrat in his political affiliations, the lessons of self-reliance, initiative

21. THE STUDENT

and capitalist *chutzpah* were ones he took to heart.

He transferred from Brevard Community College to University of South Florida, Tampa, rented an apartment with two other roommates, bought an old car and supplemented his income by delivering pizza and dyeing shoes to match wedding dresses. More importantly, he began dating. The chrysalis of self-doubt was shedding and a confident young man emerging. At times, he found relationships with Americans superficial, transient, lacking in intimacy and culturally confusing.

His room-mate invited him to "his father's wedding", quite shocking for Levis who came from a culture where divorce and remarriage were still taboo subjects. On another occasion, a friend invited him to "his parent's house." To Levis, his parents house had always been his house. But this was a society where ties with the family were respected within clear-set boundaries. The emphasis was on individual freedom, exploration and discovery. Dubai had been a closed society, not allowing him the space to think, never allowing him the opportunity to be an involved and respected citizen. Goa held few economic opportunities. America was home.

More than twenty-five years later, he still lives in Tampa, Florida with his family.

22 The young bride

AS THE COOL WINDS of February 1946 gusted over the paddy fields, a huge white *matov*, a canopy, was hastily erected outside Paulina Antoinette's house under the generous shade of an umbrella-like mango tree. The skinny, seventeen year old girl from amongst six siblings was getting married to a man she didn't know. Her fiancé, Pascoal Fernandes from the neighbouring *vaddo*, worked as a tailor in Bombay. He was a handsome youth, with a quick step about him, if a little shy and retiring. His earnings were meagre but he had prospects. His brother was in Africa. It was a good match and the Cardoso house was filled with the sort of lightness that pervades in anticipation of a new life. Paulina Antoinette was my aunt, my father's sister.

Soon after the wedding Pascoal returned to Bombay, leaving behind a pregnant Antoinette. She spent much of her time at her parent's house, doing the growing up she needed to do in order to become a wife and, soon, mother.

Months later, the shades of the *dakle salle*, the smaller reception room often used as a bedroom, were drawn. Neighbouring housewives gathered in the room and the mid-wife Ellen was called to attend to

22. THE YOUNG BRIDE

the birth. After hours of praying, reciting the rosary and labouring, Menino Fernandes screamed his way into the world. His father returned from Bombay to join in the celebrations.

Shortly, Pascoal left Goa for Kenya, leaving Antoinette in the full-bloom of pregnancy once again. Xavier Fernandes, was born in his maternal grandmother's house and didn't see his father until he was seven years old. His father often sent them presents of clothes and sweets from Africa with people who returned on holiday. All Menino and Xavier knew of their father was that he lived in a land where "sweets grew on trees." The boys grew up in a noisy household of aunts and uncles who fawned on them as first grand-children. The void of their absentee father was filled by the warmth that unfolded from their extended family. In 1956, their father returned from Nairobi to take all of them to an unknown land. They set sail on the *S. S. Karanja* from Mormugão Port, via Karachi and onto Mombasa, a diverted route because of the economic blóckade imposed by the Indian government in 1955.

The *Karanja* was one of the most celebrated ships in the British India fleet plying the Indian Ocean route. Consigned to fond memory by so many East African Goans. To the young boys, Menino and Xavier, the eleven-day voyage was an adventure; running on the deck, watching the hull of the ship cut through the deep green waters of the Indian Ocean and the excitement of having their father's undivided attention for the first time.

Antoinette was pregnant during the voyage and spent most of her days at the sick-bay. She had grown from an insecure teenage girl into a confident mother during Pascoal's long absence from Goa. She had survived child-birth and nursed her sons through sickness, angst and anxiety. Yet she didn't really know what it was to be a wife. She had left the safety of her parent's house, the mango tree she had climbed as a child, the paddy fields that skirted the narrow roads leading to the village church, sisters with whom she had stayed up late, and brothers who were possibly the only young adult male figures in her life, to live in a foreign land with a man she barely knew.

Mustering all the romantic hope that cocoons itself in a woman's heart, she steeled her nerves and set sail for Africa. Here was Kenya, populated by White settlers, Africans and Indians. She was a stranger to such diversity. She could speak neither English nor Swahili and felt isolated in this new world. She had moved from a good sized ancestral house to a much smaller dwelling. Despite the odds being stacked against her, she fell deeply in love with her husband and equally in love with Kenya. She would spend nearly twenty years in Africa, reluctantly returning only in 1974.

Long before the term "NRI grooms" became part of the lexicon, single men working in Africa and before that in Bombay, would return home to Goa to find themselves a bride. Historian Dr Teresa Albuquerque cites Ino Godinho, *In the Mission Field* (1927):

> Times were when annually brides would be brought from Malvan, Vingurla and also Goa for the purpose of marriage in Bombay and Salsette. These lasses were much appreciated for the thorough training they had undergone in their Konkan homes in agricultural and industrial pursuits. The agents engaged in this business received handsome commissions for the interesting bevy of maidens they brought from Goa and the blue mountains about the beginning of every year.[1]

The men who came to Goa, from Africa, seeking wives were slightly older gentlemen, who would invariably take young brides. Sometimes the intended bride and groom would not even have the opportunity to meet. It was almost a mail-order business with the entire arrangement made through letters of inquiry, reference and agreement.

The women, in order to facilitate their travel to Africa, would be married by civil registration. Anecdotal stories tell of how a proxy would stand in for the groom, if the groom could not travel back to Goa. Shortly following the civil ceremony, the woman would set sail for Africa having never met her husband but being wed to him for eternity. It is the courage of these young, spirited, women willing to forsake all that was familiar to them and accompany men to distant lands that enabled Goans to flourish in self-sustaining communities in the Diaspora. They were expected to bear and rear children, tutor them, impart in them Goan values and culture such as traditional cooking, singing, needle-work and prayers. With the fall of the British Empire and the return of the *Afrik'kar* or his re-emigration to other parts of the world, the Gulf groom, US Green-card holder and UK passport holder then became much sought after grooms.

Melina Tereza Conceição was just eighteen years old when she met the imposingly tall Tony Pereira at the International Youth Convention, held in Goa in 1990, organised by leading personalities

22. THE YOUNG BRIDE

spread across the Goan Diaspora. Tony was amongst the many young Goans from UK, Canada and the US attending the conference and hoping to learn more about his culture. Tony was born in Africa but his family had migrated to the US when he was a young lad. Melina was a volunteer at the Convention. There was an instant attraction, a down-to-earth simplicity about Tony, which drew her to him.

The lissome girl with the easy smile was still in college. Meeting a man and marriage were far from her mind. She is the daughter of Edward Conceição and Kate Pinheiro, from Aldona, a quaint rustic village peppered with picturesque houses obviously built on remittances from expat earnings in the north of Goa. As with most Goan parents, their expectations for their young daughter focused on education and then maybe finding a job, but Melina had set her heart on Tony. After a few years of long distance courting, Melina arrived in San Francisco on a fiancée's visa in 1994. The US K-1 fiancé(e) visa came into existence precisely to accommodate girls like Melina. Prior to the K-1, only a spouse could be sponsored into the US; but given the seriousness of marriage and the high rate of divorce in America, the government allows for a period of familiarization and adjustment, enabling a fiancé a ninety-day stay in the country, providing for much needed time to make the important decision. Leaving her family was a huge step for Melina. She had never been outside of India. But she was confident of what she was doing. She had an instinctive, gut-level feel that this was her destiny, the man of her dreams.

Melina had to adjust to a new human being who was now her husband, a new family and a new country. She was struck by America's ethnic and cultural diversity. Having grown up in a homogenised society, where everybody looked and dressed alike, this was a country of uninhibited people, in dress and attitude. It was the heady 1990s, there were women with spiked hair and men with body piercings. Despite its unfamiliarity, she felt comfortable in her new surroundings. Her more immediate concerns were growing into the role of wife and companion. She had to learn to cook and tend to the house. Domestic help was taken for granted in Goa but non-existent in the US.

She was grateful that Tony came from the same cultural background as her, and that they shared similar values and life experiences, even if they had been shaped in different parts of the world. For Goan-American men who seek girls from Goa it is this familiarity that brings comfort and consonance. The emphasis is on extended family relationships rather than nuclear units and the determination to make an honest effort in the business of marriage.

Girls arriving from Goa, have a distinct advantage. To a large extent, middle-class Goan girls are influenced by that great American export – pop-culture. They grow up listening to Bruce Springsteen, watching CNN and Bold and Beautiful. Western liberal attitudes are not shocking, at best they are mildly amusing. Their transition to American society is almost seamless.

For all the success stories, there are failures as well – more so as the complexity of human sexuality, emotional needs and intellectual compatibility grows. Goan Americans date across the racial divide. They have relationships at college and work. They bond with people who share common interests, politics and points of reference. Their sexual and intellectual expectations are influenced by these experiences. Commonality of interests and core beliefs makes for stronger relationships than commonality of culture alone.

There is something in the human psyche that resists diluting the gene-pool. It is this instinct which propels us to marry within our frame of cultural reference, people who look like us, dress like us and behave like us. Yet there is another pull that makes mankind want to spread his genes as widely as possibly. It is at best a difficult choice to be wedged between the expectations fostered by tradition and ones that are aroused by personal needs. Whatever the choice one makes, marriage is a kaleidoscope of colours that one ultimately adjusts to find the perfect picture.

23 Race relations

> Goa is a sleepy hollow of a place whose inhabitants have no greater ambition than to find employment on British territory... in addition to the natives, Goa has a considerable population of half-castes, who although black as Africans, pride themselves as having Portuguese blood in their veins. They are a pugnacious and litigious lot, and idle withal, not to mention a little weakness for alcohol. – *The Graphic*, September 27, 1890.

IT WAS WARM in the last week of November 1875, but the Portuguese Governor in Goa was not particularly preoccupied with the weather. He had been informed at the last minute by Lisbon of a possible visit to Goa by the Prince of Wales, Edward VII and that all honours must be shown to him.[1]

The Prince was touring India, perhaps with a view to better understanding this jewel in the Empire, for two years later his mother, Queen Victoria, would be crowned Empress of India. Edward himself would occupy the seat very late and very briefly in his life, being crowned Emperor in 1901. By then, a substantial number of Goans had settled in British India's principal city of Bombay.

23. RACE RELATIONS

His boat, the *Serapis*, moored just off the coast of Goa. A crowd of Goans and Portuguese gathered to greet the illustrious guest. An account of his visit appearing on the *Graphic*, December 4, 1875, read:

The Prince of Wales and the Governor of Goa on their way to the Cathedral at Old Goa, 1875, engraving from *The Illustrated London News*.

> The inhabitants – the Goanese are a mixed breed of Portuguese, Hindoos and Africans, "blacker in hue," a writer to the *Daily Telegraph* tells us "than almost any natives of the Peninsular, and very useful as cooks, interpreters, nurses and body-servants.[2]

The Press was subscribing to stereotypes of Goans which pervaded British India at the time. A more unguarded version of which comes from Richard Burton, the English explorer, when he describes Goans as "the lowest in the scale of civilised humanity,"[3] in *Goa and the Blue Mountains*. He thought of Goans as "cookboys", "dry-nurses" and "buttrels" who came to "wealthy British India" to gather rupees.*

The majority of Goans who made their way to British India filled the ranks of the working class. It was easy to cast them as ayahs, butlers and cooks, but was there possibly another self-serving reason for the perpetuation of the stereotype?

The British carried within them as much zeal for reform as did the Portuguese but it occurred to them early on that in a populous, mutinous sub-continent it would be fool-hardy to intrude on the slumber of tradition and religion. In any case, the Briton was possessed of a certain aloofness, a northern chill in his relations with the indigenous population. The British saw themselves as men of morality, altruism,

---

*"Scions of that half pariah race which yearly issues from Goa, Daman and Diu to gather Rupees as "cook-boys", dry-nurses and "buttrels" in wealthy British India." Burton R F, *The Lake Regions of Central Africa*, New York: Harper & Brother, 1860, pg 104.

the more able administrators, adjudicators of justice entrusted with the burdensome task of civilising the world, not so much through religion but more so by way of the steam engine. The Portuguese they saw as effete and their subjects the outcome of emasculated governance.

Marquess Wellesley, Governor-General of India (1798-1805), flaunted that the British governed "the most opulent flourishing part of India in which property, life, civil order and liberty are more secure... than any other country in this quarter of the globe."[4] The image of the impoverished working class, alcohol-sodden Goan, reinforced repeatedly, much like a latter-day commercial, reminded the Indian of just how grateful he should be for being colonised by a North European, Protestant power rather than an enfeebled, Southern European Catholic nation.

Racism and stereotype is not the monopoly of Western civilizations. Goans carried their own prejudice against Africans, a bias which took root in Goa itself. The Portuguese were notorious slave-traders. Much of the African population that inhabits remote corners of the world, from South America to Arabia, owes its Diaspora to the slave trade that proved so lucrative to Arab and European sea-faring powers. The African slaves brought into Goa were subjected to all the rigours and indignity that went with bondage; considered a sub-human species and auctioned in the open market at the *"O Leilão"* on the Rua Direita, the central thoroughfare of the capital city of Goa in the 17th century. Here traders haggled as belligerently over slaves as they did over horses. The younger women, mostly from Mozambique, were paraded nude, so as to entice a higher bidder.[5] Slaves were discarded if they fell ill or beaten and buried in the backyard.[6] However reprehensible life might have been as a colonised people, it couldn't possibly compare with that of being slaves. Helpless, fearful, ruthlessly uprooted from their own surroundings and sold into a life of unendurable abjection, they elicited disdain in the Goan rather than sympathy. It is part of the human condition to stand aback from those crushed and humiliated.

Stereotypes of the *khampri* prevailed: black, primitive, uncouth and uneducated. Tales of his perceived stupidity have become part of our lore. There is the often repeated story of *"Khampri Augustine"* who is told to go to Panjim and does so but does not have the presence of mind to question the purpose of his visit. The word *khampri* itself is invariably used as a pejorative either in reference to a dark complexion

23. RACE RELATIONS

or extreme stupidity.

The other encounter Goans had with Africans was of them as troops in the Portuguese garrisons. Did their ferociousness instill fear which curdled into hatred? In March 1942, the Portuguese sailboat *Zarco Gonçalves* escorting the troopship *João Belo* docked at Mormugão on its interrupted voyage to East Timor. Portuguese Timor had come under attack by the Dutch, catching Portugal off-guard and re-enforcements had been sent from her colonies in Africa. The troopship carried onboard two companies of European troops and African fighters from Mozambique. Altogether a total of a 1000 men sojourned in Goa.

Unfortunately, the living quarters assigned to the African troops did not have adequate provisions for nature calls. The men took to defecating on Goan beaches.[7] No doubt, the dark African roaming the beaches of Goa in search of a spot to relieve himself was seen as a predatory creature pouncing on unsuspecting women. There was much fear of miscegenation, a general belief that African men were incapable of controlling their lust. Calls of alert would go out if they were seen in the vicinity. Some families are rumoured to have moved residence. There were certainly sexual encounters between Africans and Goan women but they were consensual in nature. The off-spring of such unions were adopted by childless families, as *posken* or *afilhado*, or taken in by charity houses. The notion of the uncivilised and sexually unbridled African germinated on our own soil and then travelled to the plains of East Africa.

The colonization of East Africa by the British presented an unique situation; a three-tiered society. At the top of the pyramid with a share of the country's most fertile lands were the White settlers. In the middle was a tier of Indian traders, thought to be economic interlopers but tolerated to the extent the British sense of justice could accommodate. Goans were grist for the mill of Empire, the indispensable middle-agent and favoured race juxtaposed against Indians whom they weren't particularly fond of. Milling at the bottom were Africans, disenfranchised from any substantive power in their own countries.

Goans were not exempt from the colour bar which persisted in East Africa. In some shops, there were separate entrances for Whites and non-Whites, separate washrooms at the railway stations and entry to "Whites only" hotels and establishments was prohibited. Living areas were racially segregated. Upward mobility on the job front was limited. Their position was always subordinated to the British; at times bullied and their official authority questioned by anyone who happened to be White. Nonetheless they enjoyed a unique position. A relationship of absolute trust and dependency when it came to dealing with Africans; the sort of trust which exists between a parent and favourite child diminished only by the child being an unequal in the relationship.

Mervyn Maciel, who had been orphaned when the *S. S. Tilawa* was tragically torpedoed in World War II (see chapter *The War Years*), returned to Kenya after his education in India and rose to the position of District Clerk, working mostly in the Northern District Frontier. (Joseph Maciel remained in Bombay and entered the Society of Jesus seminary and, Wilfred Maciel, after further studying in the UK, returned to Kenya to become a prominent journalist.) Mervyn, author of the book *Bwana Karani*, recounted to me that often he was left in-charge of the out-post if the District Commissioner was away. He would have to visit political prisoners at a time when Kenya was making its nationalist aspirations felt, censor their mail, carry out inspections and even oversee the caning of prisoners.

Interestingly, racism's changing face was dependent not on colour but geographical terrain. A hapless Goan in British India was a valued ally in British East Africa. Michael George Power, a British District Officer who served at Kilifi and Taita Hills District, 1949-53, speaks of this symbiotic relationship. He says the Secretariat in Kenya would have "collapsed completely without the excellent Goan clerks" who worked there, describing them as honest and meticulous and according to Power, "because you never trust an African with money."[8] The British relationship with Africans was ambivalent; they thought of them as either delinquents to be patronised by paternalism or feckless, petty thieves, not to be trusted. Some Goans held fairly responsible positions of overseeing Africans subordinated to them in offices and on private estates. What effect did this role of intermediary have on Goans and their relationship with Africans?

Dr Cornel DaCosta, the sprightly academic and writer of Goan origin, was born into Kenya's complex society of imposed racial segregation and shared his views with me. Interaction between the races, he says, was minimal except in work situations and in some areas of sport. The territories were deemed to 'belong' to the Europeans whose hegemony was strongly dominant.

23. RACE RELATIONS

That the true inheritors of the territories were indeed the Africans featured little in the consciousness of the three 'races', including the Africans. The Africans mainly undertook work of a menial nature for the Europeans and Asians. In commercial establishments, they would be watchmen, gardeners, cleaners, vehicle drivers, kitchen staff and the like. The academic qualifications of the Europeans were generally unknown but they did hold the top jobs everywhere! Asians did not have actual power to effect their prejudice against the African but there was relatively little socialization outside of sport. Yet, even in sport, Cornel recalls, a Sikh hockey player who strongly expressed the view that "we Asians built up Kenya and don't see why we should give it all up to the Africans at independence."

The other contact Goans had with Africans, Cornel acknowledges, was when they employed African nannies and house servants. Often, such domestic labour had to be accommodated within the household and not many households had necessary residential provisions. In some cases, fairly good housing was available to the Goans, as employees of the East African Railways and Harbours. In such housing quarters, a room for the domestic house servant would be available for those willing to pay for such services. In general, not many had suitable accommodation even if they were willing to pay for a house servant. Domestic help usually shopped for groceries, cleaned, cooked and assisted the *'memsahib'* and, was paid on a negotiated monthly wage. In a few cases, liberal Goan employers of such domestic staff would try to teach English to the Swahili speaking employees either themselves or through evening classes if available nearby. However, most interaction with the domestic staff was in spoken Swahili with which the Goans had generally acquainted themselves in small measure. Certain African domestic workers such as from the Wakamba tribe were deemed to be more reliable and honest and were more acceptable than the Luo tribe. Inverted racism was all too prevalent, thinking of Africans as "wogs" who couldn't be trusted, although such terminology was rare.

The independence of African colonies led to the largest exodus of Indians and Goans out of Africa. Two decades after the expulsions, movie producer, Mira Nair's camera scans the picture of a headmaster standing in front of the Norman Godinho School on Buganda Road, Kampala in Uganda, founded by the philanthropic Goan, Norman Godinho. Except of course the protagonists of Mira Nair's classic film, *Mississippi Masala*, are an Indian family, no longer living in Uganda but have been forced to emigrate to Mississippi, the deep South of America. The move compels the family to examine their own racial biases against African-Americans. Denzil Washington, gives a raw performance as Demetrius Williams and sums up the bias with the classic line "you think you are better than us."

To the Indian, and by extension the Goan, the Black American is an enigma. The world media, a convent education and popular culture may acquaint the Indian to some extent with the psyche of the White America but nothing prepares him for the wounds of the Black American.

Traditionally the Blacks have been America's largest ethnic minority, now superseded by the Latinos. Having migrated to the North from the Deep South in search of employment, they are concentrated in the inner-cities of Chicago, New York, Detroit, Cleveland and Philadelphia. Sadly, they are ghettoised in these areas while the affluent White population has spread into the suburbs. It remains largely resistant to Black residential integration, although willful segregation is prohibited under the Fair Housings Act of 1968.

First generation Indians who migrated to the US, in the early 1970s and took over the 7-Eleven shops, the fast-food franchises and motel chains have progressed up the social and financial ladder. The other Indian export to America is the doctor, the foreign student and the IT engineer. He is America's richest minority with a personal income that exceeds the national average, as noted earlier. Asians in the US are the most likely ethnic minority to live in mixed-neighbourhoods away from their own ethnicity and in the plush suburbs.

The gulf between the two communities, Indian and African, is more than economic disparity. It is a fundamental difference in how aspiration is channelized. While the Indian is quiet, reclusive, submissive and ever ready to fade into the background, the Black is vocal in his protest of inequality. The Indian's belief in the virtue of a solid scholastic career, the work ethnic, marriage, strong condemnation of children born out of wedlock, self-sustaining family units, low propensity for crime and an acute embarrassment to be on welfare, mirrors the cultural ideals hailed by mainstream America. It has lead to success in a society that rewards these values. The ghettoization of Blacks and the inherent cycle of poverty that the ghetto brings has lead to a stereotype of the Black American, as most likely to fail

23. RACE RELATIONS

scholastically, exhibit a poor work ethnic, display a high incidence of promiscuity, single-parenthood and dependence on welfare. While the Indian is hailed as the "model ethnic minority" the Black is perceived as playing to his sense of victimhood and insisting on his "forty acres and a mule," a reference to compensation promised to slaves after the American Civil War of 1861.

Attitudes to race and the shaping of stereotypes are a component of collective cultural biases. They are subtly transferred from generation to generation. Conservative argument believes stereotype is based on factual information and that at every point evidence constantly reinforces the stereotype. Liberal attitudes make allowance for disparities of income and opportunity and acknowledge that, fundamentally, human beings are all the same. Is the Goan a liberal or a conservative when it comes to questions of race? Would the Goan have viewed the African-American differently had he arrived on American shores without the burden of his own viewpoint shaped by his unique history with the African?

There is little social interaction in America between the Goan community and Blacks. The odd White American is an honorary guest at Goan social functions but relationships with Blacks are conspicuous only in their absence, although among the more progressive Goans a glacial change is taking place. While inter-racial marriages between White Americans and Goans are generally a source of pride for Goan Catholic parents, between Blacks and Goans they would be a very rare if not unheard event. Conversely, to the Black American every ethnic minority entering America is seen as a direct threat to his livelihood.

Melvin was registered as a job-candidate whilst I was working in a recruitment agency in Minnesota. He had been unsuccessful for some time in finding a job and the frustration wore him down. He accused me of being racist and not forwarding his resume to prospective employers. I asked him politely if he had seen my colour lately, it wasn't very different from his.

Racism is rarely about colour. It embodies a complexity of issues, our innate human desire to dominate, to establish a pecking order and place ourselves favourably in that order, to distance ourselves from the victimised and ally with the successful. Being an African American is the hardest job Melvin has in America.

24 Colour of friendship

OUR WORLD IS RENT asunder by the politics of hate, chauvinism of the extremist and the ranting of the self-righteous; but it is redeemed by the hope of friendship. There have been few times in my life when I have become acutely and painfully conscious of my skin colour being brown. An occasion presented itself while sitting in the cafeteria at American Insurance (name changed).

I was on temporary assignment in the audio-transcription unit and my boss, Janice Krus, took me to lunch at the in-house cafeteria. There amidst a sea of White faces, I sat like a piece of brown shipwreckage, staring down into my egg and potato salad.

Back at the audio-transcription unit, comprising of seven women and one college-going lad, the atmosphere was definitely one of easy camaraderie. The type only women are capable of engineering. Not that there wasn't enough catty politics to keep the local gazette in business but it never reached the malignant proportions that dominate male corridors of power.

I was the new girl on campus and these women were oblivious to my colour. They adopted me like I had been abandoned at birth and

24. COLOUR OF FRIENDSHIP

left on the doorsteps of a nunnery. One girl was particularly enamoured by me. We would chat about the most inconsequential things; countries we hoped to visit, our mothers-in-law, our husbands, our honeymoons and our desire to have children. The fact that we had lived entire lifetimes in different countries and different cultures did not matter.

Our stories were eerily similar, if one changed the names of places and people involved. By then, George Bush had convinced the country to invade Iraq, that the threat of terror was everywhere, that "you're either with us or against us in the fight against terror." The politics of her country and my divergent views never affected our personal relationship. There were times we discussed it marginally but it was irrelevant to our friendship.

America expanded my world. It taught me that friendship can straddle cultural and racial divides. That the heart was the most malleable of muscles. Over the course of years I made many friends; our dearest Goan friends, the Cordeiros, my German friend Dr Christiana Sieler who survived World War II, and my wonderful Korean friend Gin who survived life on a rural Mennonite farm. Friendships are woven from the delicate strands of hope found in Pandora's last box.

Seven years had passed in the blink of an eye. During which time, our daughter Lauren was born. She was an American by birth and a Goan above all else. It was cold as we left for the airport, the bare ground peeping above the tufts of snow, bore the promise of spring. My daughter looked out of the car window, waving goodbye to the only world she had known. I had lived most of my life in Dubai and had never been part of it. I was not part of America either, but I was taking a part of America with me; my daughter.

Part IV

A Mighty Empire

25 My Beautiful Launderette

WE ARRIVED IN LONDON in 2008. My husband had been assigned to yet another overseas project. Our wandering lifestyle had earned us the tag of latter-day nomads. I was reminded of that journey my mother took many years ago to follow her husband to the Arabian Gulf. Much like her, I now had a child of my own, clinging to me at Heathrow Airport.

Owing to its proximity to my husband's place of work, we took up a flat on the outskirts of Greater London. Here, I suffered a cultural shock of bare-chested men with more tattoo than arm, women who made swearing into an Olympic sport and children gearing to be members of the Football Hooligan Club.

I was in a titty land of foul language and uncouth yobs. The image of Somerset Maugham's England and the idea of the quintessential English gentlemen formed by watching far too many episodes of Sir Nigel Hawthorne in *"Yes Minister"* was crumbling before my very eyes. Our slick, modern development of flats rose incongruously in the midst of red-brick houses and became my refuge in a city where people seemed to be perpetually frigid or on edge.

25. My Beautiful Launderette

Perhaps a lot had changed since Stephen Frears produced his ground-breaking film, *My Beautiful Launderette*, 1985, in which the Asian protagonist is the victim of both racial prejudice and homophobia. Perhaps right-wing extremists didn't go around smashing shop windows in 2008, but to me it was a society ill at ease with itself. Grudgingly coming to terms with diversity.

Let me not sound too strident a note on what I call racial disintegration. I have come across spectacularly good people across the globe whose generosity of spirit has literally saved my life. The British lady who decided my grocery-laden bag was too heavy for me and carried it for two blocks has to figure quite high on that list. Something in the human spirit recognizes we are all fellow-travellers on this planet. That we are not terribly different in the way we think, act and bleed. However, this spirit of understanding does not translate to communities. Whole communities remain segregated, strangers at sea, scrambling to establish identity and reinforce whatever differences exist, however superficial.

We are in full-blown celebration of Freud's "narcissism of minor differences". Investments made in trying to integrate communities are facile attempts at band-aiding this lamentable condition of segregated co-existence. The human psyche seeks mirrors for reflected racial or cultural features. How does one reconcile the need for familiarity with the fact that much societal success has been achieved through constant widening of the gene pool? Indeed the reproductive gene is designed to cast as wide a net as possible.

As I walk the streets of London, board the red double-decker buses and sit in sterile restaurants with glass facades, I can't help but notice the small, quiet lives that immigrants and ethnic minorities lead.

Doubtless, minorities have done well for themselves as doctors, barristers and permeated all levels of society. I don't mean to purge them of their status in British society. But a substantial mass are disenfranchised from mainstream society, still floundering on its periphery, unrepresented in politics and often misrepresented by the print media, leading segregated lives in the Southalls of the UK. They are immigrants in perpetuity, robotic and purposeless save for the expediency of survival. These people have learnt to ask little and to fade away when trouble looms large, as it often does for them. I can imagine the lives of these invisible people in the 1960s when racism was almost a badge of honour and there persisted an imagined threat to British identity.

As late as 1979, Southall witnessed bloody race-riots, when the neo-Nazi National Front (NF) tried to hold a public meeting during an election campaign in a predominantly Asian community. According to its constitution, the British National Party (BNP) which is consistently anti-immigration, advocates "firm but voluntary incentives for immigrants and their descendants to return home."[1]

In 1997, the Goan Welfare Association was invited by the group Resistance to distribute leaflets to homes in the Merton area, to counter the propaganda and lies peddled by the BNP. That Asian communities persevered, under these circumstances, is testimony only to the resilience of the human spirit and its need to survive against all odds.

My initial opinion of Britain would mollify over the course of time, if for no other reason than the fact that it had opened its doors and provided opportunity to so many Goans. According to the 1901 Census, there were 139 Goans in London, most of whom would have been a floating population of *tarvottis*. The numbers have certainly grown since then, although official estimates do not exist because they are now part of the larger Indian community for census purposes.

Britain is now home to second and third-generation Goans who think of themselves as Goan-English. In the words of one second-generation Goan, "I consider myself to be a bit of both, Goan and English. I am influenced by the English at school and my life in the Performing Arts, but I still maintain my Goan background and will never deny my Goan identity, of which I am very proud but equally proud to be British."

The Goan's relationship with the Briton begins on a ship.

26 Setting sail with the English

> Darkies from the Deep... There are full-blooded negroes from Gambia, and half-caste Portuguese from Goa... neither easy to be distinguished... nor capable of being understood by any Englishman. – *Daily News*, England, May 29, 1872

SOMETIME IN THE late 1800s, able-bodied Costa Santan embarked on a career at sea, which had him working on the ship, *Warterm*.[1] Possibly in his twenties and through the help of an agent or *Ghat Sarhang* as they were called in Bombay, he landed a job sailing with the English.

London's Dockland area has been transformed in recent years by development projects. Here amidst gleaming towers of glass and steel, with elegant yachts moored along waterways that rip inlands, I find it hard to imagine the rat-infested squalor that pervaded between mast and mist at turn of 19th century England. Yet, this is precisely where Santan landed.

It was winter and he was not keeping well. Weary, cold, possibly suffering from a chest congestion, malaria, cholera, yellow fever or any number of accidents that likely befell seamen, he made his way

26. SETTING SAIL WITH THE ENGLISH

to a sailor-town around the docks. Hilton Docker (1809) a medical doctor appointed to tend to seamen wrote in a letter to the Shipping Committee of the East India Company:

> The natives of India who come to this country are mostly of bad constitutions. Numbers are landed sick from the ships, where they have been ill a great part of the voyage... those who are landed healthy are of course exposed to the same danger of climate and season; and in addition almost all of them give way to every excess in drinking, debauchery and contract...[2]

Little evidence is left today of the important role the localities of Limehouse, Wapping and Shadwell played, as sailor-towns. Wapping, once made the historian John Stow (1525-1605) rant and call it "a continual street or filthy strait passage with alleys of small tenements or cottages built, inhabited by sailors' victuallers."[3] These lodgings put a roof above Asian seafarers' heads, as they waited for a ship-master to engage their services for the return journey home. Crew were not bound by a contract and had to secure work by themselves for the return journey home.

Strangers' Home for Asiatic Seamen. Engraving from *The Illustrated London News*, 1870.

Some of the original houses of the early 19th century still line-up shoulder to shoulder, on either side of narrow alleys criss-crossing through Wapping and Shadwell. Walking through these narrow alleys, Santan would have watched Chinese men smoking opium in the dark lodgings known as "joints", foreign-smelling food hanging from the rafters, soliciting prostitutes scouring the streets and Asian seamen milling about peddling knick-knacks to keep body and soul together.

Mortality rates from disease, venereal amongst them, were high. Conditions were so wretched that it caused an outcry in Victorian England. In 1857, the "Strangers' Home for Asiatic Seamen" was built on West India Dock Road, to assist with boarding. In 1872, some 23 men from Bombay and Goa resided at the Strangers' Home.[4] Despite the improvement in the dwellings provided to Asian sea-farers, as late as in 1920, health inspectors condemned the *"godowns"* used by P&O liners to house their sailors while docked.

In a world of racial inequality, Santan was engaged because he cost much less than an English seaman. The 1901 census puts the wages for a British seaman between £3 to £4 pounds per journey, while an Indian might be paid between 15 to 20 rupees, about a £1 (In 1898, 15 rupees was pegged to a £1.) Wages were usually paid once the ship had docked but if the seamen was engaged on another ship for the return journey, then wages were handed over to the new shipmaster. *

But frequently, Asian seamen were abandoned by their shipmasters once they docked until mid-twentieth century legislation bound ships to ensure continuous employment.

Onboard the ship, Santan Costa was a steward attached to the saloon of the ship, the *Topaz*. Goans were rarely employed below deck. They were almost always engaged either as cooks or stewards. British captains depended tremendously on them to look after their comforts while at sea just as they might have depended on a butler or a valet back in England.

In 1957, Captain Baillie of P&O liner wrote: "I have never failed to appreciate the cleanliness, discipline and comfort of our ships in which the deck hands are *lascars* and the stewards mostly Goanese".[5] *Tarvottis* enjoyed a fair amount of privilege onboard ships. Cooks were paid higher wages than their African or Indian counterparts. They were accommodated separately from their Indian counterparts and a differentiation maintained between Indian seamen who were generically called *lascari* and the Goans referred to simply as Goanese. †

But life at sea was hard, and the ship was often a jutting splinter of racial discord amongst crew members. English seamen saw them as servile, obsequious and damned useless in cold weather.

To the English sailor, the poorly paid Indian seafarer was a threat to his own livelihood. Beatings were common onboard ships. A Se-

---

*"In the ordinary case of the man being subsequently engaged on another ship for return to India, the wages should be handed over to the master of that ship for payment when the man is finally discharged in India." – A letter to the Secretary, Board of Trade, dated October 1912, 25, National Archives Kew, BT 15/62.

†In a British House of Commons debate (1899), the President of the Board of Trade asks incredulously, "Does the Honourable Gentleman say that these Goanese Christians live and sleep in the same space area as the Mohammedan lascars do?" *Hansard*, House of Commons Debate, March 28, 1899 vol 69 cc 661-8 661, 666

bastian Dias who was hired in June 1915 died of a heart-attack just eight months later, while at sea.[6] Joaquim Souza, who was engaged onboard the *Baron Balfour* in 1914, committed suicide nine months into the voyage.[7] An 1802 report on two ships, the *Union* and *Perseverance*, gave such graphic details of brutal conditions onboard that the Committee of Shipping could not "help shuddering at the inhumanity of those in charge."[8]

Sailing with men at such close quarters for months on end meant fights onboard the ships were frequent. Gangs onboard ships were usually divided along racial lines. There was a fair degree of hostility between Indian and Far Eastern crew. Goans kept to themselves.

An article which appeared on the Port of London Authority (PLA) Monthly 13th of December 1957, states:

> The Goans are more clannish and less inclined to shore excursions. When two or three ships that carry these nationals are in the Port together, a play or a concert may sometimes be produced by the Goans on board one of the vessels. The script is written by the more talented among them and the music is provided by what is usually an excellent amateur orchestra. Rehearsed with infinite patience, these concerts offer surprisingly good entertainment which may last for four or five hours....
>
> The Roman Catholic Goanese have an "altar peak," with its own small altar, aboard every ship in which they serve. During the voyage, if there is no priest on board, they choose one of their own number to conduct the prayers.[9]

Although social taboos largely prevented upper-caste Hindu Goans from embarking on a career at sea, Dinkar Nadkarni, born in 1900, was employed onboard the *S.S. Rizwani*, as a medical officer.[10] The surname can be traced to *nadkarni*, the occupation of a clerk involved in the collection of taxes. This man would have hailed from an orthodox, upper-caste, Hindu family. If indeed he did put out to sea, it was a statement of his own independence. It is more likely that he tended to the sick only after they landed at port. There were also Konkani-speaking Muslims from Ratnagiri on board British ships. A Jainoo Ebraim from Ratnagiri set sail on the *Worsley Hall*, in 1914.[11]

It was very rare that wives were deserted by *tarvotti* husbands who stayed on in England. It was more common for wives to lose their husbands to the sea; a C. Continho who sailed onboard the *Okara*, drowned in 1914 at the tender age of 20.[12] Nonetheless, Historical-

Geographer Clifford Pereira, Fellow of the Royal Geographical Society and author of *The Hidden Black & Asian History of Bexley*, has found records of a few Goans who settled in the port-towns of England. These sailors were possibly the earliest Goan immigrants to the UK.

Santan might have wanted to return to Goa, to the loving arms of a wife and family. He might have colluded with a Goan cook onboard and put aside salted and cured meats which he would take as presents for his family. A small token for the lonely lives the sea and separation wrought upon them. Sadly, Santan Costa, died on January 5, 1915, at the Seamen's Hospital, Greenwich, London of "consumption", which today is known as tuberculosis. He was forty-seven years old at the time.

Setting sail with the British also took the Goan to other parts of their Empire, notably East Africa.

27 Early days in Uganda

> It must be noted, that wherever Goans are found either in Africa or India, they form proud, independent and exclusive communities. – Author Evelyn Waugh in *The Times*, March 24, 1954.

IT COULD BE SAID the colonization of Uganda began in 1860 with Captain Hanning Speke's second expedition into the interiors of Africa. Uganda, he declared was "better cultivated and better governed than any other."[1] Speke's description of Uganda, given at the Royal Institution of Great Britain, on the evening of June 23, 1863 was most colourful:

> Their princes had large harems of women, their progeny most numerous. When a King dies all his sons are burnt except his successor and two others who are kept in case of accident until the coronation, after which one is pensioned off and the other banished to Unyoro. Untidiness in dress is a capital crime, except if the offender possesses sufficient riches to pay an enormous fine. Ingratitude or even neglecting to thank a person, for a benefit conferred,

27. EARLY DAYS IN UGANDA

is punishable. The Court customs are also curious, no one is allowed to stand before the King and to touch him or look at one of his women, is death. They believe implicitly in magic and the evil eye, and the Kings are always attended by a certain number of women crowned with dead lizards and bearing bowls of plantain wine in their hands.[2]

The early European explorer of this ilk returned with fanciful images of Africa, which filled the dimly-lit dining halls of Victorian England, the more outlandish the better. These images, from a completely Orientalist point of view, fired the English imagination and increased their resolve to "civilize" the Dark Continent.

Into this kingdom came men from the Church Missionary Society with Bibles in their hands, men who wanted to put an end to the marauding Arabs trading in slaves, men intoxicated with the smell of the coffee bean and blinded by the white of its ivory tusks, men who built forts in the name of the Imperial British East Africa Company, who came with gun-powder and hoisted the Union Jack and finally came men with a meter gauge, single-line track and built the railway from Mombasa to the eastern shores of Lake Victoria.

Uganda, an area of 93,981 square miles, a sizable amount of it open water and swamp land, infested by the mosquito and tsetse fly, had to be tamed if it was going to be of any commercial value to the British. Without effective transportation into the interiors, it was a veritable waste land but with an effective transport system to move cargoes from the interior to the nearby port of Mombasa, it could be transformed.

There was agricultural land that lay uncultivated and unpopulated plains which had potential to become a home to European populations.[3] The problem was finding cheap labour to undertake this overwhelming project of laying track across 657 miles from Mombasa to Lake Victoria. Land which was afflicted with the worst epidemics of malaria, dysentery and undetermined disease ravaging men and beast alike, in part desert and in part home to various African tribes.

Almost from the onset it was determined that India would support the railway venture by supplying *coolies* to do the earth work. Under the provisions of the India Emigration Act XXI of 1883, indentured labour was brought in from India to build the railway. At the tail end of 1895, George Whitehouse, the Chief Engineer, arrived in Mombasa to commence the project.[4] By then, 1,100 "*coolies* and artisans" had arrived from India, most of them Muslims, who the British felt served a dual purpose of also being able to fend of potential attacks from the African natives.[5]

There were clerical positions to be filled with the railways; keeping track of site provisions, handling petty-cash, book-keeping and post-office responsibilities. Tasks which needed "trustworthy, God-fearing men". It was these positions that brought Goans to Uganda in the early half of the 20th century.

The Indian Civil Services, proved to be excellent recruiting grounds, on a rare but not unprecedented occasion their service in Uganda counted as an extension of their service in India. The more competent clerks were then sent to recruit staff in India, which put at a further advantage the Christians of Bombay, swelling their numbers in East Africa.

The big draw was the medical, food and living quarters provided which meant the salary in its entirety could be sent back home to the family. There were others who arrived with the bravado of entrepreneurship, seeking to make good on business opportunities. J. A. Nazareth had the contract for catering to the Uganda Railways, both for the food served onboard the train as well as the railway restaurants.[6] Cooks working at these restaurants also tended to be Goan.

Goans congregated in the townships of Kampala, the commercial capital, and Entebbe, the seat of government at the time, both cities bordering the huge water body of Lake Victoria. The colonial climate in Uganda was more relaxed than other parts of Africa, not given to sharp racial injustices or numbing poverty. Nonetheless, Uganda was not immune from a peculiarity of African colonization, which created a three-tiered society, with the Whites at the top, the Asians namely Indians and Goans in the middle and the Africans at the bottom of this pyramid. Possibly nowhere in the world has the indigenous population been so disenfranchised and twice removed first by Europeans and then by Indians, from any substantive power in their own countries.

The Indians some considered to be "junior partners" in this colonization and the African's initial formation into associations and unions was to counter Indians who they saw as crowding in on opportunities in the Civil Services, the coffee plantations and the retail trade.[7] Their overwhelming Indo-phobia and the sting of their eventual betrayal of the Asian must be mitigated when viewed through the lens of their own pain and struggle.

Writer Armando Rodrigues was born in Uganda in 1930. Apart from spending some time in India to further his education, he spent most of his adult life there until he emigrated to Canada in 1969. He gave me an eye-witness account of life in Uganda in the 1930s. Residential areas were segregated amongst the Whites, Asians and Africans. Like everyone else, they lived in houses made from clay with thatched roofs and gauze on the windows and doors to keep out the insects. The clay would heat up in the summer months causing fissures and becoming a sanctuary for vermin. Later, corrugated iron roofing made an appearance. Sanitation and sewage were primitive. Night-soil porters transported the offending contents in an ox-driven tanker. Rain-water was harvested for drinking, cooking and bathing. The lifestyle was not given to luxury but the goodness of the earth provided them fruits, vegetables, meat and dairy.

Goan housewives busied themselves with the children, while Africans worked as domestics, eagerly learning to cook *sorpotel*, *vindaloo* and *xacuti*. Dinner was served at the table. The women's primary responsibility was the home. Goans were functional in English, the women less so and right from the start an emphasis was placed on learning as much English as quickly as possible. It was obvious to them that their chances of distinguishing themselves in a British colony were tied to proficiency in the English language. Konkani and Portuguese receded into the background.

Surviving Uganda was another matter altogether. The country, particularly near the Lake, was infested with mosquitoes. Malaria and its subsequent slide into Blackwater fever were rife. In 1903, there were 13 cases of Blackwater fever "amongst Europeans, Goans and Indians," of which four proved fatal.[8] Still, they made their peace with the environment, with big-jawed crocodiles and slithering snakes, even having monkeys as pets.

The population of Goans in Uganda was meagre but certainly it was adequate enough to form an association of sorts which would bring the community together. Perhaps as a token of appreciation for the retinue of Goan clerks in the East African Civil Services, the British provided the land for the club house at the "peppercorn" rent of Rupee 1 for 49 years.

The emigrating Goan did not come from a tradition of clubs. The true blue-blooded clubs and gymkhanas belonged to the world of the British colonial officers and settlers. To the British, contact with the "native" was limited to domestic servants. Their world was exclusive and not to be sullied by non-White social inter-mingling. Exclusive clubs and gymkhanas with tennis courts and swimming pools had sprung up all over the Empire.

In a *World of Difference*, Philip W. Porter writes: "In East Africa, the first structure established in any colonial administrative settlement was usually the Club, where colonial officers and their families would relax, drink their 'sun-downers' after work and reinforce their various prejudices."[9] This idea of exclusivity, cohesion and community fit in well with the Goan psyche and the first Uganda Goan club, originally named the Goa-Portuguese Institute, later renamed the Entebbe Goan Institute, came into being on April 24, 1905 with A. J. Reggo as Convener and President and James De Silva as Secretary.

The Goan clubs of East Africa would fracture along caste lines to accommodate their own strident notions of exclusivity, although even within the confines imposed by caste there were noble men, like Sebastian "PCSC" Nazareth, president of the Entebbe Goan Institute five times, who tried their best to veer away from this inherited system of exclusion.

Clubs and close-knit associations of this sort which facilitate a sense of belonging, a shared sense of values, social contact and a common culture, usually engender sub-cultures, a spontaneous outpouring of collective energy which finds release in the discovery of something entirely new, be it music, literature or art. Yet, the Goan Club of East Africa cannot claim any such success. There are East African Goans who deride the club as a superfluous aspect of their lives where men and women met to gossip, to engage in class and caste prejudice and to celebrate the superficial.

However Ugandan-born, Peter Nazareth, son of PCSC Nazareth and author of *The General is Up*, sees the club in an entirely different light and acknowledged in correspondence with me the vital role played by the institutes. The Goan Institutes, he says were the center of the Goan social, sporting and religious life. The Entebbe Goan Institute had a reading room, mostly for newspapers and magazines and it also had beautifully bound books from way back. Even more important, the institute was a dynamo for living change. The events of the country affected the club, and were in turn affected by what happened in the institute.

Although the clubs never gave birth to any great movements, it had a transformative effective; a slow Anglicising of Goan society had begun making them more compatible with the environment of East Africa. Armando Rodrigues dwelt on the social changes the club engineered.

The club was their second home. There was no closing time for the bar. Sundowners (dances) were held every month, as was Housie. Weddings and anniversaries were celebrated at the Club, so was Christmas. Concerts and Konkani plays were organised frequently by the Jolly Boys. Marshall Fernandes was a good violinist, Ishmael Francis played the drums, Beatriz Almeida, later to become Armando's mother-in-law, played the piano. After work got over at 4 pm, they would dash home for tea and then to the club. Ladies played badminton and cards, men played tennis, field hockey, cards, carrom and volleyball. After that, they quenched their thirst at the bar, with the usual camaraderie of "my round or your round." Favourite drinks were Bell's beer, Nile beer or Scotch and soda. Other diversions were fishing, hunting, walks and picnics in the famous Botanical Gardens. They were a close-knit community.

The lack of appropriate educational institutions posed a problem. In 1928, Georgina Rodrigues was possibly the only Goan lady in Uganda with two years of university education. A handful of Goan children were old enough for primary education and she volunteered her services. By 1930, the swell in the number of students prompted the government to fund a school. Violet Lobo was to become its first headmistress. The school was supported by the Entebbe Goan Institute, who made an annual donation and was eventually named the Entebbe Goan School. Later Norman Godinho – believed to be one of the richest Goans of the time, with interests in cine theatres and sisal estates – would fund the renowned Norman Godinho School.

By 1931, the number of Goans had risen to 1,124.[10] E. L Scott, the then Chief Secretary to the Government of Uganda (1932), came to be of the opinion that "the Goans in Uganda, in my days, were certainly a most industrious and well conducted community, devout Roman Catholics and as loyal to the British Empire as any British subjects."[11] But despite the respect Goans had earned, this was still a colony where the British operated in a position of superiority, accepting this to be the natural order of things, their role defined as "not only the trustee for the development and advance in the civilization of the African but the trustee for the world of very rich territories."[12] And nowhere did Imperial privilege and prerogative, come more to the forefront that at the work-place.

A report for the East African Commission (1929) noted that "the clerical staff was almost entirely Indian, chiefly Goanese."[13] Armando Rodrigues described the working relationship as that of "master and servant". One man who seriously challenged the dynamics of this relationship was John Francis Fernandez, a Mangalorean.[14]

John was an unlikely hero. He came to East Africa in 1901, to work with the Uganda Railways as a clerk. He was obviously a strong and independent personality, said to garner the respect of those who worked under him. He served as a head-clerk in the outposts of Kisumu and under Sir Geoffrey Archer on the Marsabit Expedition, assisting him greatly in the triangulation of the Northern Frontier District. Geoffrey Archer went on to become Governor of Somaliland and then of Uganda in 1922.

John was decorated with the General Services Medal and the Nandi Clasp but his position continued to be that of book-keeper. In 1923, he was transferred to Uganda, where he further distinguished himself in exemplary service. Towards the end of his service, in 1932, he took up cudgels on his own behalf and challenged the notion that tacitly upheld racial inequality within the Civil Services. Among other things he wanted his designation to be changed from Book-keeper to that of Accountant and the adjective "Asiatic" which qualified his position, to be dropped. He felt strongly that in Uganda it had the "same significance as nigger".[15]

Alone, tiny in the face of bureaucracy and racism, he nonetheless, soldiered on. His case would be deliberated for over two years in the corridors of colonial power. He proved his mettle in an interview with Sir George Tomlinson, Assistant Under Secretary of State, Colonial Office, when he refused to accept a medal of honour. He insisted he had asked for bread and they were giving him metal.

Sir Bernard Henry Bourdillon, Governor of Uganda (1932-1935), was adamant not to entertain any possibility of conceding to Fernandez's demands, having taken a dislike to him and labelling him as "difficult." In any case, Bourdillon insisted he did not wish to go against the "long-established limitation of the sphere of the Asiatics in the Public Service." When political pressure began to mount from England, he denied that Asians were withheld from promotion merely because of their race and insisted that "the Asiatic branch of service have not displayed the capacity, nor submitted applications, for such advancement" and that the "Asiatic staff has not been able to produce men of sufficiently outstanding qualifications"[16]. Fernandez, however, found support in his immediate supervisors, the Honours Department and even in the Colonial Office itself, without which the case would never have advanced to the point that it did. The composite, organic and often conflicting nature not just of Colonial Africa but of human societies is played out in the unfolding drama of this case. On the one hand there are men determined to uphold an inequitable *status quo* and other men stoked by their conscience want to move the moral *zeitgeist* of the times ahead. Ironically, Fernandez was estranged from the Asian community. Rebelling against the established practice of not socialising with the Africans, Fernandez had married an African woman.

Incidents such as these did not mean life was without redemption. There is little doubt, that Goans in the East African Civil Services enjoyed their position. Within the confines that race wrought unto them, there was still room for growth.

W. A. Coutinho, who had joined in 1912 as a Fourth Grade clerk, earning Shillings 960 per year, retired as a First Grade clerk in 1927, earning at the time Shillings 6,120 per annum, a not inconsiderable amount. His immediate supervisor signed off on a pension of Shillings 1,701 per year with the acknowledgment that Coutinho had worked "indefatigably and uncomplainingly."[17]

From approximately 1891 upto 1926, one Indian rupee exchanged for one shilling and four pence; thereafter the Rupee was slightly devalued. By the 1930s, a Goan clerk would earn between Rs 350-450 per month in East Africa, while his counterpart in Goa was earning Rs 250 as late as in the 1960s.

It might have been an unequal relationship but it was also, in the best British tradition, a paternalistic one. Here at last was structure, order and appreciation in the life of the Goan, allowing him longevity of employment, security that extended to his grave and beyond as pensions reverted to the wife if he passed away. More importantly, he wasn't entirely stifled, he had opportunity to be competitive and rise in the ranks. As early as 1928, there were eleven "Super Scale" and six "Special Grade" posts created so that clerks of exceptional ability may compete for them.[18] No Goan however could rise to the post of Officer in the early half of the 20th century. By the 1940s, Antu Rodrigues had risen to a commendable position in an administrative capacity.

The rights of the Asian Civil Service clerk were to some extent represented and protected by the Uganda Asiatic Civil Service Association, which was in operation from the 1920s, and in which Goans played prominent roles as board members. Its main concerns were pay, housing, pensions, medical facilities and work environment. In the main, the association was seen as a "toothless tiger" unable in any tangible way to alter the course of management decisions. It was however instrumental in safe-guarding the widows and orphans pension scheme.

The Civil Service was marked by disparity at both ends. At the apex was the inequality of the Asian to the European, and at the other end was the gap between Africans and Asians. When in 1940 a proposal came into effect to regularise the scales and put the African on par with the Asian, the Asiatic Civil Service Association objected. In a letter to Secretary of State to the Colonies signed by joint signatories, J.M.S Azavedo and Peter I. Pereira, they stated the proposal was "an attempt to degrade most unjustly the status of the Asiatic in the Civil Service."[19]

On the face of it, this seemed like inverted Goan racism but the historical reality was while revisions attempted to improve the plight of the African, they usually ended by disadvantaging the Asian. Azavedo also served as president of the Goan Entebbe Institute in 1944, 1949 and 1955 and Pereira in 1951. These men were distinguished most prominently by their ability to converse in the Queens' English which made them the obvious choice in positions which required skillful negotiation with the British.

In 1956, the Commission for East African Civil Services, headed by Sir David Lidbury and which subsequently became known as the "Lidbury Commission" adopted, in principle, the concept of equal pay for equal work in the East African Civil Service sector. Although, as was often the case with the British, certain "allowances" ensured them of a higher earning. The Commission reinforced what had already been acknowledged for some years prior to its finding, that barriers to upward mobility be removed and the work-force be primarily

27. Early Days in Uganda

recruited from amongst Africans, thus signaling the phasing out of Goans from the Civil Services.

At the time of Independence, the British government had signaled their willingness to compensate the Asian civil clerk with a lump sum payment of £4,000 and the European £8,000. Three members of the Asiatic Civil Service Association travelled to London for the final negotiations but returned empty-handed, leaving the Goan Civil Servant feeling wounded, deserted and betrayed.

Initially at least, the removal of the colour bar meant upward mobility for a lot of Goans. Ferdinand Rodrigues, Alvaro Collaço, Eleuterio Sequeira, Reginald Dias and Armando Rodrigues reached positions that were previously entirely the domain of the British. Alvaro Collaço rose to the position of Acting Head of the Budget Department, Ministry of Finance and Ferdinand Rodrigues in 1972 became Under Secretary, President's Office, as well as decorated with a Knight Commander of the Order of St. Gregory the Great. Armando who had started out as a clerk in 1947 became the C.E.O(E) of the government's Ministry of Works, Communication and Housing.

Life had indeed come full circle. John Francis Fernandez had fought so valiantly just for the designation of Accountant and lost on the premise that an Asian could not fill such a position, but when the racial ceiling on upward mobility finally came crashing down, the Asian spirit and intellect soared to new heights.

Ironically, despite the pervasiveness of Africanisation, empirical evidence points to the Goan population increasing in Uganda during the 1960s, estimated to be 5,350, and possibly at its peak. It would be another decade for Uganda's Goans to realise that 90 days was too short a time to pack-up a life-time of memories and bid farewell to the country they loved.†*

---

*In August of 1972, the Asians of Uganda were given 90 days by Idi Ami to leave the country. The vast majority of them emigrated to the United Kingdom and Canada.

28 The Goan man of Kenya

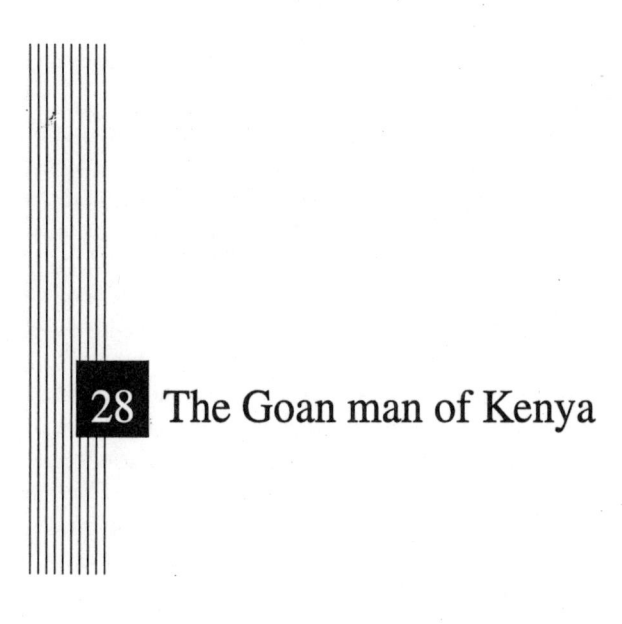

> There is a saying in Nairobi, 'The keys of all the White men's safes are in the pockets of the Goans'. They are a trustworthy community. – The Earl of Lytton, in the House of Lords, November 28, 1963.

> To the Indians of Kenya. Owed so much, repaid so ill. — J. M. Nazareth, dedication in his book *Brown Man, Black Country*.

KENYA BORDERS UGANDA and conveniently located along its south-easterly coast lies the port of Mombasa, which had long served as a major refuelling port for the sea-route between Europe and Asia. By the mid-twentieth century, Kenya would become home to the largest Goan population in the Diaspora.

An interesting first-hand account of life in remote outposts of Kenya is left for us by the Mangalorean clerk, John Francis Fernandez.

John migrated to East Africa in 1901 (see chapter *Early days in Uganda*) and recalls in a letter to the Secretary of State for the Colonies, having his evening meals eaten sitting cross-legged on his bed in order to prevent mosquito bites and "the myriads of lake flies" getting into his plate of soup. Water was always scarce and that which was available was usually "highly brackish, tasted like soap suds and flavoured with rhino and other animal matter."[1]

There were Goan-run shops in the solitary, isolated outposts of the interiors, where a congregation of three or four provision stores of rusty corrugated iron constituted a town, sitting snakes put in an appearance in their out-houses and other reptilian encounters awaited on the way to work. Willy Pereira had a shop in Garba Tula, a remote outpost in northern Kenya. Willy was pivotal to Garba Tula. Besides supply provisions, he did everything from running lorries to collecting the mail.

Despite the deprivations, Goans persevered and grew into tightly-knit communities. One reason for their cohesion was the pattern of residential segregation that persisted throughout British East Africa. In Nairobi, Parklands, Pangani and Eastleigh were marked as the Asian areas while Pumwani, Kariokor and Donholm were the African areas. Europeans occupied the more salubrious north-westerly areas.[2]

In Eastleigh, quite a few Goan tailors and carpenters lived in boarding or "bachelor" houses. Whole families housed in single rooms in soulless large tenements. Some were lucky to have an attached kitchen. Others cooked in the enclosed concrete compound or in their rooms on a *jiko ya makaa*, a charcoal stove, leaving the doors open for ventilation. Toilet facilities were communal. A few common taps provided cold water but bath water was heated on the stove in recycled kerosene tins. Those Goans who worked in government departments were provided accommodation. The railway quarters, often called *landies* because they were built near railway landings, particularly were the envy of Kenya. Bungalow type row houses fronted by verandas and grassy patches of land. The back of the house looked in on another row of houses; an ideal community environment for young children and wives.

Mombasa was a relaxed coastal town and much more ethnically diversified than Nairobi. Goans lived in several areas: Macupa, Hobley Road, Ganjoni where the Goan High School was located and Queensway. There were Goans just above Kilindini harbor, Makadara and Old Port and, a few outside the island in the Port Ritz area. The parishioners of the Holy Ghost Cathedral were predominantly Goan. The community's sense of ethnic identity was continually reinforced within the small confines of the island. A 1921 census put the number of Goans in Kenya at 2,000.[3] Another indicator of their presence and prominence is given by the Revenue Collection data of 1931. They paid 7% of the total non-native poll-tax, a direct, per head tax with the intent of raising revenue for public expenditure. Interestingly, they paid 12.3% of the total revenue from consumption of wines and spirits.[4] They had an enormous fondness for brandy and out-stripped consumption of both the European and Indian communities.

In Kenya besides being employed in large numbers with the Civil Services, Goans were engaged in trade. Dr Cornel DaCosta, whose memories of Kenya go back to the 1940s, vividly described to me the many thriving Goan businesses in operation. The two St. Rose brothers, who had studied pharmacy in the United Kingdom, ran a large Edward St. Rose & Co. store in Mombasa.

Cornel remembers an interesting incident that transpired in the store. Frank Banham, a school-headmaster, having purchased a pair of sunglasses, decided to return them several weeks later. St. Rose was having none of it and refused. Banham crushed the spindly glasses and threw them at St. Rose's bewildered face. St. Rose took him to court where the presiding judge remarked that Banham had acted "more like a schoolboy than a headmaster", and ordered him to pay damages to St. Rose. Other Goan stores were those run by S. Francis Dias and a haberdashery owned by the Monteiro family. C.P.V. Rodrigues owned a plush liquor store, while Cunha & Son traded in religious artifacts. There were numerous tailoring shops which did exceedingly well for themselves.

By 1948, the number of Goans[5] had risen to 7,159, a swell which prompted Dr Antonines C. L de Souza to ask searching questions about their role in Kenya. Through to 1945, Dr Souza took an active part in the East African Indian National Congress, rising to the ranks of vice-president. When, in keeping with the traditions of the Congress, he stood for President, he was however humiliatingly defeated by A. B. Patel. This defeat, which he took to be ethnically motivated by him being a Catholic Goan, left him embittered towards Indian politics, whereupon he severed his ties with the Indian Congress and began concentrating on the Goans as an individual community. In 1952, an editorial of *Goan Voice*, Kenya, of which A. C. L. de Souza was founder and editor, posed the question:

> Where does the Goan young man stand in this conflict between the old and the new, the spiritual and the material, the permanent and the evanescent? What is his place to be in the complex

28. THE GOAN MAN OF KENYA

society of East Africa, his contribution to its progress and his justification for an honorable place in it?[6]

The Goan young man was wedged between White supremacy and alienation from native Africans. Indeed, he was isolated even from Indians, to whom he was a fish-eating Portuguese national. Robert G. Gregory, in *East Africa: The Asians' Political Role*, writes: "Many Goans were quick to learn English, adopt European dress even for women, live and eat in European style. The Goan clerks in government service were conspicuous in joining Europeans on the cricket field after work... and became 'more British than the English.'"[7]

The Civil Services, a seemingly Western lifestyle, Christianity and an unwavering loyalty to the Empire had made the Goan a buffer between indigenous populations and the British, perhaps even a pawn between the Indian community and the British. If he was uncertain about his role and future in Kenya, then he was equally uncertain about his role in the affairs of Goa.

* * *

In 1955, Barrister Joaquim M. Nazareth Q. C. tried to register the Goa Liberation Association, later renamed the East African Goan National Association. Born of the village of Moira, lying in the north of Goa, Nazareth had for the most part kept away from Goan politics in Kenya.

In his memoirs, titled *Brown Man, Black Country*, he writes: "The Goan in me had receded into the background and the Indian part of me had come to the fore. I could identity myself only as an Indian, for Goa was an unknown, an almost invisible speck in the vast maze of India."[8] In Kenya, he had the honour of being the second Asian to be appointed Queen's Council.

The medium-built, intellectual was given to quiet moral and legal deliberations rather than frivolous gaiety. He was a somewhat alienated man, thought of more as a 'Bombay Goan', having spent his formative years there, graduating from the University of Bombay with a first-class-first and winning the St. Xavier's College Gold Medal. He rarely put in an appearance for Goan social functions, rather preferring to keep to a coterie of like-minded and politically-driven men. His austere principles, perhaps, did not serve him well in politics which called for more pragmatic choices to be made. Nonetheless, he would eventually bring the "Quit Goa" movement to the forefront of Goan consciousness in Kenya.

The Portuguese had no jurisdiction in Kenya, but were keen to portray the Goans there as being entirely sympathetic to Portugal. There can be no contesting that a sizable number of them were in favour of Portugal's continued presence in Goa. The British, who kept minor surveillance on the Goan community, acknowledged in an intelligence summary:

> The East African Goan National Association continues to agitate against Portuguese rule in Goa. It is difficult, as yet, to assess the extent to which the Association has the support of Goans in East Africa. It seems that a substantial minority wish to attain independence for Goa, not realising that this would almost inevitably be followed by the absorption of the territory by India.[9]

The newspaper *Globe*, under the editorial supervision of M. I. Fernandes, was so stridently anti-Indian, that it was rebuked by the Indian Commissioner. Even the East African Goan National Association, whatever the personal feelings of its membership might have been, maintained publicly that "for an agreed period, Goa shall remain a separate State and that its territorial integrity shall always be respected unless and until Goans shall freely decide to merge with India."[10]

On the afternoon of November 16, 1955, the Portuguese Ambassador called on Sir Harold Caccia, Deputy Under-Secretary of State, Foreign Office, to convince him to discourage what they called a "self-styled" and "subversive organization" headed by the "instigator" Nazareth.[11] The British had their own reasons for distrusting Nazareth. He was formerly the President of the Kenya Indian Congress (1950-52), some of whom were sympathetic to African nationalist aspirations. Sir Evelyn Baring, the broadly-built Governor of Kenya (1952-59), believed the Indian Commissioner's office had "inspired" the formation of the Goan National Association, and knew it had contributed 600 shillings towards its expenses.[12]

The other members were Eclito D'Souza as Vice President, P. M. Rebello as Hon. Treasurer and Rosário Da Gama Pinto, as proposed Secretary who was employed at the time with the Ministry of Community Development, came particularly under the radar of suspicion. His brother Pio Gama Pinto was closely associated with Kenya's own nationalist figures and detained by the British, under Operation Anvil, initiated in 1952 to stem the Mau Mau rebellion, a formidable movement seeking Kenyan independence. The British in Kenya refused to register the association. Governor Baring explained his reasons to Alan Lennox-Boyd, Secretary of State for the Colonies. The intentions of the association, he felt, were "clearly inflammatory", hostile and offensive to a "friendly colonial power, Portugal" who they had referred to as a fascist dictatorship. Its utterances "immoderate and abusive".[13]

The association claimed that Goans in Kenya were afraid to become members for fear of reprisals when they went back to Goa.* There might have been merit to this assertion. Angelo Faria, son of Albert Faria a pro-independence activist and president of the Goan Community, Mombasa, spent his youth in Kenya. In correspondence with me, Angelo contends that the contribution to the Liberation of Goa from Goans in Kenya was at best marginal. The community had a *sossegado* mentality towards developments in Goa, which they visited on "home leave" every three to four years and to which they periodically remitted money. The small pro-India faction led by J.M. Nazareth was juxtaposed against a pro-Portuguese faction represented by the G.O.A and led by Dr. A.C.L de Souza, appealing to religious and cultural fears. The tentacles of the caste system had permeated every sphere of Goan society in Kenya, ultimately seeping into its political fabric. What seemed like political ideological differences on the face of it, had their genesis in caste rivalries between the two leading Goan figures.

Albert Faria, Angelo's father, had much earlier in 1950 become a victim of an over-zealous pro-Portuguese lobbyist. Albert had attached his name on a felicitation telegram to Pandit Nehru on India's independence. Two years later whilst on a visit to Goa, he was arrested at Mormugão harbour, allegedly at the instigation of a fellow Goan in the higher echelons of the Portuguese Consul-General offices in Kenya. He was held in detention for ten days before being released on bail. He jumped bail and returned to Africa, but was sentenced to a long term of penal servitude *in absentia*. This order was rescinded by José de Neiva, Portuguese Consul General in Nairobi, when he found no basis for the arrest action.

---

*"Goans hesitate to become members of the association because they fear that they will be victimised by the Portuguese authorities when they go to Goa." Kenya Goans Call for "Quit Goa", *The Colonial Times*, Kenya, October 29, 1955.

Amidst the political intrigues of Africa and those of Goa, life continued unabated and consumed by the trivial for most Goans in Kenya. Weddings carried on with much pomp at the Holy Ghost Cathedral. Cardinal Deniel issued a twelve-point decree in which women had to wear sleeves "at least to their elbows". Nairobi's top band, The Revelers, played at dances held at the gymkhana. It was the end of an era, only no one knew it as yet.

In 1958, Dr A.C.L de Souza, passed away. He didn't live to see almost 10,000 Goans leave Kenya following its independence in 1963. He was spared the sad realization that the young Goan man of his time had no definitive role at all to play in Kenya's future nor an honorable place in it. Yet the seeds of hope, aspiration and the pursuit of intellectual curiosity that he had planted in the Goans of Kenya bore fruit elsewhere. A certain amount of foresight on his part had made him implore Goans to give up their Portuguese nationality and take up British passports. Some returned to Goa, now free and firmly a part of India. The vast majority emigrated to the United Kingdom and Canada.

29 Emma Gama Pinto

> If you consider my past justifies your expectations of a good citizen of Kenya who has the true interests of the masses of this country at heart, then I request you to vote for me. – Letter from Pio Gama Pinto to KANU members of the House of Representatives, Nairobi, May 29, 1963.

YOUNG EMMA DIAS awaited the arrival of the man from Suswa Road. The meeting had been arranged through her twin-sister Joyce and the man's brother, Rosário. When he finally arrived, Emma noticed he had a slight stoop and walked with his shoulders bent forward. Perhaps to disguise his nervousness, he began talking about the population statistics of Jamshedpur, Emma's home town in India. The man in question was Pio Gama Pinto.

The Goan of Kenya was largely divorced from the politics of Kenya. Kenya's politics affected him only to the extent of his continued future in the colony. Given that an independent Africa would jeopardise his livelihood, the Goan was at best ambivalent to notions of an independent Kenya and at worst tacitly supportive of Britain's continued engagement.

29. EMMA GAMA PINTO

Despite the general apathy which existed between Goans and native Africans, and even between the larger Indian community and the indigenous population, there were in Kenya's history a few dedicated Indians who embraced the cause of Kenya's own nationalist aspirations. Jawaharlal Nehru was a staunch advocate for the independence of African colonies and supported the cause in whatever capacity he could at the international level. One political activist fiercely committed to Kenya's independence, was Goan-born Pio Gama Pinto; tall, arresting in his presence and intense.

In 1953, the year Emma came to Nairobi, Governor Evelyn Baring stood before the Kenya Legislative Council and, in his opening speech, convinced them of Kenya's prosperity.[1] He spoke of a rising national income from £53 million in 1947 to about £107 million in 1952. Unfortunately this prosperity had not permeated to the African. Instead, it was evidence of the wide abyss that existed between native Africans and White settlers. Kenya was in the grip of a crisis. A growing Kikuyu population had put pressure on land, the most fertile of which was occupied by White settlers, rendering vast sections of Africans landless or as impoverished "squatters". This resentment found expression in a return to tribal Kikuyu loyalties and gave birth to the Mau Mau insurgency.

To the African, Mau Mau was the militant voice of nationalist aspirations. To the White settler, it was a vulgar and brutal attack on their way of life. Savage atrocities to be condemned and its leaders annihilated. Emma had landed at a perilous time; Kenya was under a state of Emergency. Little did she know that she, herself, would spend a good deal of time writing to Governor Baring.

Emma and Pio began courting. Having done brief stints as a journalist with the *Colonial Times* and the *Daily Chronicle*, Pio was now employed by the East African Indian National Congress. He worked diligently in a small room of the Desai Memorial Library, writing articles and petitions, raising awareness of the injustice of the Emergency and money for detainees. He was instrumental in revising the Land Reform Act. The Indian High Commissioner, Apa Pant, gifted Pio with a typewriter and stationery from his office.[2]

One of Pio's many associates was Makhan Singh, who along with Fred Kubai had been engaged in trade union activities. They had tried to register the East African Trade Unions Congress in May of 1949. The Kenya government could not find adequate reason to reject the application but did so nonetheless, citing Makhan Singh "had all the characteristics of a Communist party member."[3] It was an effective way to disqualify people who raised unsettling questions about equality in an unequal country. This label of Communist was one that had stuck to Pio as well, something Emma found unpalatable. She confronted Pio and told him that she was not interested in being associated with a Communist. Pio appeared at her doorsteps with a box of chocolates and an offer to discuss the issue with a priest.

On January 9, 1954, the couple wed at Parklands Catholic Church. It was a large wedding, mostly friends from the groom's side. J. M. Nazareth raised the toast. Emma's parents had flown in from India. The next day the groom and a few guests suffered a bout of food poisoning. A seven-year-old girl succumbed. It was perhaps a somber foreshadowing of events to unfold.

Four months after the wedding, Nairobi was cordoned off by police. Operation Anvil, under General Erskine, had commenced. It was an attempt to "clean-up" the city of "subversives and undesirables." On the first day of the operation, the Indian Commissioner's office in the Grogan Road area became a target. At mid-day, a group of British soldiers entered the offices, held staff at gun-point, threatening to shoot and forced open cabinets with confidential files. Seeing the African staff in the office disperse, they gave chase using filthy language, breaking down doors and claiming loudly that the Indian Commissioner's office was a Mau Mau office.[4] The African staff, all nominal employees of the Indian Commission, were arrested without cause and taken away. Although, the government apologised to the Commissioner the next day claiming it to be a mistake, the British clearly perceived a sympathetic attitude towards the Mau Mau in certain Indian political circles. For the most part, the Indian community remained apathetic and in some instances offered loud condemnation of the Mau Mau.

Emma and Pio settled into domesticity, coming to terms with Emma's lack of culinary skills and Pio's busy schedule. Pio didn't want Emma to waste her life at home and encouraged her to work. She landed a job as a junior secretary at International Aeradio Limited (IAL), a British engineering firm at Nairobi West Airport. Four weeks into her job, she received a call. Pio had been arrested under the broad sweep of Operation Anvil. She rushed to Nairobi prison, where she was met by the prominent Goan lawyer, Fitz Remédios Santana de Souza. Just two years earlier, Fitz was part of the defence team for the "Kapenguria six" among which was Jomo Kenyatta, the charismatic nationalist leader who was eventually to become independent Kenya's first Prime Minister, but at the time stood accused of inciting the Mau Mau rebellion. Fitz and his wife Romola would become lifelong friends of Emma. Pio spent barely ten minutes with her outside the prison reception area, near the gates, assuring her that he would be home soon. He believed it had all been a mistake which would get sorted out. It would be the last time she was to see him for nearly four years.

Five months into their marriage, Pio was taken from Emma. He was sent to Mombasa's Fort Jesus prison and then to Takwa Detention Camp on Manda Island, a hot, inhospitable island off the east coast of Kenya, often scorched without the relief of rain. When the International Red Cross team of Dr Marcel Junod and Dr Jean-Maurice Rubli visited Takwa, they saw the detention huts set in the hollows of the dunes, denying detainees the benefit of sea-breeze, making it all the more airless and intolerable.

The Kenya government believed the Mau Mau was a disease. Camps were justified as a means to "mental" rehabilitation. Detainees were segregated into those who were inclined to rehabilitation, meaning those who co-operated, and those branded as "hard-core." Pio was considered "hard-core" and kept away from the main camp population. Beatings were common in the camps. Conditions were cramped and unsanitary with filthy latrines and overflowing night-soil buckets, resulting in frequent outbreaks of typhoid, tuberculosis and dysentery.[5] Pellagra, a vitamin deficiency, and scurvy, due to dietary frugalities, were rampant. One of Pio's tasks was to empty night-soil onto the beach, where he sometimes found turtle eggs with which he supplemented his diet. At one point, Pio was assigned chores in the canteen. He smuggled food rations to share with fellow detainees. Years later, when he was released, he rarely spoke about his time in detention. He escaped much of the physical brutality meted out to Kenyan inmates but the experience left him traumatised nonetheless and he confided to Emma that he had seriously considered suicide. Ultimately it was the sufferings of these detainees that pricked the British public conscience and genuinely opened up the debate for Kenya's independence.

For the most part, Emma was by herself and would need to muster all her inner reserves to survive. She did not have any contact with Pio. Her written pleas to Governor Baring, went unanswered. It would be almost two years before she was allowed to write to him. For a while, Anton and Ema Gama Pinto, Pio's parents, moved to Nairobi from Nyeri, to be of assistance to Emma. The Gama Pinto ancestry can be traced to Carrem, Porvorim in Goa. Emma continued in her job at IAL and even overcame Kenya's notorious colour bar which existed in most companies. In her last year at IAL, she found herself to be the only Asian invited to a dinner-party hosted by the managing director from London, at a "Whites-only" hotel.

Then in January of 1958, Pio was released from detention and transferred to Kabarnet, to be held under Restriction Orders, a sort of house-arrest under supervision of District Commissioner, Butler. Pio was the only inmate in a single-room house. If Pio was to be exiled, Emma decided to join him. She, under police escort, made the ten-hour trek from Nairobi to Kabarnet, a feat which earned her the respect of the District Commissioner and his wife. She stayed with Pio, initially in the small dwelling but later in a two-bedroom house constructed especially for them. Here in misty Kabarnet, where Pio and Emma rediscovered each other, their first child Linda was conceived. After nearly two years at Kabarnet, in October 1959, Pio was at last declared a non-threat to security and released just in time for the birth of their second daughter, Malusha.

Kenya woke up to independence on December 12, 1963. Pio initially stayed away from the fray of African politics. He was always of the opinion that Africans should have the loudest say in the running of their country. Nonetheless, he concentrated his energies in working behind the scenes, shaping political opinion, fund-raising, assisting ex-detainees and setting up the Lumumba Institute. He renewed his ties with Fred Kubai and set about strengthening the position of trade unions. On a trip to India, to celebrate the end of colonial rule in Goa, he met with Nehru in New Delhi and convinced him to fund a Swahili newspaper, thus establishing the *Sauti Ya Mwafrica*. Later at Emma's insistence, Pio stood for a Parliamentary seat, and was voted in as a Specially Elected Member of the House of Representatives. Kenya was keen to reciprocate its love.

Politics in post-colonial Kenya was riddled with corruption. A rift had developed between Jomo Kenyatta, and a more radical group lead by Vice-President Oginga Odinga and supported by Pio. Perhaps the last furious row between Pio and Kenyatta, at the legislative building, witnessed from afar by Fitz de Souza, had sealed Pio's fate.

On February 25, 1965, Emma received a call while at work from her mother, to tell her that Pio had been attacked. Shots had rung out into the mid-morning quiet of Nairobi's Lower Kabete Road. An African man approached Pio, whilst he was in his car with his daughter, Tereskha, greeting him with "*Jambo, Bwana*" and a bullet. Emma hurried home, only to find Pio still in the car. Someone had put a blanket over Pio's pale bullet-ridden body. A vain attempt to cover Kenya's quivering collective shame and guilt. Pio had given his life to the Kenya he loved so much, becoming her first martyr after independence. Eleven years into their marriage, Pio was once again taken from Emma.

Emma moved to Canada two years later after the assassination of Pio and dedicated her life to single-handedly raising three girls. She currently resides in Ottawa, Canada. On October 17, 2008, Emma Gama Pinto received a First Day Cover Kenyan stamp depicting Pio. The series of four stamps are titled "Heroes of Kenya". Included on the stamp are Oginga Odinga, Pio Gama Pinto, Tom Mboya and Ronald Ngala.

30 Expulsion from Malawi

> We had no time to sell our house and we were allowed to bring out £300 a person. — Goan refugee from Malawi to the *Times* reporter Penny Haslemere, May 19, 1976.

ANTHONY FERNANDES WAS arrested on April 21, 1976, and taken to Chichiri police station.[1] Several Goans were already at Chichiri when he arrived. Martin Gwede, Head of Special Branch, informed them that they were being held for "acts of subversion, immorality and arrogance".

After a brief discussion amongst themselves, they decided in all humility to seek forgiveness from His Excellency the Life President of the Republic of Malaŵi, Ngwazi Dr Hastings Kamuzu Banda. But if they thought their ordeal would soon be over, they were wrong. It was just beginning. They were herded onto a truck and taken to Malawi's infamous Mulanje prison which rests on the border between Malawi and Mozambique.

As they trundled into the darkness at night on open trucks, their thoughts might have turned to the journalists, academics, cabinet ministers, teachers and Jehovah's Witnesses who had disappeared in

30. EXPULSION FROM MALAWI

Malawi's prisons. By the early 1970s, Malawi had over 700 political detainees.[2] At this point, the Goans had no idea what had prompted this detention. About 200 Goan men were imprisoned at Mulanje.

Malawi, formerly known as Nyasaland, then a British protectorate, is a tiny land-locked African state wedged between Tanzania, Zambia and Mozambique. The British settled mostly in the Shire Highlands but apart from a tobacco crop, the area yielded little else. In 1964, Malawi became an independent state. Its new constitution made it a single-party state. Dr Hastings Kamuzu Banda as head of the ruling Malawi Congress Party, declared himself President for life. What followed was a reign of fear and intimidation by a man consumed by his own sense of grandeur.

Gabriel Louzado, who had represented Malawi in badminton at the 1974 Commonwealth Games, was the first Goan to be arrested.[3] In correspondence with me, Gabriel detailed the events leading up to the arrest and his detention. A friend of his had flown into Malawi and the two of them were sitting at the Goan Club, having a drink late into the night on April 12, 1976. The club was empty save for the two friends chatting away and the staff tending to them. Hastings Banda had just finished one of his interminable speeches on the radio and was being cheered by the Mbumba Women's League, when Gabriel requested the bartender to switch the radio to light FM. The bartender reported the incident to the authorities, misrepresenting it entirely and accusing Gabriel of insolently ordering him to switch off the radio while the speech was going on. This trifling incident was to have grave repercussions for the Goan community.

An early mention of Goans in the Nyasa lake region was by Doctor Livingstone. In a letter dated April 9, 1872, addressed to James Gordon Bennett, the newspaper tycoon who sent Stanley White to find Livingstone, he writes of the German explorer Dr Albrecht Roscher having with him Goan servants as he reached Lake Nyasa, now Lake Malawi.[4] Tragically, Roscher was murdered during this expedition and it was his Goan servants that gave details to the British authorities.

Whether these Goans resided in the Lake Nyasa area or had been recruited in Zanzibar or from Mozambique is not known. Certainly there were Goans in the interiors of that region. Livingstone met a Goan priest in 1862, stationed at Tete, which borders Malawi to the southeast, managing a remote mission outpost of the Portuguese[5] and also in the area were two Goan religious educators imparting instruction to European students.[6]

Mozambique, which neighbours Malawi, had been under Portuguese influence since the 16th century and home to a not insignificant Goan population, many of them traders who had spread into the interiors. In 1908, the British government began constructing a railway that would connect Blantyre, the main town of Malawi, with Chiromo in the south, finally winding its way to the port of Portuguese Mozambique.[7] The Goan settlement in Mozambique, ventured into Malawi to work on railway jobs.

The community grew by encouraging friends and family from Goa to join those pioneering souls who had set up homes. They would arrive by sea at the Port of Beira in Mozambique and from there make their way by train to the townships of Malawi. By the mid-twentieth century, a thriving Goan community had established itself in the main towns of Blantyre and Limbe, 11 kms east of Blantyre, with workshops for the Malawi Railways. Quite a few Goan families were scattered in the rural areas. Eventually, it grew to be a tight-knit community of about 500 people.

Malawi was considerably poorer than Kenya or Uganda, its main townships, undeveloped without even a cinema house for entertainment. In the capital of Blantyre, Goans worked in the European-owned tobacco companies, civil services and in the railways, some even as train-drivers. In the rural areas they had family-run shops, either a tailoring outfit or a general stores. which used the front-end to vendor the goods whilst the back-rooms were living quarters.

Unlike Kenya, where sheer numbers had distinguished the Goans into a distinct group, here Goans blended with the larger Indian community. They had a peripheral connection to Goans in other parts of East Africa, which they used for arranging marriages and other social contacts.

Like all colonial East African territories, life was segregated into three tiers with the British at the top, the Africans at the base and the Asians shuttling in between the two. Despite the inequity of their lives, Goans were deeply rooted in Malawi and its generous laid-back spirit of living. Their children went to the Catholic-run Our Lady of Wisdom School in Limbe or the Indian school run by Mrs Saprani. Those who wanted to pursue higher studies usually returned to India. Boys often took over the running of the family-owned businesses. For

30. Expulsion from Malawi

the most part, life centered around the Goan Club in Limbe. After-work hours were spent in the pleasant company of fellow Goans playing cards, bingo or enjoying a game of badminton. The club was a community space for organising tournaments, dances and used as a reception hall for many a Goan wedding.

The first rumblings of change came as Malawi marched towards independence in the early 1960s. Independence of African states throughout the continent usually brought uncertainty for Asian communities. The Indians were the traders, money-lenders, middle-rung administrative white collar workers. The Africans strongly believed they were being swindled by Indians. The monopolisation of retail trade, interest rates perceived to be usurious, wage differentials in commercial establishments were to them stolen opportunities. Much of the post-independence wrath and disappointment in not making the grand leap after independence into prosperity was directed at Asians. There were dictatorial despots who inflamed these anti-Asian feelings and promised redress. The extent to which the fate of these Goans was predetermined, can be judged from statements made by Hastings Banda in 1959: "If they interfere in politics, they will be told to clear out. We will boycott their stores and they know what that means – bankruptcy."[8] The idea of boycotting Indian shops was almost an African *cliché*. In 1959, violent riots in Malawi targeted Asian shops, commonly called *dukan* or *dukas* across Africa. Once Malawi gained independence it aggressively pursued a policy of Africanization, with Banda allegedly saying: "As far as I know, there is no Malawian trading either in Bombay, Madras or anywhere else in India."[9]

In Malawi, the anti-Asian sentiment was compounded by Hastings Banda being a deeply troubled, dictatorial megalomaniac. Under his leadership, Malawians would have to tread lightly, ever conscious of not offending their President. No person could have a ceremonial picture bigger than Banda's gracing a wall. Nor could one have a title more impressive than his of President. The Goan Club could no longer have a President, they had to have a Chairman. Women were forbidden to wear pants or skirts above their knees. Men could not keep their hair long.

On April 12, 1976, the Goan Club would unwittingly become center-stage for Banda's delusions of grandeur. Following Gabriel's arrest on charges of subversion and insolence for switching off the radio, other members of the club, including its chairman were rounded up and taken to Chichiri police station and from there to Mulanje prison. Gabriel was incarcerated at Zomba prison some 40 miles to the north. There was no justification given for their arrests except that they had been holding subversive meetings. Gwede, the Head of Special Branch, told them he could do what he wished with them. Most of the men had been taken abruptly, without any warning, arriving at Mulanje prison unprepared and in a state of shock.[10]

Prison conditions were abysmal. They were given one blanket for every three people to share, made to sleep on the concrete floor, allowed to shower once a day but were not given a towel. The food, being an African diet, was unpalatable to the Goans. There were two tiny cells which housed all the inmates; closed and without proper ventilation, some of the men began suffering from bronchitis and asthma. On the third day, they were stripped of whatever money or belongings they had on them and served with a 28-day detention order. Within days, the men were covered in lice, suffering from malaria and malnutrition. Two had to be hospitalized. After two weeks in detention, they were released but declared Prohibited Immigrants; they had forty-eight hours to leave the country. Meanwhile all sorts of rumours were swirling within the Goan community making their way to major news publications. *The Times* of London, cited a wedding party at the Goan club as being responsible. That they had not halted their celebrations while Banda's speech was being aired.[11] Another rumour circulating was that a Goan had beaten up his African domestic help and had been reported to the authorities.

What Banda had not counted on was that this incident would create a diplomatic storm. The Goans, save for a few families who were Portuguese nationals, were all UK passport holders. The sudden arrival in the UK on May 16, 1976, of 61 Goans, prompted a nervous reaction in Britain, being as usual wary about accommodating Asian expulsions from Africa.[12] The UK threatened to cut off much needed aid to Malawi if mass expulsions continued, aid which in that year itself had amounted to £9 million.[13] With the world watching, Banda made a public retreat, declaring in a speech on May 29, 1976:

> There is no cause of friction between us and the Europeans. Between us and the Asians. The only Europeans, Asians, we do not welcome here are the arrogant, the crooks, the subservient. That Club was closed because members of that Club were deliberately engaging in subversion. They were deliberately acting arrogantly and I'll tell you why. The British government has

219

30. Expulsion from Malawi

> agreed to take as many Asians as possible. But for the past two or three years, a number of Asians here, who are too much in a hurry to go to Britain, they deliberately engaged in subversion, arrogance, even to the point of beating Africans, in order to get deported because they know that once they are deported the British Government will have to take them in... no government can tolerate open subversion, arrogance and speaking evil of the government to Africans openly like that, no, government can stand that.[14]

The precariousness of life in Malawi was to visit Martin Gwede himself, the man who had claimed he had the fate of Goans at Chichiri prison in his hand. A year later, he was sentenced to death for plotting to assassinate Banda, a sentence later commuted.

Some 270 Goans ultimately made their way from Malawi to London in 1976, uprooted from their lives on a whim.

31 Onwards to England

> I consider that, if they wish to leave Kenya, they should return to their countries of origin – India and Pakistan, which certainly would not refuse them admission. – Duncan Sandys, House of Commons debate on Commonwealth Immigrants' Bill, Feb 27, 1968

THERE IS A MOMENT in every nation's history when it renews itself and moves forth reinvigorated. For Britain, this moment was the 1960s. Amidst broad cultural changes which swept across the country, the decade saw the collapse of its empire in Africa. A collapse which would bring to the forefront questions about its very nationhood and redefine its national identity.

Perhaps it was always understood that Asians in Africa were citizens without a country. There was never any love lost between Africans and Indians. Paul Theroux, in *Hating the Asians*, writes that, to the African: "the *wahindi* was responsible for flagrant racism, the failure of African socialism and progress, all the bad driving and motor accidents, sins of pride, envy, scandal, gluttony and lust, monopoly business... a high birth rate and bad food."[1] Independence of African

31. ONWARDS TO ENGLAND

countries perched the Asian on a perilous ledge. Africanization in commercial establishments, termination of trade licenses, *coups d'etat* or even a shift in the political wind were used as excuses to go on a rampage, burn Asian shops, loot, pillage and assault. It was against a back-drop of inverted racism that the stranded Goan made his way to England in the 1960s.

Britain was in turmoil about its own future. On July 20, 1957, British Prime Minister, Harold Macmillan told a Tory rally in Bedford that "most of our people have never had it so good." Interestingly, the rally was to mark 25 years of service by Alan Lennox-Boyd, Colonial Secretary (1954-59). Lennox-Boyd's brand of Right wing politics and aversion to constitutional reform in the colonies had made him a detested figure, particularly in Kenya. Macmillan on the other hand recognised that England's economy could no longer be propped-up by colonies. His legacy was wrenching open the doors to the decolonization of Africa. A move which opened the floodgates for an Asian exodus out of Africa.

The Conservative anthem of "never had it so good" was wearing thin as the overheated economy of the 1950s gave way to the bust of the 1960s. It was paralysed by trade unions with an average of 2,521 strikes per year and held hostage to an acute housing shortage, the degree and pathos of which was best encapsulated in a drama called "Cathy Come Home." The documentary-like drama portrayed the life of an urban couple who move progressively – but rather quickly – from unemployment to homelessness and destitution. To this toxic cocktail of squalid inner cities, an economy tethering on recession and a housing crisis was added an influx of lost, displaced, bewildered Asians fast fleeing from former African colonies.

More than being just a dilemma on how best to physically accommodate and socially integrate them into Britain, the English were presented with a moral quandary as to what their legal and ethical obligations were to people who were clearly not "White British" and yet British citizens. Labour MP Peter Mahon vehemently argued, at a House of Commons debate in 1968: "These people have no rights recognised by the Governments of India or Pakistan. They are British citizens, carrying British passports issued by the British High Commissioner. Our end then, is to deprive citizens of fundamental rights. What is worse, we are breaking our word. It is a shameful betrayal."[2]

Juxtaposed against that sense of honour was a Britain, ruddy-faced, scrubbed clean of the grime of Victorian England and victorious after World War II, furiously opposed to "darkies" coming in by the shipload. Landladies still put out signs on their windows saying "No Coloureds allowed." The war had reignited nationalist fervour, a distrust of foreigners and a closing of ranks. The sheer numbers arriving were beginning to overwhelm the nation. Amidst a flurry of race and immigration politics, by 1968, a voucher system was put into effect allowing a quota of 1,500 Asian families per year who were "British Citizens Overseas". Incredibly, India too restricted entry to those East African Indians wanting to return in the wake of African Indophobia.

The Goans who came to Britain did not have a strong affinity to Goa. They had lived most, if not all, of their lives in East Africa. Generally, these were middle-class Goans or at least Goans with middle-class aspirations, the product of a good education system. Goa had few opportunities to offer this cadre of teachers, clerks from the Civil Services and banking sector. They did not find it hard to get absorbed in the workforce in the United Kingdom. Dr Cornel DaCosta arrived in 1962, as a young student from Mombasa, Kenya. He bears the measured gait and eloquence of the typical English professor and has always emphasised the need for Goan communities to assimilate into the mainstream society. He gave me a first-hand account of 1960s Britain.

Work was plentiful, he says, but the main concern was accommodation. In general, the availability of accommodation got better as people understood where best to establish themselves. Often, this was as close to those already in Britain. A sizable number of Goans settled in Tooting and Tooting Bec, the Manor House area and Newham. Tooting lies to the South of London and is typical of an ethnically diverse London suburb, where shops named Polski Mart co-exist with Amal Fried Chicken and The Kebab Factory, white-clad butchers hang exotic meats in their windows and, melamine dishes and plastic buckets find themselves overflowing from Pound shops onto the sidewalks. Goans found comfort and familiarity in the area, home to many first-generation immigrant communities.

The overall numbers were not terribly significant, and Goans were indistinguishable from other Indians or Pakistanis. Goa was not yet on the tourist map, ignorance amongst the Whites was of a high order. In Cornel's opinion, they had a marked lack of curiosity about the new settlers or their former background.

31. Onwards to England

The plenitude of opportunity in the United Kingdom and the reality that it was quite capable of absorbing the numbers emerging from Africa did not spare the new immigrants from being resented. The British have never been congenial to foreigners. Dominic Sandbrook, in his book, *Never Had it so Good*, writes: "The British built their imperial identity by contrasting their own virtues with the supposed wickedness, indolence, infantilism and corruption of their subjugated colonial peoples. Racial stereotypes were central to the British outlook during the heyday of the Empire."[3] Faced with the suddenness of this influx of "coloured" people, there was a resurgence of White British national pride and a palpable fear that it was under assault.

Earlier in 1958, things had come to a head in Notting Hill. Unemployment, disillusionment, boredom and the summer heat proved to be all the trigger it needed for a trifling incident at a pub to turn into a riot of "nigger hunting", vandalising and burning homes. The clashes between the mostly West Indian population and a working class White population were dismissed as delinquent adolescent behaviour by the media, but the seeds of hate were liberally sprinkled on fertile soil. They left an indelible mark on British politics where the race card played well and played often got results. In 1964, Conservative MP Peter Griffiths campaigned in Smethwick for the general election with the slogan: "If you want a nigger for a neighbour, vote Labour." He won.

Dr Edward Raymond D'Sa who first came to the UK from Kenya as a student shares an honest moment with me. He suspects Goans muddled through, not wanting to be seen complaining. They pretended that racism happened to Indians and not Goans. They found consolation in church attendance and endless dances.

When discrimination was not overt it existed in its subtler shades. One Goan remembers being called for an interview because of his European sounding name but when he got to the offices, there was a visible look of disappointment on the face of the interviewer to discover he was Asian.

Amidst a sense of fear and threat to the British national identity, there emerged the British sense of justice and fair play and found its voice in the liberal press and Labour party politics. Then Labour Home Secretary, Roy Jenkins, in a 1966 speech, radically altered the commonly held notions of assimilation, urging that integration need not be "a flattening process of assimilation but equal opportunity, accompanied by cultural diversity in an atmosphere of mutual tolerance."

Goans found a different type of segregation in the United Kingdom: that of class. White British saw Asians as replacements for working class British. Asians found themselves pigeon-holed, their expectations and aspirations for their children as future accountants and doctors, laughed at as being ridiculous and unrealistic. Asians for their part, had visions of their children going to school in *propah* blazers and ties, becoming members of country clubs, living in chocolate-box cottages with rose gardens, but in reality they lived cheek by jowl in run-down, crowded city centers, with working class British; a wide chasm persisting between expectation and reality. Getting job references to start a career was difficult. Their qualifications were either worth less or discredited altogether.

Eventually, what greatly aided Goans was Britain's much touted welfare system in housing and health-care. Some even managed to arrange for housing through the welfare system before they arrived in the UK. They were confusing times, turbulent times setting the stage for what it meant to be British in the 20th century and through it all, the newly arrived East African Goans were struggling to find their own feet, let alone their own voice.

Goans sought comfort in community and once again, as in East Africa, the Club House became a metaphor for the community. The East African Catholic Society was formed in 1962, operating from Manor House in North London. Its focus right from the start was to acquire a property and build a club house. Meanwhile dances were held in a church hall near Oxford Circus and Porchester Hall in Queensway, Bayswater. In 1982, respectable premises were found in the predominantly White neighbourhood of Ravensbourne, Kent for a club house. Formerly owned by *The Times* newspaper, it consisted of a four-bedroom caretaker's bungalow and sprawling six acres of playing fields.[4] The location proved to be unwise. The club house burnt down. There were whispers of it being arson with distinct racial overtones. Even though the club house did not survive, the Goan Overseas Association did and it continuously endeavours to represent the community.

Flávio Gracias, the tall, instantly likeable man, has been involved with the G.O.A since 1985 in one capacity or the other. Over the last decade, it has grown under his tireless leadership as president. The

31. ONWARDS TO ENGLAND

association is a life-line for Goans in the United Kingdom. It provides a sense of continuity and ameliorates the gnawing isolation and feeling of abandonment that often plagues immigrants in Western societies.

A lot of the immigrant Goans from East Africa were young men and women on the threshold of their own sexual maturity, thrust into the "Swinging Sixties". This, after all, was the age of the mini-skirt, beehive hairdos, bell-bottom pants and the Pill; of sexual experimentation; drugs and rock 'n' roll; a generation bent on pushing the boundaries of limitation hitherto imposed on them through culturisation.

Goans were not part of this revolution but were influenced by it nonetheless. They had moved from a fairly parochial background to the more libertine climes of Britain. In East Africa, they had an identity that was tied into their parents or even their grandparents back in Goa. In Britain, they discovered the heady delights of anonymity, and anonymity can transform human beings in the most magnificent ways. It freed them from the confines imposed by cultural norms, to experiment sexually, intellectually and emotionally. It was an intoxicating world of dating without chaperones, a few even ventured into interracial dating, finding the allure of British women fascinating. These relationships rarely if ever culminated in a union. There was a blurring of class, caste and colour boundaries. Africans, for instance, were not their menials who had served them at the dinner table but co-workers to be respected.

On the whole, there wasn't assimilation into White British society. They led parallel lives. Brushing against each other on the streets. The sterile relationships at work did not spill over in friendship outside of the office. But the meat-eating, beer drinking, church-going, rock 'n' roll loving Goan may have had an easier time of his transition into an England of Sunday roasts, Christmas pageants and *Coronation Street* soap-opera lives.

East African Goans are an amalgam of being Goans by origin, of having spent their childhood in Africa, of arriving in the UK in the prime of their lives and having to adapt to English moors. In England, community is defined not by physical proximity but rather by a nebulous concept of cultural kinship. Culture, like all living organisms, is not immune from Darwinian evolution. Ultimately, a sub-culture develops which in itself is distinct. They have, for instance, largely lost touch with Konkani as their mother tongue. Having grown up in the townships of Nairobi, Mombasa and Kampala, they are townspeople, well-read and well-spoken. While the Catholic Goan from Goa still maintains a fondness for things Portuguese, the East African Goan is more inclined to be an Anglophile and Anglicised. At times, he finds the Goan from Goa perplexing; distanced by years of separated lives, held in kinship only by a dim memory.

East African Goans are testimony that culture cannot become solidified in time. It seizes upon chance and circumstance to shape itself and exists on a continuum of experience. Yet threads of commonality – a shared sense of history, beliefs, values, food and music – weave in and out of the larger whole, forming a nebulous nucleus of kinship and solidarity.

32 Freedom fighters in London

> I regard it as very unattractive and undesirable that we should put ourselves in the position of having to defend, or being bound to defend, the interests of Portugal in Goa. – British Labour politician and president of the Stop the War Coalition Wedgewood Benn, in the House of Commons, July 1, 1958.

THE QUESTION OF GOA would take center-stage during the mid-twentieth century. That a tiny dot of land should come to dominate the political landscape of the mid-1950s seems incredible in hindsight. But Goa was to become a proxy for major world players and in no small way touch on issues of sovereignty, nationality, aggression and integrity.

To India, Goa had become a colonial 'pimple'. To Portugal, the last stand of an emasculated power.

Goa yielded little to Portugal but it was an Olympian mascot of its former glory. The gatepost of its sea-trade into Asia where the best of its virtuous and adventurous men had wandered, conquered and prospered. Into this fray were new players on the world stage – Western democracies who saw Indian posturing as an assault on

32. FREEDOM FIGHTERS IN LONDON

sovereign territory and willful neglect of international law. The Soviet Union played in India's quarter with rhetoric in the Soviet mouthpiece *Pravda*. Britain was compromised. Her sympathies lay mid-way between its oldest European ally, Portugal, and its former colony and member of the Commonwealth, India. Much as loyalties were divided across the international arena, so did emotions run high on both sides of the fray for the Goans in London.

Following India's own independence in 1947, the 51 year old, Vengalil Krishnan Krishna Menon, a central figure in the freedom struggle and closely associated with Nehru, was posted as High Commissioner to Britain. He took office at India House in Aldwych. In the grand old tradition of the original India House at Highgate, North London, which had nurtured so many Indian radicals amongst London's Indian student population, he began enflaming young East African Goan students to agitate for Goa's liberation. India House at Aldwych is on a busy street opposite the historic Waldorf Hotel. Just to its side, throughout the 1950s, was a restaurant run by a Goan manager and frequented by Goans.

Menon shared an acquaintance with the Goan-born artist, Francis Newton Souza. Indeed Souza sustained himself in those lean years through Menon's patronage and Menon had arranged for him to have an exhibition at the embassy. It's difficult to know what the tea-totaling, vegetarian, non-smoking bachelor had in common with the Bohemian Souza fueled by sexual excess and drink, apart from their strong Left-wing leanings. Certainly both had a literary streak in them, for Souza was soon to publish his piece, *Nirvana of a Maggot* (1955) and Menon had worked as an editor at the Bodley Head Press and later became the first editor at Pelican Books. Menon had other Goans close to him who shared a desire to see a free Goa – an opera singer by the name of Aurora worked for the Indian High Commission; the short, stocky-built lawyer João Cabral and students like Anthony Remédios who was completing his civil engineering degree and who subsequently began assisting the Indian High Commission with translation of Portuguese documents.

João Cabral had solidified the support in London for a free Goa into a fledging group, the Goa League, based at 77 Dean Street, London. The name was strikingly similar to the nationalist India League, whose precursor had been the Home Rule for India League, formed in Britain in 1916. Krishna Menon himself had been secretary of India

League from 1929 and the driving force behind its operations.

Maria Aurora Couto in *Goa: A Daughter's Story*, writes of Lúcio de Miranda, a professor of mathematics who upon fleeing Portugal because of an inflammatory speech he made in support of a liberated Goa, made his way to London where he formed the Goa League.[1] Lúcio, Cabral and a medico named Denis, might have all worked together. Cabral was the secretary and Denis the chairman. I had been put in touch with Anthony Remédios, later to become secretary, through a mutual acquaintance. It was in corresponding with him that I pieced together this part of our history. Remédios was a little reticent about sharing his memories, pleading old age. Little did I know then, he was suffering from ill-health and sadly passed away on April 16, 2009, even as this book was being written.

Flyer by The Goa League for a public meeting in London, 1956, to address the issue of Goa's Liberation. Courtesy the late Anthony Remédios.

Remédios came from the heart of colonial Africa where racial segregation was rife. His father had emigrated to Salisbury, now Harare, which was then part of Southern Rhodesia, in 1900. The family was fairly prosperous, running numerous business enterprises including a general dealers shop, soft drink factory and a bakery. Regardless, segregation was a way of life and after finishing his sixth standard in a "coloured" school, there was no further education available to a "coloured", so his father sent him to Portuguese Mozambique to study Portuguese.

Later, Anthony travelled to Cape Town, South Africa, to further his education. If Harare had been prone to racial segregation, South Africa would prove to an education in humiliation for the eighteen-year-old Remédios. Here, Africans and Indians suffered the worst sort of degradation, being denied any semblance of equality with the White man. To the South African, every Indian was a "coolie" regardless of his occupation. In 1948, Daniel François Malan came to power and formally instituted "Apartheid" (or separateness), a system of legal racial segregation enforced by the National Party government in South Africa between 1948 and 1994. These early injustices constructed by the very mechanism of White supremacy had a deep and lasting impact on Remédios and shaped his political world-view.

The Goa League held its first meeting at Earl's Court near Central London, in 1956. By this time Menon had left London and been appointed to the General Assembly of the United Nations. Many of the students attending lived around the London area renting bed-sits for £2 per week. About 80 Goans gathered to attend that first meeting. Remédios along with Francis Newton Souza's then wife, Maria, cooked *sorpatel* in the basement of a building for those Goans in attendance. The attractive and articulate Maria was a dynamic woman, not just the consort of the well-known artist but a woman in her own right, a *couturier* whose clients included the higher echelons of the diplomatic circles. At the time, João Cabral was holding a Portuguese passport. The Portuguese embassy complained to the British that a Portuguese passport holder was engaging in political activities. Cabral resigned as secretary and Remédios, who was holding a British passport, took over the reins. Most Goans in Britain remained oblivious of the Goa League's activities. Even those that attended the meeting did so more out of curiosity than commitment.

When Dr Ram Hegde and Purushottam Kakodkar, both political activists agitating for Goa's Liberation and detained by the Portuguese, were released, they arrived in London on their way back to Goa. A reception was arranged for them by the Goa League at Canning Town, near London's Dockland area. To bolster the attendance, Anthony scoured the Docklands, looking for ships with a Goan crew.

Another meeting took place on June 18, 1956 to commemorate the *satyagrah* movement. It was a cloudy day; at around eight that evening, as twilight spread across a summer sky, Member of Parliament, Wedgewood Benn, or Wedgy Benn as he was known, was scheduled to be the keynote speaker. Wedgewood was a confirmed Socialist in UK political circles, sympathetic to the Goa League's pro-India stance and had argued vociferously in the House of Commons, against Britain offering any military help to Portugal to defend against India. The third speaker scheduled for that day was Joseph Murumbi, a member of the Movement for Colonial Freedom and later to become Kenya's second bi-racial Vice-President of Goan-Kenyan parentage.

The *Manchester Guardian* newspaper perhaps echoed public sentiment, when it stated, on August 5, 1954, "Only one solution of India's dispute with Portugal can be satisfactory. That is the incorporation of Goa in India by peaceful means and with goodwill." Lord Swinton, as Secretary of State for Commonwealth Relations, and Selwyn Lloyd in his capacity as Minister of State for Foreign Affairs, presented a joint Cabinet paper outlining Britain's high-wire act of balancing its obligation to respond if Portugal invoked a *casus foederis*, a call for assistance based on its Alliance treaty, and its responsibilities to India as a member of the Commonwealth.[2]

On December 12, 1961, the British convened a secret meeting. The Lord Privy Seal confirmed Portugal had "formally invoked the assistance of the United Kingdom government, under the terms of the Agreement of 1899, in defending Goa against aggression from India."[3] Britain politely declined.

Krishna Menon who had earlier invested at least some of his frenetic energy into galvanising support for a free Goa in London, was also ultimately responsible in his capacity as Minister for Defense in India, for sending in troops into Goa, an act which played heavily on Nehru's conscience and caused a permanent dent in his image on the international front. Menon was convinced that Portugal would soon make the issue of Goa one of sovereignty over her "overseas territories" which might well have resulted in a long and lengthy legal battle over semantics.[4] Persistent press reports that Portugal was planning a defense treaty with Pakistan plagued Menon. In 1959, Remédios left England and returned to India to see if he could further aid in the Liberation movement.

Soon after Goa became part of India, another voice in the Diaspora made itself vocal, the Goa Freedom Movement or *Movimento Pro-Goa*.[5] Its genesis lay in a conference held in 1963, in the biting cold of a Paris winter at the magnificent Palais D'Orsay. The genuine angst expressed in Paris gave birth to the Goa Freedom Movement as an association of like-minded people, however nebulous its membership. The conference was spearheaded by Mirabeau Gama-Rose, chairman of the Goan Association, Kenya, which immediately following Goa's absorption into India had started a campaign demanding "self-determination" for Goans. Certainly, the list of thirty-three or so delegates that made up the conference in Paris was impressive. A group of eloquent, Goan intellectuals from the far-flung corners of Brazil and Macau, to Mozambique and the Arabian Gulf. Carlos Oliveira Pegado was the lone attendee from Goa. Mirabeau belonged to that generation, closely associated with the Portuguese Consulate in Nairobi. He was a practicing lawyer who would become a central figure in Nairobi, following Kenya's Independence. The main thrust of Mirabeau's opening speech was the evolution of Goa into a distinct entity, visibly European in content and one that needed to emerge as a self-governing body.

António da Fonseca, as the secretary-general, eventually came to be the force behind the Goa Freedom Movement. António came from the bedrock of Kenyan Goans, who felt strongly about autonomy for Goa. He had been attached to the East African Command (2nd Echelon) of the army in Kenya, where traditionally a distinction was maintained between Indians and Goans.

The momentum certainly seemed to be on their side. Five days after the conference in Paris, the association were granted a hearing at the Trusteeship Committee of the United Nation's General Assembly.[6] Four delegates – António da Fonseca, Wolfang de Souza, Professor Leo de Souza and Romeo da Silva – flew to New York. At about eleven in the morning of December 10, 1963, they appeared before the committee to make their petition on behalf of Goa.

The main agenda that day was Portugal's continued possession of colonies in Africa. They had been granted a hearing with the understanding that they would contribute to the subject of "self-determination" for these colonies. When their own agenda, which was quite sympathetic to Portugal, became transparent, African delegates in the committee called for their petition to be stricken off the record. The reason a record of it survives in the UN is because the US and some European allies voted against it being stricken. The group would find some solace in the US, through individuals like the Massachusetts Republican Congressmen Keith Hastings. They had a private hearing with Hastings a week later. Hastings was keen to pursue this line of defiance against India's perceived aggression against Goa, which he believed, should not "go unchallenged."

On April 26, 1965, a three-man delegation again led by António, were given a patient hearing in London with the Asian Parliamentary Sub-Committee, under the chairmanship of Anthony Royle, to present their case for self-determination.[7] Royle, a shrewd Conservative MP from Richmond, Surrey, was possibly aware of the lack of any substantive support for the movement, evidenced by his question: "What support does the Goa Freedom Movement have of Goans and what is its membership?"

The courage of all these Goans, whether they subscribed to the Goa League or the Goa Freedom Movement, has to be admired for one thing that is uncontested is their love for Goa. Was theirs a nobler world? Our most noble acts carry the imprint of self-serving motives.

Long after the doors had closed on all the Portuguese garrisons in Goa, the flag had been folded and sent back, Goa had been declared a Union territory of India and then a full-fledged state; long after Portugal's memory grew dim; the Goan remained connected to Britain. Ironically, for a good many Goans, it would be Portugal that would open the doors to employment in Britain in the 21st century.

33 Salubritas et Industria

SWINDON DOESN'T LOOK LIKE a factory town. It is lush green with swathes of agricultural land, the streets lined with houses not given to prosperity but neither to the grime associated with industrial hubs. At the dawn of the 21st century, Swindon became home to a substantial number of Goans who have made their way to the UK by virtue of a Portuguese passport.

I met Agnelo de Mello at his home in Swindon. Sporting an Islander shirt, he exuded all the charm of a Goan. Much like the Biblical patriarch Abraham, Agnelo, an ex-president of the Goan Swindon Association, contends he is the genesis of the growing Goan tribe in Swindon. Having moved here from the Gulf some twenty years ago, he knew the then manager of the Rover assembly plant and was instrumental in getting assembly-line work for Goans. From this humble seedling, a mighty tree has grown.

As per the 2001 UK Census, Swindon had a population of 180,061 of which 2.1% were of Asian descent. Senior Catholic priest Monsignor Twomey estimates the influx of Goans in recent years to be in the region of 8,000.[1] Although this figure is hard to verify, Swindon

33. SALUBRITAS ET INDUSTRIA

has possibly the most robust concentration of Goans in a single area. The Monsignor's predominantly Irish Catholic parish has now been replaced by Goans. A large percentage of them are from Siridao, Goa Velha and Agassim.

Portugal affords Goans the right to Portuguese nationality. Prior to the Liberation of Goa in 1961, Goans were Portuguese nationals. Portugal has left this option open to Goans born before 1961 and up to three generations henceforth. With Portugal being a member of the European Union, holders of Portuguese passports can move freely within member states of the EU. One of the big draws of this mobility of labour is Goans now have access to UK labour markets.

Swindon is an industrial estate, home to companies such as Honda, BMW and Faccenda, one of UK's largest chicken processing plants. It is in factories such as these that Goans find employment. Inability to communicate in English has been an impediment and condemned many to low-skilled jobs on the assembly line. In the spiraling 2007 recession, those hardest hit were the ones unable to speak in English. Life is not only hard but competitive as well. Amongst native Swindonians, there is a feeling that an influx of immigrants including the Poles and Brazilians are taking over their jobs. In 2004, rocks were hurled at a coach carrying ethnic minority workers from a Faccenda factory. Later in the year, coaches used to bus workers were vandalized. Faccenda, the chicken processing unit, which provided employment to at least 100 Goans, often came under attack for using cheap, immigrant labour. Goans earn between £5.52 and £6.00 per hour. It's difficult to make ends meet in the UK with a minimum-wage job.

Goans live in the town center along Manchester Road, Elmina Road and Broad Street. A major worry for any new arrival to the UK is housing and rent. A *kudd*-system, a sort of family-run hostel has been set up to ease the pain of initial rent payments. Families who arrived early on in Swindon, invested in houses and have now converted parts of these houses into rooms for rent. The average monthly rent is between £250 to £400 per month. These cramped living conditions have at times earned the ire of their neighbours. The large amounts of garbage generated and the resultant pestilence is seen as a health hazard. Doubtless, the entry of new immigrants is always viewed from a jaundiced perspective and a lot of problems that were already in existence in Swindon are now likely to be blamed on the new arrival.

The Swindon migration is unique in one respect. These were not young men setting out to explore unknown worlds, as in Africa and the Gulf. Many who emigrated to Swindon, did so in their fifties, with full-fledged families. They come from a working class background, without a strong academic resume. Some have had difficulties adjusting to life in the UK. The cultural difference, the lack of extended family support and at times the inherent racism of British society towards new comers has doubtless led some to question their move. But despite these hindrances, Goans find their new life offers their children opportunities they could not easily avail of back in Goa.

Veena and her family migrated to Swindon seven years ago. She works at the Churchfields School, where quite a few Goan students attend. The transition from Goa to Swindon for these children is not always an easy one, says Veena, but the school provides a supportive atmosphere. Initially, Goan students would leave the world of academics after finishing their O-Levels (Secondary school level or 10th standard equivalent) and take up jobs, but now she finds many going on to university. Some have preformed so well, they are part of the school's "Top Set". Veena tells me children are encouraged, whether their aptitude is in drama, music, art or academics.

The story of new immigrants is as timeless as Swindon's chalk hills. The hopes and aspirations these families have for their children is the propeller that enables them to endure life in all its severity. Life does not stand still, it is a continuum. The earliest waves of Goan immigrants into Swindon have already established themselves. They have taken out mortgages on houses and put down roots in their community. They are on their way to leading comfortable lives. Swindon's motto is "*Salubritas et Industria*", meaning health and industry.

Goans in Swindon enjoy both.

34 Growing up Goan-British

IN THE 1980s, a new band burst onto the UK pop scene. It was Culture Club, headed by an androgynous lead singer, Boy George, whose bizarre dress sense was as much a statement as his music. In many ways, Culture Club epitomised that decade. If the music of the 1960s had defined that generation's need to explore its sexuality and engage in honest conversations about the Vietnam War, Women's Rights and Civil Rights, then the 1980s were an examination of The Self. An exploration and acceptance of one's own individuality.

The Goans who had come to the UK in the 1960s from East Africa gave birth to a generation that came of age in 1980s Britain. Although Goans had spent a lifetime in Africa, they were never Africans and though they had British passports which eventually enabled them to come to the UK, they were never British. Being Goan was the only identity they acknowledged. However much it may have evolved on account of its experiences in the Diaspora, it was not grafted onto the stem of another identity. Their children, growing up in Britain would be the first to encounter a hyphenated identity, that of being Goan-British. One might expect this situation to have produced a cultural schizophrenia of sorts. Instead it has produced a generation who have seamlessly synthesised both cultures and emerged confident in who they are as a group.

Alison Braganza's parents emigrated from Nairobi in 1971. She was born in the UK and grew up in a predominantly White middle-class neighbourhood. She was formerly the PR and Events Manager for the Young London Goans Society (YLGS) alongside its Managing Director, Magdalena D'Souza. The group came into existence in 2000, with the intention of bringing the young Goans of London together. Alison and Maggie, as they are known to friends, come in contact with a lot of Goans of their generation. Alison in a lot of ways is the epitome of a young, British lass; self-assured, brimming with confidence, ambitious with her personal and professional life and yet she is profoundly aware that she is a Goan as well. She was just eight years old when a particular incident made her realise she was different.

She was in primary school and they were painting portraits. Everyone had mixed flesh colour paints. Alison went ahead and painted her flesh the same pink colour as everyone else. Her teacher quietly pointed out that she should have painted her skin brown. Alison though, does not have any issues with being different. Two things have specifically made her realise she is different from the mainstream. The huge gatherings for birthdays, christenings, communions and weddings. She noticed early on that this was not the case with the other children in her school. The only other girl who had similar experiences was an Italian. Alison's family would attend a lot of dances and community events organised by the G.O.A. This sense of community was markedly different from her peers.

Both Alison and Maggie went to predominantly White schools. Their early experiences in life were shaped by a very English environment. Goan adolescents grow up acquainting themselves with the Bronte sisters at school and listening to the Pet Shop Boys at home. How much exposure Goans have to their own community depends on where they live. Those that live in North London or Swindon, where there is a higher concentration of Goans, can expect to form childhood friends with other Goan children. For most Goans though, their early friendships cut across the racial divide, more so for children who attend Catholic schools. Being Catholic has been an added bonus for Goans. It qualifies them for admission in much sought after Catholic schools, which have a stellar reputation both in terms of academic achievement and high standards of discipline.

The 1980s was the decade of Thatcherism, propagating the virtues of a free-market economy, self-reliance and – some may argue – rampant materialism back into the stream of public consciousness. The British are slavishly individualistic and while the Goan embraces individualism, he also draws strength from family and community. Speaking to Maggie, I realise how important some of the cultural anchors identified with being a Goan are to her, such as religion and the coming together of the community whenever something happens, whether good or bad. She is Catholic and sees that as another marker of her identity.

To what extent Goan cultural organizations have been able to fulfill the needs of these young Goans is debatable. There is the reality that as each successive generation of Goan children gets more assimilated into the mainstream society, the cultural appeal of these organisations diminishes. They are seen as anachronistic and not addressing issues relevant to second-generation Goan-British. Associations such as the Young London Goans Society (YLGS) and Fenny Fever have sprung up to cater to the needs of the younger generation and are somewhat "chaperoned" by the older Goan Association.

Adolescence inevitably means having to wade through questions about sexuality and relationships. The Eighties was the decade of big hair and even bigger sexual appetites. Sexually explicit music videos and television programmes made their way onto the screen. Whether media in anyway influences behaviour or merely reflects current trends has been a long-standing debate, but certainly in very subtle ways it condones certain behaviours. According to the Office of National Statistics (ONS), the number of teen pregnancies rose sharply in the 1980s.[1] By 1998 there were 41,089 teen pregnancies in England. Since then the rate has been declining possibly on account of better information and contraception made available, although Britain still faces the largest number of teen pregnancies in Europe. The challenge for Goan parents in the UK is very often having to be honest about issues of peer pressure, consensual sex and the emotional lives of their children in a liberal, Western democracy.

Eddie Fernandes, editor and owner of Goanvoice UK, moved from Kenya to the UK in the 1960s. He is father to two sons raised in the UK. In East Africa, he says, there was no mingling with other races. Even coming to the UK did not significantly change this dynamic.

There was interaction at work but those relationships did not extend to socialising elsewhere. Children now grow up in a multi-cultural society in a truer sense of the word. They go to culturally diverse schools, socialise with their friends after school but they come home to a monoculture. This creates tension at times, causing a schism in parental relationships.

Alison had a couple of English boyfriends in adolescence but adulthood brought more nagging questions as to what she was really looking for in relationships. Questions of her own personal identity plagued her. She joined the Young London Goans Society and got more involved with the community. She eventually began dating a Goan man. The relationship felt comfortable, relaxed and familiar right from the beginning, the culture was the same and so was the religion.

Racism is another issue still very present in British society. Certainly the days of "nigger-hunting" have passed but racial bullying at school persists and so does subtle discrimination at work. One young Goan student wrote to me saying, "I definitely feel that racism persists in the UK. I blame this on the media for corrupting minds and portraying stereotypes. Everyday incidents of racism occur be they physical, verbal or emotional, intentional or not."

In a 2002 survey conducted by *She* magazine, in partnership with the Commission for Race Equality (CRE), based solely on a sample of women respondents, 64% felt that race limits a choice of career and 67% felt it limited career progression.[2] Alison works as a fund-raising and marketing assistant for a charity and Maggie is a history teacher. Both the girls say they have not experienced discrimination at work. It is largely up to the individual to make an effort and go the extra mile but certainly neither of them feel they have been denied opportunities because of their race.

Perhaps being Christian has helped Goans ease their assimilation in a White Christian British society. Similarity of religion mollifies the sting of British racism. A Home Office Research Study, conducted in 2001, noted people are more likely to be discriminated against if religious affiliation became apparent through dress or custom; a "visible difference" from the mainstream. Hindus, Muslims, Sikhs and Jews reported a higher degree of discrimination.[3] One respondent to the study wrote: "If you're a Hindu you have problems, if you're a Hindu with a dot, you have more problems."

Britain has made great strides in its battle against intolerance though. British author of Goan origin, Edna Fernandes writes in *Holy Warriors*:

> Britain, a mongrel nation that assimilated invaders and refugees and emerged stronger for it, lived up to its tradition of absorbing newcomers, going through the phases of suspicion and insecurity to something approaching tolerance and accommodation... India was no longer the place of the Raj and Kiplingesque elephant rides through jungle morning mist. It had melded with British identity to create a distinct Indo-British character – Punjabi, Gujarati, Konkani with a British accent.[4]

Edna grew up in Britain but told me in conversation the atmosphere at home was definitely Goan. Something in the way she engages people in conversation, her warmth and congeniality are distinctly Goan.

In a modest survey carried out in 1996 by Dr Edward D'Sa, statistician and former editor of *Goan Digest*, three-quarters of Goan respondents said they did not feel assimilated into mainstream British society. A lot may have changed in the intervening years. Second and third generation Goans have come of age since then and feel more assimilated than their parents. But there has also been a resurgence of the Goan identity. Their parents, while in Africa, had a long-distance relationship with Goa, returning every four or five years on holiday. They maintained their links by waiting for letters and stories of Goa that would arrive by ship, carried by returning holiday-makers. Over the course of the years, Goa became almost a mythical entity, one which bound them but whose affairs were distant. The situation for their children in England is slightly different. Alison feels strongly about her Goan identity. She says if somebody asked her, she wouldn't say she's British. She would say she was Goan and the only time she acknowledges that she is British is if she has to fill out a form. She doesn't look at English people and think she's one of them.

Frequent travel from London to Goa, improved communication and the profusion of Internet-based information groups have all helped Goans in the Diaspora come in closer contact. The interest in Goa though is superficial. They remain ignorant and disinterested in its political and economic present and divorced from its ground realities. With each successive generation, a sense of being British overpowers. Goa recedes into a solitary recess of the subconscious. The evolution of one's personal and collective identity cannot be artificially halted. But this very process of evolution engages in questions about what identity itself is.

Perhaps when we attempt to define Goan identity, it behooves us to look beyond its cultural baubles of food, song and dance. Perhaps our identity should be defined by our more intrinsic values of tolerance, fortitude, perseverance, a low propensity for crime, a reputation for honesty, trust-worthiness and liberal-minded attitude. These qualities have transcended above all and survived in the Goan Diaspora, across continents.

35 Love, friendship and farewell

IN 1897, A TALL gangly man, of aristocratic bearing, left the village of Guirim, lying to the north of Goa along what is now the highway connecting Panjim with Mapuçá. He set sail from Bombay to Aden, and then in a German boat for the port of Zanzibar, arriving in Mombasa on *dhow*. Possessed of a steely determination, he walked from Mombasa to Baringo, a distance of over 600 kilometres. Peter Nicholas Zuzarte,[1] could not possibly have anticipated the adventure that lay ahead.

He came from a family of considerable wealth. The ancestral house was resplendently lit up with chandeliers and, as was the privilege of the elite, it had an attached chapel, graced with jewelled ornaments. A priest adept in Latin, Portuguese and Greek tended to the spiritual and administrative needs of the household. This wealth did little to quell the wanderlust in young Peter. He applied for a job as a clerk with Mackinnon Mackenzie, a recruiting firm in Bombay.

On reaching Baringo in the lush, agricultural Rift Valley Province, he clerked for a while for Geoffrey Archer, who later became Governor of Somaliland. He moved frequently, finally settling in Londiani,

35. LOVE, FRIENDSHIP AND FAREWELL

and opening up his own shop, the *Londiani Trading Company*, in an area generally reserved for Europeans, quite isolated for its only other neighbour was the post-office. The shop, built of corrugated iron, with its family quarters at the back, surrounded by Peter's rose garden and guarded by his pet dogs, did very well, which might have caused racial rancour in rural Kenya.

While in the Rift Valley, he had met a Maasai woman, the daughter of a *Laibon*, a medicine man and spiritual leader in East African society, a man of some daring who had incited the Maasai to rebel against the British on more than one occasion. Although the woman barely knew of a world beyond the Rift Valley, she could speak in several languages including English and Hindi. What was the attraction between an African woman and a Goan man? Both their respective communities would have frowned on such an arrangement. It was not uncommon for Goan men to bed *hampulem,* African women. Stories of these living arrangements were whispered back in Goa, but the unions never culminated in marriage. When it came time to choosing a wife, they travelled home in search of one.

In any case, love seems to have blossomed in the Rift valley for the union gave birth to Joseph Murumbi-Zuzarte in 1911, who would go on to become independent Kenya's second Vice-President. What forces wrought havoc on his parents' relationship is difficult to say, but it seems to have been as lonely and isolated from humanity as their shop. Years later Murumbi recalled having no one to play with as a child except his father, mother and their dogs. The relationship fizzled out shortly afterwards and Peter Zuzarte met Ezalda Clara Albuquerque, the woman he would marry.

Ezalda, from the village of Candolim, which lies along the coast of North Goa's Bardez taluka, was as spirited as she was courageous, often seen riding the plains of East Africa on horseback or a tractor to make house-calls as a midwife. Sadly, she was trapped in an unhappy marriage despite bearing her husband nine children. Perhaps the marriage had disintegrated completely when she met Peter, for reportedly Anthony showed a distinct lack of interest in taking care of the family. Peter and she began courting. He bringing her books to woo her, a gesture which sealed a life-long passion for literature for them both. Murumbi went to live with his new family when his father married. To the already existing nine children, three more siblings would be added in due course, Portia, Peter and Zelia who died young.

In 1929, Peter and Ezalda were drawn into an incident which rocked the very foundations of the Goan community in Kenya. John Dias, Ezalda's son by her previous marriage, was shot dead in the streets of Nakuru.

John Dias, was a mild-mannered young boy who in 1929 took up a job at a hotel in Nakuru run by Bernard Joseph Potter.[2] John and Potter's twenty-year-old daughter fell in love, a star-crossed match if ever there was one, which ended tragically for all concerned. On the night of September 11, 1929, an enraged Potter learned of his daughter's relationship with Dias. Potter was an ex-soldier, who came to Kenya just two years earlier and after a brief stint working as a storekeeper at the Camberwell Board of Guardians, became the manager of a hotel. Potter was by some accounts, typical of the very chauvinistic White settler mindset, surrounded by drink-sodden individuals, who might have goaded him on about his daughter's relationship with a "coloured" man. A definite taboo in segregated colonial Kenya. The next morning, Potter saw Dias in the market and later claiming that he was overwhelmed with emotion, shot him dead with the revolver he always had at hand.

The cold-blooded shooting sent shock-waves across Kenya and its racial implications were not lost on the Goan community. They etched it onto their collective consciousness, a cautionary tale not to bite of the forbidden fruit, relayed from generation to generation becoming apocryphal in time.

To the credit of the British justice system, Potter was sentenced to ten years imprisonment, the longest sentence ever meted out to a White in Kenya at the time. In large part this justice was the result of Peter and Ezalda's tireless battle with the authorities in seeking redress.

For the most part, Peter Zuzarte was separated from his children. He had sent them to India to further their education. Joseph Murumbi left at the tender age of six to attend the Good Shepherd School Convent and later the St. Joseph's High School, both in Bangalore. At twelve years he moved to St. Pancras European Boys High School in Bellary, an immensely impoverished district of what is today the State of Karnataka, then predominantly dependent on agriculture. He was a fellow boarder along with Eddie Pereira, another Goan activist of Kenya.

It was at this time, Murumbi's father began experiencing financial

35. LOVE, FRIENDSHIP AND FAREWELL

difficulties. While he was away on a short trip to Nairobi, miscreants set fire to his shop. Racial jealousies had sprouted and given rise to tension. The shop was not insured and he lost everything. There was no money left in the family, none to fund Joseph's education; but by then the young Murumbi had made an impression on the Principal, Father Callenberg, who stepped in and covered his fees.

Murumbi worked for sometime in India, first as a clerk in a garage and later at Burmah Shell Oil Storage and Distributing Company, the forebearer of Bharat Petroleum. He also volunteered for famine relief work in the South of India. No doubt this experience would shape his world-views and prepare him for the role he would eventually assume. At one point he did a stint at an ice-factory.

In 1933, twenty-two year old Murumbi, who had inherited his father's longish face, returned to Kenya. He joined his father in running the market-garden he had set up at Kampi-ya-Moto.

According to a published interview with Anne Thurston, Murumbi admits that it was his father who prompted him to visit his mother and establish contact with the Maasai. Peter felt they were in greater need of his assistance than Asians.

Joseph now assumed Murumbi as his family name.[3] Two years later, his father lay dying in Lower Molo. Murumbi barely knew his father as an adult, he had done his growing up in India but Peter had often visited his children, taking them on trips to Goa. Murumbi rushed to Peter's side, trying to shift him to a hospital. Peter refused, sensing the end was nigh. On his death-bed, he bequeath his book and stamp collection to Murumbi, which he grew into the magnificent Murumbi collection, now an important part of Kenya's cultural heritage housed in a gallery in Nairobi, Kenya.

After his father's death, his heart was no longer in the business. He closed shop and travelled to the more populous township of Nairobi looking for work. There he joined the Medical Department as a clerk. At the onset of World War II, he enlisted with the British Military administration in Somalia. He started out as a typist and was eventually promoted to Deputy Controller of Imports and Exports.

Returning to Kenya after the war, Murumbi and another Goan, Pio Gama Pinto, would become political soul mates. Despite Pio being sixteen years Murumbi's junior, he nonetheless became Murumbi's political ideologue. In the fifties, Pio and Emma Gama Pinto found themselves living next to Cecilia, Murumbi first wife and his son Joe, in Mrs Fitz de Souza's large house.[4] Pio and Murumbi were founding members of the K.A.U Study Circle, of which Murumbi was Secretary, which filled the political vacuum during Jomo Kenyatta's long years in prison. With the clouds of a crackdown on nationalist aspirations looming large in Kenya, Pio and the Indian Commissioner, Apa Pant helped Murumbi leave Kenya. In April of 1953, it was arranged for Murumbi to tour India, Egypt and the UK, with an African delegation to impress upon the situation in Kenya and to muster support. Murumbi "with his quiet manner and Western clothing" is said to have made an impression. While in India, his accompanying delegate Oginga Odinga made it clear to the press, that in the eyes of the African, the Indian was no better than the White settlers of Kenya.[5] Murumbi didn't return to Kenya but stayed on in the UK instead, for the next nine years. When Pio himself was incarcerated for his support of the Mau Mau rebellion, Emma discovered she had no rent money.[6] Pio had secretly been paying Cecilia Murumbi's rent as well. Although most of Pio's private papers were destroyed, one particularly warm letter sent to Murumbi in 1961, while he was still in London, does survive. His warm salutation of "my dear Joe" is telling of their close relationship, although evidently circumstances had not allowed them to correspond with any great regularity. Pio, assures Murumbi that he need not worry about his safety and that he had infact kept in contact with most of those who had previously been detained in Kenyan prison camps, reassuring him that he (Murumbi) too would soon be in a position to return to Kenya. As it turned out, Murumbi returned the following year and immediately joined the Kenya African National Union, (KANU) as Secretary to Jomo Kenyatta. KANU won the 1963 general elections and Joseph Murumbi became the party's Minister of State. In May of 1966, he was appointed Vice President of Kenya. It is hard to imagine that a boy born to a Goan father, who did much of his growing up in India, would become Kenya's second Vice-President binding Goa and Kenya in inadvertent kinship.

Pio and Murumbi's shared bond, however close, was premised on entirely different personalities. While Pio supported the Mau Mau movement, at the risk of his own life, Murumbi denied any involvement with it.[7] Pio was a staunch socialist while Murumbi was an astute businessman, seeing trade as a virtue in itself and not bound by moral quandary. When he left the fray of politics, he became Chairman of a subsidiary established in Kenya by Rothsmans who had major hold-

35. Love, Friendship and Farewell

ings in South Africa. Kenya observed a total boycott of goods from South Africa. Asked about Rothsmans' association with South Africa, he is reported to have said he had "no qualms" and that: "trade must go on."[8] Pio was the firebrand, consumed by frenetic energy, passionate and intense, driven by his inner principles. Murumbi was the public figure of Kenya, the one the British called its moderate face. He had the composure of an English gentlemen, influenced in this respect by his long years in England. His second wife Sheila was English. Pio and Murumbi were a polar constellation, both lighting up the Kenyan sky. Both Murumbi and Pio are only posthumously celebrated by the Goan community. To those who didn't know him personally, Murumbi was an African. To others he was a half-breed, the off-spring of a taboo relationship. Pio was a "communist", an unknowable, whose politics they didn't particularly care for.

In later years, Pio and Murumbi lived a short distance from each other. The day Pio was assassinated, it was Murumbi that Emma reached out to first. They arrived together to find Pio still in the car, his dead body covered in a blanket and their toddler daughter, Tereska, crouched in the backseat. They took the pale Pio inside the house, so pale that Emma remarked on it. Neither one of them had had the opportunity to bid Pio farewell; husband, father and life-long friend.

Murumbi asked to be buried alongside Pio, upon his own death. The City Park Cemetery, Nairobi, where Pio is buried was full at the time of his demise in 1990. The nearest place they could find was just outside the cemetery. The two of them lie barely 10 yards away from each other. In Kenya, close to each other, where their hearts always belonged.

The history of human beings is fraught with prejudice and segregation from that which is different from us. Yet from this fray of hate and suspicion, the heart can also gracefully reach out and forever change the landscape of humanity. It is reassuring for mankind that from disparate histories, life can intertwine and form a single thread of friendship, union and off-spring.

The people who came before us, who extended their hearts to people who did not quite look like us, the lovers who died for their love, the friends who remained chained by threads of loyalty; they changed the world. Ultimately it is the compassion of the human heart that evolves society. It takes us nearer to a purer truth, creates in us an amnesia of past historical hurt and creates new life which ventures forth.

36 A debt of gratitude

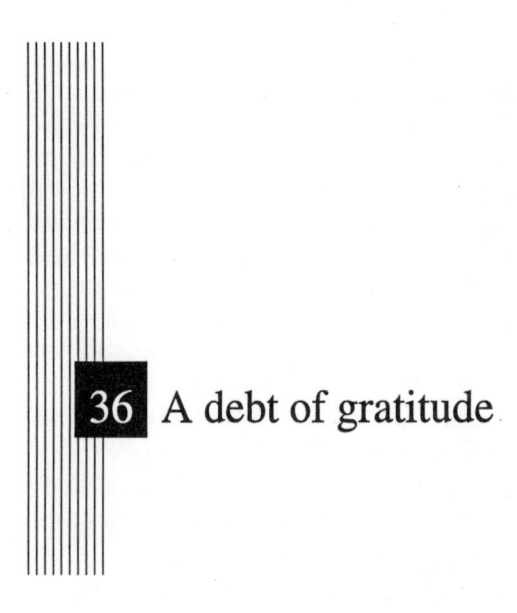

THIS BOOK WOULD not have been possible without Eddie and Lira Fernandes, both librarians living in London. They embraced this project as if it was their own, throwing open their vast resources of research material and contacts. Eddie, who edits the goanvoice.org.uk website, was a tremendous source of information for time-periods which I can only visit as a tourist.

Goa-based journalist-writer-publisher Frederick Noronha was the first to moot the idea that I pen my experiences in the Diaspora. His constant encouragement formed a kind of discipline in me even when doubts crawled into the hollows of my mind. Academic consultant on the project, Jason Keith Fernandes, wagered me to rise to the challenge after doing a first-read and providing an unflinching critique.

My mother, Helen Cardoso, was a goldmine of first-hand information, whom I mined unscrupulously. My father, Roque Cardoso, and my uncle Lenny Gomes, filled in huge gaps about mid-century Goa as seen through the eyes of people who lived in its villages. All three have spent their entire adult lives in the Arabian Gulf. My mother-in-law Thelma do Rosário Carvalho was helpful, being a Portuguese

36. A DEBT OF GRATITUDE

teacher by profession.

Long-time friend Dr Basílio Monteiro, associate professor at St. John's University, New York, helped set up interviews in America and we bounced ideas off each other about Christianity in Goa. I am indebted to Historical-Geographer Clifford (Cliff) J. Pereira, a Fellow of the Geographical Society and author of *The View from Shooters Hill: The Hidden Black & Asian History of Bexley*, for patiently answering my questions, selflessly sharing his own research and directing me to relevant archives. Angelo Faria, retired senior member, International Monetary Fund and the East African Service Organisation, was a font of information on Kenya and the intricate web of relationships which persisted in Colonial Africa. His first hand accounts of some larger-than-life personalities in Kenya was invaluable.

I cannot express enough gratitude to Cliff, Angelo, Lira and Eddie who read and re-read chapters, especially aspects dealing with Africa.

More than anything, this book has been a community project. The enthusiasm of the community in contributing personal anecdotes was endearing. In order of input, special mention to:

Mervyn Maciel, senior retired official from the Colonial Civil Services of Kenya, author of *Bwana Karani*, now living in the UK, who was tireless in providing me with information and sending me cuttings and photographs of Africa, taking me back in time; Anthony Fernandes and Possedonio Tovar Dias, both close friends of my parents from Dubai; Dr João Carlos Fillipe de Melo, Ras Al Khaimah; Pamela Fernandes, Dubai; Father Michael Victor Cardoz of the Arabian Vicarage, Dubai; Doreen Martins, teacher from St. Mary's School, Dubai; Concie Lobo, brother of John Lobo, Dubai; Carmon Santos, community leader in Kuwait; the Guiaos of Peekskill, New York; Victor Rangel-Ribeiro, author of the novel *Tivolem* and *Loving Ayesha and Other Stories*; Monsignor Nicholas Soares, New York; Levis and Gary Cardoso, my brothers who live in Florida; Benegal Pereira, son of the nationalist freedom fighter Eddie Pereira, New Hampshire, who has been actively involved in linking the Asian-African Diaspora through cyber initiatives such as Namaskar-Africana-L; Melina Pereira, San Diego; Armando Rodrigues, a writer and master of the anecdote, who gave me an eye-witness account of life in Uganda in 1930s; Canada-based Emma Gama Pinto, widow of Independent Kenya's first marytr Pio Gama Pinto; Felix Pereira, head of the UK Malawi Goans and Gabriel Louzado, ex-Malawi now resident in UK.

A special thanks to Dr Cornel DaCosta, adjunct Professor of Education, Florida State University, London Center. He grew up in Kenya and then migrated to the UK as a young student, and provided fascinating insights into life in Africa. Also to Dr Ed D'Sa, statistician and founder-editor of the earlier published *Goan Digest*, UK; the Rhodesian-born Anthony Remédios, then secretary of the Goa League formed in the London of the 1950s, who sadly passed away in Mumbai even while I was still in the process of completing the book; Angelo D'Mello, ex-president of the Goan Swindon Association; Geraldo Oliveira, Swindon, UK; Alison Braganza, ex-PR and Events Manager of the Young London Goans Society; Maggie D'Souza, Managing Director Young London Goans Society; Xavier Fernandes, my cousin who lives in Southampton, UK and Lawrence Fernandes, his son; Jennifer Price-Pereira, niece of the bi-racial Goan Joseph Murumbi, Kenya's second Vice-President; and Seraphino Antao, renowed sportsman.

I'd be remiss if I didn't mention the helpful staff at the British Library, King's Cross, the Colindale newspaper library and the National Archives at Kew, members of the online volunteer-run network Goanet at goanet.org, the academic cyber-forum Goa-Research-Net at Yahoogroups.com, africana-orientalia also at Yahoogroups.com, and Rene Barreto, president of World Goa Day, for putting out my requests at various forums at different points of time.

The historians of Goa, who have selflessly dedicated their lives to chronicling Goa's history, deserve special thanks. Of your work I have drunk deeply and madly, and yet never quite enough. Others have kept the stories of Goa alive through the oral tradition. My thanks to historians Dr Teotonio Rosário de Sousa and Dr Fatima Gracias, for doing a read of the chapter *An Alliance of Sorts* and to Prof Paul Melo Castro of the University of Leeds for his feedback on Portuguese text.

Last but not least, sources who talked to me on condition of anonymity, particularly one from Malawi. I am grateful for their candid disclosures. They know who they are, and deserve my sincere thanks.

By way of an aside, I have retained some words as they are written in the original documents. They may be offensive to our twenty-first century sensibilities, but to alter them would be to dilute the essence of the specific time periods. The picture on the front-cover is of the Railway Goan Institute orchestra, dating back to 1920; a caption hand-

36. A DEBT OF GRATITUDE

written on it is apparently misleading as the Railway Goan Institute was based in Nairobi, and not Uganda.

Finally, no thank you would be complete without acknowledging the two people who are my life, Savio Carvalho and my muse, Lauren Carvalho, thank you for your patience.

Selma Carvalho
London, June 2010

37 Notes

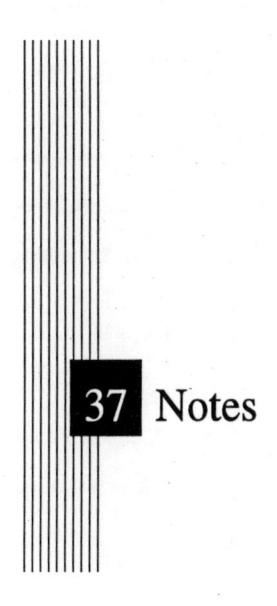

BL = British Library, St. Pancras-King's Cross, UK
NA= National Archives, Kew, UK
TT = *The Times* of London
IWM = Imperial War Museum
All websites mentioned were last accessed on May 7, 2010.

A BRIEF INTRODUCTION

1. Menezes A, *The Cradle of My Dreams: Selected writings of Armando Menezes*, Chennai, India: 2 Casa Goa, 2002, p 196.
2. De Souza, T R, *Medieval Goa: A socio-economic history*. Goa: Goa1556. 2009/1979. p 29 of the 2009 edition.
3. Assis Correia L. *Goa: Through the Mists of History from 10,000 BC – AD 1958*, Goa: Maureen Publishers Pvt Ltd., 2006, p 282.
4 The cabinet council, *TT*, October 1, 1880. A mention is made of the ice-factories run by Goans in Zanzibar.

AN ALLIANCE... OF SORTS

1. NA, SP 89/72 Secretaries of State: State foreign papers. 1772. folio p 114.
2. Boxer C.R. *The Portuguese Seaborne Empire 1415-1825*, London: Hutchinson, 1969, p 181.

3. NA, SP 89/72, Secretaries of State: State foreign papers, 1772. folio p. 113

4. Boxer C. R, *The Portuguese Seaborne Empire: 1415-1825*, London : Hutchinson, 1969, p 181-189.

5. NA, SP89/72, Secretaries of State: State foreign papers, 1772, letter is an enclosure folio p 237.

6. Boxer C. R, *The Portuguese Seaborne Empire: 1415-1825*, London : Hutchinson, 1969, chp The Pobaline Dictatorship and its aftermath.

7. NA, UK, SP 89/73, Secretary of State: State Papers, Portugal, 1772. Folio p 22-25.

8. Danvers F C. *The Portuguese in India: Being a History of Rise and Decline of their Eastern Empire*, Delhi: B R Publishing Corp, Delhi reprint, 2006, p 438. Danvers includes abstract of Census of 1776 in his book.

9. NA, UK SP 87/74, Secretary of State: State Papers, Portugal, 1774. Folio p 31.

10. Ibid, folio p 31-35.

11. Marques P. L , *The British Occupation of Goa, 1799-1815*, Lisbon: British Historical Society of Portugal, 1994, p 65.

12. England, *Glasgow Herald*, January 7, 1857, reported that the King of Portugal would exchange Goa in liquidation of an old debt and for a province in Europe.

13. The Possession of Goa, *Morning Chronicle*, January 30, 1857. *The Bombay Telegraph* as quoted in the *Chronicle*.

14. *Hansard*, HC Deb 01 July 1880 vol 253 cc1249-50

15. Great Britain and Portugal, *TT*, Jan 13, 1892. "The government of India found it to their interest to offer the Portuguese government only one lakh rupee as indemnity for working the salt-pans instead of all four lakhs as formerly. This money was all absorbed in the payment of interest due to the Mormugão railway."

16. *Poona District Gazetteer*, Vol XVIII (1885) Population: Christians.

17. IWM, 3972.

18. *Poona District Gazetteer*, Vol XVIII (1885) Population: Christians

19. *Bombay Gazetteer*, Bombay Town & Island, Volume 1, 1909 Communication and Trade: Factories.

20. NA, FO96/189, Bombay: Goan Community, 1901. Loose item in box.

21. India and the King-Emperor, *TT*, December 02, 1911.

22. *Bombay Gazetteer*, Bombay Town & Island , Vol 1, 1909 Communication and Trade.

23. *Bombay Gazetteer*, Bombay Town & Island, Vol 1, 1909, Foreign Trade, 420.

24. NA, CO536/218, Uganda, 1946-1949, foreword on the report "A Development Plan for Uganda" by E. B. Worthington. Loose booklet in box.

A QUIET REBELLION

1. Sandberg, G A Recent visit to Goa, 1890, BL, shelfmark ORW.1986.a 5557.

2. Esteves, S. *This is Goa*, Bombay: Source Publishers Pvt., Ltd. 1983. This description draws on the details provided by Esteves Sartos but also combines my own experiences.

3. A Christmas in Goa, *TT*, December 23, 1961. Correspondent recalls his Christmas spent there over 30 years ago.

4. *Illustrated Guide to Goa*, 1931, The Times of India, Bombay: Times of India Press, p 47.

5. Da Costa F J, (1896) *Jacob e Dulce*, translated from Portuguese into English by Alvaro Noronha Da Costa, (2004), New Delhi: Sahitya Akademi, 2004. His writing

first appeared as *Notas a lápis* in the daily *O Ultramar*, later compiled into a novel, *Jacob e Dulce*, and released in 1896.

6. ibid, letter from J A Ismael Gracias, addendum.

7. Assis Correia L., *Goa: Through the Mists of History from 10,000 BC-AD 1958*, Goa: Maureen Publishers, 2006 p 313-316.

8. Marini, E. *Goa as I saw it*, Switzerland: Sauberlin & Pfeiffer. S.A. Vevey,1957.

9. Kosambi, D. D. *The village communities in the Old Conquests of Goa*, Bombay: *Journal of the University of Bombay*, xv, no. 4 1947.

10. Vanjari S., Feudal land tenure system in Goa, *Economic and Political Weekly*, Vol 3, No. 22, June 1, 1968.

11. Kosambi, D. D. *The village communities in the Old Conquests of Goa*, Bombay: *Journal of the University of Bombay*, xv, no. 4 1947.

12. De Souza, T R, (2009), *Medieval Goa: A socio-economic history*. Goa: Goa,1556, 2009/1979. p 35 of the 2009 edition.

13. De Souza T R, Goan Agrarian Economy in Crisis, *Itihas*, 1976.

14. Couto M A, *Goa: A Daughter's Story*, New Delhi: Penguin Books India, 2005 p 139

15. NA, CAB/24/2, Importation of Labour from abroad, 1916.

16. Assis Correia L, *Goa: Through the Mists of History from 10,000 BC – AD 1958*, Goa: Maureen Publishers, 2006 p 282.

17. NA, ADM1/21202, Service of Goanese with Royal Navy, 1937-1945. Report on Recruitment and Conditions of Service.

18. Assis Correia L., *Goa: Through the Mists of History from 10,000 BC – AD 1958*, Goa:Maureen Publishers, 2006, p 283.

19. Richard B. F. Papers published in *Journal of the Royal Geographical Society of London*, Vol. 29, (1859), p 16.

20. British Colonisation in East Africa, *Liverpool Mercury*, June 7, 1895. See also, Civilising Zanzibar with the brandy bottle, T*he Pall Mall Gazette*, June 16, 1885.

21. Ancestry.com, US Department of Labour forms, List or Manifest of Aliens Employed on the vessel as members of crew onboard the *S.S. Croyden*. Names are as they appear on manifest some of which may have been corrupted by the English captains who wrote them.

22. NA, BT15/84, Havana Consul-General, Expenses incurred in connection with maintenance of Goanese seamen on their release from prison, 1928.

23. NA, ADM1/21202, Service of Goanese with Royal Navy, 1937-1945. Report on Recruitment and Conditions of Service.

24. HC (*Hansard*) Debate April 10, 1907 vol 172 c200. European and Native populations at Nairobi. (8a) East Africa as well as *The Times*, January 30, 1923 ("A Census taken at the end of 1921 gave the details of non-native inhabitants of the colony, Europeans, 10,000; Arabs, 10,000; Indians, 22,000; and Goans, 2,000").

25. Telegrams, *The Times*, July 20, 1931 (re "preliminary results of the census of non-natives of Tanganyika territory, taken in April, show that... Europeans 8,163, Indians 23,288, Goans 1,727"). See also House of Commons debate, *Hansard* ref, HC Deb 27 March 1935 vol 299 cc1887-8.

26. Stopford, J G, *What Africa can do for White men*, Oxford University Press, 1902, p 58 "Goanese cooks from India require £2 13s to £3 10 s per month. African cook requires £1 to £1-7s per month."

27. Tanganyika, The Policy of the Government, *TT*, May 21, 1921.

28. ibid

29. The Administrative problem in Equatorial Africa, *TT*, October 1, 1901.

30. BL, shelfmark: IOR/L/PS/12/4445, Coll 42/20, Protection of Portuguese Indians in Persia.
31. Ibid.

THE WAR YEARS

1. NA, FO 371/31136, Conditions in Portuguese India, 1942. Intelligence summary dated June 6, 1942 p 2.
2. BL, MSS EUR F 226/4, Bremner, Alice: India during the Raj, 1942.
3. NA, FO 371/31136, Conditions in Portuguese India, 1942. Intelligence summary dated June 6, 1942.
4. BL, MSS EUR F 226/4, Bremner, Alice: India during the Raj, 1942. The description of Archbishop José de Costa Nunes is provided by Alice Bremner.
5. NA, FO 371/26837, Attitude of Portuguese India, 1940-1941. Intelligence summary dated December 17, 1940. This physical description is provided by Claude Bremner.
6. Assis Correia L. *Goa: Through the Mists of History from 10,000 BC – AD 1958*, Goa:Maureen Publishers, 2006, p 313-316.
7. NA FO 371/31136, Conditions in Portuguese India, 1942. Intelligence summary dated circa end February 1942.
8. ibid, February 15, 1942.
9. ibid, March 31, 1942.
10. Refugees from Burma, *TT*, 5th May 1942.
11. NA, CO 323/1627/8, Goan Portuguese Nationals, 1939. Letter from Government House Nairobi to Secretary of State for the Colonies, dated June 8, 1939.
12. Goan School Mombasa 75th Anniversary Souvenir brochure, p 42.
13. Information on the Maciel family, provided by surviving son Mervyn Maciel, residing in UK.
14. *S.S. Tilawa* Memorial website: http://sstilawa.com/
15. List of fatalities at: http://www.convoyweb.org.uk/oskms/mem/45_1.htm
16. Commonwealth War Graves Commission website: http://www.cwgc.org/, Goan sailors commemorated by Bombay/Chittagong 1939-1945, War memorial.
17. Ibid.
18. NA, ADM 1/21202, Service of Goanese with Royal Navy, 1937-47
19. Ibid.
20. NA, FO 371/31136, Conditions in Portuguese India, 1942, Intelligence summary dated September 1, 1942.
21. Ibid.
22. ibid, August 16, 1942.
23. ibid, June 30, 1942.

THE RED BOOK

1. *Goa: Goan Point of View*, London: Goa League Publication, London, 1956.
2. *The Times of India Illustrated Guide to Goa* Bombay: The Times of India Press, 1931, p 51.
3. Ibid P 52.
4. Marini, E. (1957) *Goa as I saw it,* Switzerland: Sauberling & Pfeiffer S.A. Vevey, 1957 p 169.

5. NA, DO 189/347, Economic Implications following Indian occupation of Goa, 1961-1963. P 39. A substantive Confidential Report was compiled by the British government. Among those interviewed in Goa at the time were Mr José António Gouveia, President of the Management Committee of the Goa Chamber of Commerce, Dr Redualdo da Costa, President do Junta Comercia Externo, Mr & Mrs M J Bhatia of Althertons & Jacobs, V. M. Salgaocar, V. Pinto of Obras Publicas, Robert Hepp, agent for Volkswagen in Goa, and Mr Chowgule.

6. Ibid. P 46.

7. ibid. P 45.

8. NA, SP 89/73, Secretary of State: State Papers, Portugal, 1782, letter from Robert Walpole to Earl of Rochford dated July 1, 1772: "I understand a great part of what the Queen of Portugal receives issues out of the Revenue of Goa."

9. *Picturesque Goa, Guide to Goa* (1952), Goa: Goa Press. The names of these establishments have been taken from the advertisements on this guide.

10. NA, DO 189/347, Economic Implications following Indian occupation of Goa, 1961-1963. p 33.

11. NA, DO 189/347, Economic Implications following Indian occupation of Goa, 1961-1963, I.P.B.A Report on India, VII, Goa, April 1962.

12. NA, DO 189/347, Economic Implications following Indian occupation of Goa, 1961-1963. p 18.

13. Ibid, p 18-25. The Handbook for India's import policy is called the Red Book, although it later years a green border was added to its cover to denote a more liberal policy.

14. Ibid. (as per *Government Gazette, Botelim Official*, Government of Goa, Daman and Diu, Notice)

15. Couto M A, *Goa: A Daughter's Story*, New Delhi: Penguin Books India, 2005, p 70.

16. Goa, Daman & Diu Goa: Department of Information and Tourism, Government of Goa, 1964 p 8.

17. Saksena R. N, *Goa: Into the Mainstream*, Abhinav Publications, 2003, p 80-86.

18. ibid, p 87.

19. Indian compromise on Prohibition, *TT*, November 7, 1968.

20. NA, DO 189/437, Economic Implications following Indian occupation of Goa, 1961-1963.

21. *Goa Migration Study 2008*, conducted by the State of Goa, India. p 38.

AN ILLICIT PAST

1. Maitland A, *Wilfred Thesiger: The life of the great explorer*, London: Harper Press, 2006, see chapters Prelude to Arabia and Arabian Sands.

2. Ibid, p 270

3. Boxer C. R. *The Portuguese Seaborne Empire: 1415-1825*, London: Hutchinson, 1969, p 46.

4. Gracias, F, *Health and Hygiene in Colonial Goa*, New Delhi: Concept Publishing Co, 1994 p 105.

5. BL, IOR/L/E/7/1365, file 4933, Indian Hemp.

6. Chatterjee I. & Eaton R. M, *Slavery and South Asian History*, Indiana: Indiana University Press, 2006 p 246.

7. NA, FO371/185547, Gold Smuggling, 1966. Confidential report on gold Smuggling from Dubai to India, January 19, 1966, P 2.

37. NOTES

8. ibid

9. NA, FO 371/31136, Conditions in Portuguese India, 1942, Intelligence summary, February 15, 1942.

10. NA, FO 371/34682, Conditions in Portuguese India, 1942, Intelligence summary, January 31, 1943.

11. Smuggling and Port Rashid, *TT*, June 21, 1977.

12. India to control gold holdings, *TT*, January 10, 1963.

13. NA, FO371/185547, Gold Smuggling, 1966. Confidential report on gold smuggling from Dubai to India, January 19, 1966. P 4.

14. NA, FO 371/148977, Economic Development in Trucial States. 1960. Annex to Persian Gulf Annual Economic Report for 1960.

15. Gold smuggling boosts Dubai economy, *TT*, March 3, 1969.

16. NA, FO 371/174741, Illegal immigrants, 1964. Report on Pakistani vessel "*Al-Fatah*" February 4, 1964.

17. NA, FCO 8/1272, Immigration Control, 1968 Jan01-1969 Dec 31. Telegram re Indian Dhow Fatih Salama, April 22, 1969.

18. NA, FCO 8/1272, Immigration Control, 1968 Jan01-1969 Dec 31, Confidential letter by D J McCarthy, April 14, 1969.

THE DAWN OF A NEW ERA

1. NA, FO 371/132624, Ruling Family in Trucial States: death of Ruler of Dubai, 1958. Letter from Political Agent, September 29, 1958

2. Ibid.

3. Ibid

4. Ibid Telegram from Dubai Political Agent, September, 12, 1958.

5. Ibid. Letter from Foreign Office to Bahrain Resident's Office, September 18, 1958, (quote, "There seems little doubt that we will recognise Rashid.")

6. NA, FCO 8/1510, Annual Review for Dubai and the Northern Trucial States 1970, 1970 Jan 01-1971 Dec 31. Report by Political Agent, J. L. Bullard. December 10, 1970.

7. NA, FO371/185581, Ruler of Dubai, 1966. Letter from Political Agent, May 19, 1966.

8. Ibid.

9. Britain's burden in Arabia, *TT* August 22, 1957.

10. NA, UK, FCO 8/877, Establishment of English Speaking School in Dubai, 1968. Brief report on Dubai includes population statistics.

11. NA, UK FCO 8/892, Dubai off-shore concessions and harbour project, 1967. Telegram from Foreign Office, May 4, 1967, ("Following pressure from Continental and Mehdi Tajir, B P have now agreed to a declaration that oil has been discovered.")

12. Malcolm McBain interviewing Sir Archie Lamb, at his home. Transcript of interview at:http://www.chu.cam.ac.uk/archives/collections/BDOHP/Lamb.pdf

13. NA, UK FCO 8/892, Dubai off-shore concessions and Harbour project, 1967

EARLY ARRIVALS IN THE EMIRATES

1. NA, FO 371/174742, Political Agents Impressions of Dubai, 1964. October 1, 1964.

2. NA. FCO 8/1270, Dubai Trade licences ordinance, 1969 Jan 01-1969 Dec 31. Copy of Dubai Municipality Resolution no. 155, 13th Session – April 10, 1966. (English translation).

3. Al-Suwaidi, A. Finance of International Trade in the Gulf, BRILL, 1994 p 15,16.

4. The history of Jashanmals at their website, http://www.jashanmal.ae/cgi-local/ps.pl?/aboutus

5. NA, FO 1016/854, Arabisation in Dubai, 1966. Documents labour conditions in UAE at the time stating administrative deficiencies.

6. Dubai oil expected in 30-60 days, *TT*, May 30, 1969.

7. NA, FCO 8/1510, Annual Review for Dubai and the Northern Trucial States, Report by Political Agent, J. L. Bullard. December 10, 1970.

THE M.V. DARA

1. NA, BT 239/479, MV Dara: Explosion caused by bomb, 1961-1962. Although this incident is known in the Gulf, it would have been impossible to retell with any amount of accuracy, without input from several newspaper stories of the time, and if I had not fortuitously gained access to the detailed files kept about the incident by the British. These files (*The Dara*) now rest at the National Archives in Kew, Richmond, UK. Here I chanced upon Joseph Michael Phillip Fernandes' personal account of that day, as well as the testimonies of several survivors including Captain Charles Elson and Officer Jordan.

2. By another stroke of incredible luck, I was then able to interview Joe's wife, Pamela Fernandes, to gain further insight into the role played by Joe.

3. This description of the bomb explosion is by Captain Charles Elson.

OF FAITH AND LEARNING

1. Assis Correia L, *Goa: Through the Mists of History from 10,000 BC-AD 1958*, Goa:Maureen Publishers,2006, p. 13

2. From the text of a speech given by journalist Rajdeep Sardesai at a seminar on Goan identity, titled Gomant Vishwa Sammelan, on January 3, 2005.http://www.mail-archive.com/goanet@goanet.org/msg21007.html

3. Kosambi, D. D, The village communities in the Old Conquests of Goa, Bombay: *Journal of the University of Bombay*, xv, no. 4 1947, p 67.

4. The Indian High School in Dubai, Wikipedia entry: http://en.wikipedia.org/wiki/The_Indian_High_School,_Dubai

5. History of Dubai English Speaking School from their website: http://www.dessdxb.com/information/history.html

6. NA, FCO 8/877, Establishment of English Speaking School in Dubai. 1967-1968. Letter from S. J. Nuttal, July 1967, (re: Saudi Cultural Mission).

7. NA, UK, FCO 8/877, Establishment of English Speaking School in Dubai. 1967-1968. Constitution of the English Speaking school of Dubai. (1967).

AFRIK'KAR, DUBAI'KAR, GOEM'KAR

1. BL, IOR/L/PS/12/4461, Portuguese India Consular Diaries, correspondence by M.R.A Baig, February 1, 1947.

2. Kenya franchise, TT, October 19, 1923

3. IWM, ref: 4741

4. IWM, ref: 3972
5. This is anecdotal information provided by Eddie Fernandes who spent many summers as a young boy at the Ewart Grogan sisal estates.
6. 3. NA, CAB/24/230, Report on Financial Question in Kenya by Lord Moyne, 1932.
7. Goanet news item archived at: http://www.mail-archive.com/goanet-news@lists.goanet.org/msg01367.html
8. NA, CO 323/1627/8, Goan Portuguese Nationals. 1939.
9. NA, CO822/151/3, Goan communities: Position in East Africa. Letter from Goans Overseas Association dated August 24, 1950.
10. NA, CO 822/151/3, Goan communities: Position in East Africa. Memo from P. Rogers dated June 16, 1950
11. Ibid.
12. Condition in Goa, *TT*, March 24, 1954.

DISPARATE, UNEQUAL SOCIETY

1. NA, FO 1016/854, Progress of Arabisation in Dubai, 1966
2. NA, LAB 13/1509, Persian Gulf, 1961. Letter from British Embassy, Beirut to Foreign Office, September 1, 1961, p 2.
3. NA, LAB 13/1509, Persian Gulf, 1961. Letter from British Embassy, Beirut to Foreign Office, September 26, 1961, encl: draft of Abu Dhabi state, Labour Law.

THE GULFKAR

1. http://www.uaeinteract.com/docs/-Statistics_Centre_Dubais_population_is_1,241,000/21925.htm
2. Menezes, A, *The Cradle of my Dreams: Selected writings of Armando Menezes*, Chennai, India: 2 Casa Goa, 2002, p 113-115.
3. Ibid.
4. Da Costa, F. *Jacob e Dulce*, translated by Alvaro Noronha da Costa, New Delhi: Sahitya Akademi, 2004, p 28.

HOMELESS IN UTOPIA

1. Weiner, M. *International Migration and Development: Indians in the Persian Gulf*, New York: Population Council, 1982.
2. NA, FCO 8/1272, Immigration control in Dubai, 1968-1969. Letter from Political Agent, Dubai to D. J. McCarthy, Foreign and Commonwealth Office, dated April 14, 1969.
3. Deportation of 40 nationalists from Kuwait, *TT*, May 12, 1966.

A LAND OF IMMIGRANTS

1. Emigration, Comforts on the Voyage, *TT*, May 6, 1835.
2. Emigration to North American colonies, *TT*, July 7, 1857.
3. Ancestry.com, US Department of Labour forms, List or manifest of aliens employed on the vessel as members of crew onboard the *Kentucky*. Names are as they appear on manifest some of which may have been corrupted by the English captains who wrote them.

4. San Francisco Bay strike, *Reno Evening Gazette*, May 28, 1934

5. Ancestry.com, Niagara Falls, NY, border crossing card and list or manifest of alien passengers applying for admission, US Dept of Labor. Silvester Fillepe De Souza was married to Leopoldina De Souza. Although in one document, he is listed as East Indian, this term was commonly used for Indian to distinguish them from American Indians. He is listed as a Portuguese national born in Goa, in the rest of his documentation. He landed in Montreal on August 5, 1917.

6. The Immigration Act of 1924 (The Johnson-Reed Act), US Dept of State, website: http://www.state.gov/r/pa/ho/time/id/87718.htm The act was finally repealed in 1952 but prior to that an accommodation was made in 1946, authorising the entry of Asian Indians into America based on a quota system.

7. BL, UK, IOR/L/E/7/1372, Indians in the USA.

8. US and Asiatic Seamen, *TT*, February 4, 1927.

The chapter is based on an interview with Bertha Guiao, wife of Dominic Guiao, from Peekskill, New York and information provided by Anthony Cornell D'Costa, Peekskill.

THE EXILED INTELLECTUAL

1. Da Costa F J, *Jacob e Dulce*, translated from Portuguese into English by Alvaro Noronha Da Costa, (2004), New Delhi: Sahitya Akademi, 1896, p 193.

2. Couto M A, *Goa: A Daughter's Story*, New Delhi: Penguin Books India. 2005, p. 356. See chp La Grande illusion for an elaboration on this theme.

3. Menezes, A, *The Cradle of my Dreams: Selected writings of Armando Menezes*, Chennai, India: 2 Casa Goa. 2002, p. 126.

4. Ibid. p. 100-102, see also chp The cradle of my dreams.

5. Ibid. p 28.

6. US Census Bureau, Dept of Justice, Immigration & Naturalization, Annual Report, 1957. Immigrants admitted by country of birth, year 1956.

7. US Census Bureau, Dept of Labor, Bureau of Labor Statistics, Employment and Earnings (report prepared in year 1957), Non Agricultural Employment by Industry (1956).

8. Work of five young artists, *TT*, August 4, 1955.

9. Painter who insists on making himself felt, *TT*, November 22, 1962.

10. Interview available online: http://www.pifmagazine.com/SID/28/?page=1&

11. Rangel-Riberiro V., essay available online: http://www.mail-archive.com/-goanet-news@lists.goanet.org/msg00969.html

HEATHENDOM, CHRISTENDOM

1. Emile Marini, *Goa, as I saw it*, Switzerland: Sauberlin & Pfeiffer S.A. Vevey, 1956, p 147.

2. Olivinho J F Gomes, *The Religious Orders in Goa*, Goa: Konkani Sorospot Prakashan, 2003, p 45.

3. Portuguese pretensions in India, *TT*, July 18, 1892, a reference is made to Zaleski's work titled, *Voyage à Celyon et aux Indes*.

THE INDEPENDENT GOAN

37. NOTES

1. Carson, C. et al *Eyes on the Prize Civil Rights Reader* (revised edition) London: Penguin, 1987, p 492.
2. Indian Americans watch as Bush visits their native land, ABC news online, March 1, 2006 at: http://abcnews.go.com/International/story?id=1673762&page=1

THE STUDENT

1. Reagan inauguration launched with a bang, *TT*, January 19, 1981.
2. US expect 4.5% growth, *TT*, December 22, 1983.
3. Down and out in the soup kitchen queue, *TT*, December 17, 1983.

THE YOUNG BRIDE

1. Alburquerque, Teresa, citing Ino Godinho, "In the Mission Field", (1927) available online: http://www.goacom.com/goanow/2000/janfeb/looking.html

RACE RELATIONS

1. The Prince of Wales in India, Visit to Goa, *Hampshire Telegraph*, December 1, 1875.
2. The Prince in India, *The Graphic*, December 4, 1875.
3. Burton R, *Goa and the Blue Mountains*, London: Richard Bentley, 1851, p 103
4. James L, *Raj: The making and unmaking of British India*, London: Little, Brown and Company, 1997, p 152
5. Penrose, B, *Goa – Rainho do Oriente*, Portugal: University of Coimbra, 1960, p 67.
6. Gracias, F, *Health and Hygiene in Colonial Goa*, New Delhi: Concept Publishing Co, 1994.
7. NA. FO 371/31136, Conditions in Portuguese India, 1942. British Consul to the Undersecretary to the Government of India. letter dated June 23, 1942. p 2
8. IWM ref 12931.

MY BEAUTIFUL LAUNDERETTE

1. BNP Wikipedia page.

SETTING SAIL WITH THE BRITISH

1. NA, BT 334/65, Register of Deceased Seamen. 1915.
2. Myers, Norma, *Reconstructing the Black Past: Blacks in Britain*, UK: Routledge, 1996 p 111.
3. This passage appears in A Survey of London by John Stow, penned in 1598. Wikipedia entry.
4. Strangers Home for Asiatics, *TT*, May 29, 1873.

5. Lascars onboard the Dunera, Portcities London website available online at:
http://www.portcities.org.uk/london/server/show/conMediaFile.4096/Lascars-on-board-the-Dunera.html
6. NA, BT 334/65, Register of Deceased Seamen. 1915.
7. Ibid

8. The First Asians in Britain: British attitude toward immigrant community at : http://www.fathom.com/course/21701766/session3.html

9. Lighterman, A pattern of Loyalty, P.L.A Monthly, 1957, available online at: http://www.lascars.co.uk/pladec1957.html

10. National Archives, Kew, UK, BT 372/465/112: R258213 NADKARNI D 02/10/1900 GOA, 1913-1972.

11. NA, BT 334/65, Register of Deceased Seamen. 1915.

12. Ibid

EARLY DAYS IN UGANDA

1. The Source of the Nile, *TT*, June 24, 1863.

2. ibid

3. The Commercial value of Africa, *TT*, February 15, 1896.

4. The Uganda Railway, *TT*, May 22, 1896.

5. Ibid

6. D'Souza B, *Harnessing the Trade Winds*, Kenya: Zand Graphics Ltd., 2008, p 158.

7. Ed. Eyoh d. et al, *Encyclopedia of Twentieth Century African History*, UK: Routledge, 1998 p. 397.

8. The Uganda Protectorate, *TT*, December 24, 1903.

9. Porter P W & Sheppard E. S, *A World of Difference: Society, Nature, Development*. New York: Guilford, 1998, p. 340.

10. NA, CO822/151/3, Goan communities: Position in E Africa

11. Ibid. Minor remark on correspondence from Colonial Office, Kenya, by E. L. Scott, dated June 12, 1950.

12. The East Africa Report, *TT*, May 6, 1925.

13. NA, CAB 24/201, 1929. Report on East African Commission, January 17, 1929, p 27.

14. NA, CO536/177/ part nos: 20, 10, 7 & 9, Uganda: Original Correspondence, 1933, letter from John Fernandez to Secretary of State for the Colonies, dated January 31, 1932.

15. Ibid, letter from John Fernandez to Asst. Under-Secretary of State, Colonial office, dated August 8, 1932.

16. Ibid, letter from Governor Bernard Bourdillon to Tomlinson, Asst. Under-Secretary of State, Colonial office, dated July 6, 1933.

17. NA, CO 536/148/3, Uganda Original correspondence: Pensions and Gratuities for non-Europeans, W. A. Coutinho, 1927-1928.

18. NA, CO 536/184/3, Uganda Original correspondence: J A E DeSouza, 1935.

19. NA, CO 536/205/8, Uganda Original correspondence: Local Civil Service, 1938. Letter from Uganda Asiatic Civil Service Association to Secretary of State for the Colonies, May 1, 1940. Signed signatories, J.M.S Azavedo and Peter I. Pereira.

Some information about the Association and people involved obtained through oral anecdote.

THE GOAN MAN OF KENYA

1. NA, CO536/177/ part nos: 20, 10, 7 & 9, Uganda: Original Correspondence, 1933, letter from John Fernandez to Secretary of State for the Colonies, dated January 31, 1932.

2. Akumu O. A. K & Olima W. H.A, *The dynamics and implications of racial segregation in Nairobi*, Kenya: University of Nairobi, 2007 p 88.

3. East Africa, *TT*, January 30, 1923 ("A Census taken at the end of 1921, gave the details of non-native inhabitants of the Colony, Europeans, 10,000; Arabs, 10,000; Indians, 22,000; and Goans, 2,000").

4. NA, UK, CAB/24/230, 1932. Report on Financial Question in Kenya by Lord Moyne, (June 1932), Summary of Revenue collected in 1931, Schedule 2.

5. NA, CO 822/151/3, Goan communities: Position of in East Africa. 1950.

6. The British (Newspaper) Library, Colindale, UK, MC1737, *The Goan Voice*, Kenya. These are just six holdings, from Jan to Aug 1958, but a back-dated reference is made to an editorial of 1952.

7. Gregory, R. (1981), *Co-operation and collaboration in Colonial East Africa: The Asians' Political Role, 1890-1964*, Oxford: Oxford University press on behalf of the Royal African Society, p 261.

8. Nazareth, J. M, *Brown Man, Black Country*, New Delhi: Tidings Publications, 1981. J M Nazareth's son Larry Nazareth suggested I source this book, as he felt it represented his father best "in his own words."

9. National Archives, Kew, UK, CO 822/845, East African Goan National Association in Kenya, 1955-1956, Extract from Kenya Special branch, HQ Intelligence summary.

10. Kenya Goans Call for "Quit Goa", *The Colonial Times*, October 29, 1955.

11. NA, UK, FO 371/113511, East Africa Goa Liberation Association, 1955. (i) Aide Memoire from the Portuguese Representative in London to the British Diplomat, Sir Harold Caccia. Stated therein, "Reference has been made to the name of a Mr. J. M. Nazareth, a solicitor, who would be one of the instigators of the projected subversive organisation." (ii) Note from Sir Harold Caccia, Deputy Under-Secretary of State, Foreign Office, November 16, 1955. Stated therein, "The Portuguese Ambassador called this afternoon to say that his Government had heard that efforts were being made in Kenya to establish a self-styled 'East Africa Goa Liberation Association'."

12. NA, CO 822/845, East African Goan National Association in Kenya, 1955-1956. Telegram from the Governor of Kenya to the Secretary of State for the Colonies, December 17, 1955. Stated therein, "You maybe interested to know that it is now confirmed that a contribution of Shs. 600/- towards the expenses of the Goan National Association was made from the Indian Commissioner's Officer.......The General Secretary, one R. G. Pinto, is a brother of the Pinto detained for Mau Mau activities."

13. NA, CO 822/845, East African Goan National Association in Kenya, 1955-1956. Telegram from the Governor of Kenya to Secretary of State for the Colonies, April, 16, 1956.

EMMA GAMA PINTO

1. NA, CO 822/547, Speech of Governor of Kenya, 1953.

2. Emma Gama Pinto's unpublished biography which she generously made available to me.

3. NA, CO 533/566/6, Legislation: East African Trade Union Congress, 1950. Telegram from Governor of Kenya to Secretary of State for the Colonies, October, 20, 1950, p 2.

4. NA, DO 35/5229, *Search of Indian Commissioner's office in Nairobi during round-up of Mau Mau suspects*. 1954.

5. NA, UK, CO 822/1258, Visit of International Committee of Red Cross to detention camps in Kenya, 1956-1964.
See also, Anderson, D, *Histories of the Hanged*, London: W. W. Norton & Co, 2005. and Majdalany, F, *State of Emergency, the Full Story of Mau Mau*, Boston: Houghton Mifflin,1963.

EXPULSION FROM MALAWI

1. NA. FCO 50/567, *Position of Goanese community in Malawi*, 1976 Jan 01- 1976 Dec 31. Note for file by Stanley Relton, May 11, 1976.
2. Chirwa V R, *Fearless fighter: an autobiography*, London: Zed Books, 2007 See foreword by Malcolm Smart.
3. Gabriel Louzado made available to me his account of the events that transpired that day. His account has been largely corroborated by the file FCO 50/567, NA.
4. Dr Livingstone, *TT*, April 11, 1874.
5. *Irish Monty*, Irish Jesuit Province, Vol 18 No. 200 Feb 1890, letter from Livingstone to Rev James Russell D. D. 29 December, 1862.
6. Adams H R, *The weaver boy who became a missionary*, London: Hodder and Stoughton, 1874, p 216
7. Pryor, F, *Malawi and Madagascar*, Oxford: Oxford University Press, 1990, p 30.
8. Between Black and White, *Time* U.S, April 27, 1959. http://www.time.com/time/magazine/article/0,9171,811044-2,00.html
9. Patel N. (2007), A quest for identity: the Asian minority in Africa, Switzerland: Institut du Fédéralisme Fribourg Suisse, p 12. Pdf of article available online: http://www.federalism.ch/files/documents//Patel_FINAL%20VERSION.pdf
10. NA. FCO 50/567, *Position of Goanese community in Malawi*, 1976 Jan 01- 1976 Dec 31. Note for file by Stanley Relton, May 11, 1976. Conditions at Mulanje prison are described by Anthony Fernandes in this file. Felix Pereira, who was imprisoned gave me an eye-witness account as well.
11. MPs fear mass expulsions of Asians from Malawi, *TT*, May 18, 1976.
12. No general expulsions of Malawi Asians likely, *TT*, May 17, 1976.
13. Aid warning to Malawi over expulsions, *TT*, May 19, 1976.
14. NA. FCO 50/567, *Position of Goanese community in Malawi*, 1976 Jan 01- 1976 Dec 31. British High Commission (Lilongwe, Malawi), *Goanese Expulsions*, extract of President Banda's speech, May 29, 1976

ONWARDS TO ENGLAND

1. Theroux, P., *Hating the Asians*, Transitions, No.33, Oct-Nov 1967,
2. House of Commons (Hansard) debate, 27 February 1968 vol 759 cc1241-368
3. Sandbrook, D, *Never had it so good*, United Kingdom: Abacus, 2006.
4. Goan Association, 40th Anniversary, souvenir copy.

FREEDOM-FIGHTERS IN LONDON

1. Couto M A, *Goa: A Daughter's Story*, New Delhi: Penguin Books India, 2005, p 397.
2. National Archives, Kew, UK, FO 371/112199, Portuguese Possessions in India, 1954. Draft of joint cabinet paper by Lord Swinton and Selwyn Lloyd, April 25, 1954.

3. NA, CAB/128/35, 1961. Cabinet meeting, December 12, 1961.
4. Nevrekar V, *A Peep into the Past*, Goa: Rajhauns Vitaran, 1997, p. 89.
5. *Nehru's Aggression Condemned*, A Goa Freedom Movement publication detailing the Paris Conference held 3-5th December, 1963.
6. *Goan Petitioners in the United Nations*, A Goa Freedom Movement publication detailing the petition in the United Nations on December 10, 1963.
7. *The Voice of Goa in the House of Commons*, A Goa Freedom Movement publication (circa 1966).

See also, *Goa – Goan point of view*, The Goa League publication (1956), *Indian Imperialism – A law unto itself*, A Goa Freedom Movement publication (circa 1963-66).

Salubritas et Industria

1. Large numbers expected for mass at Christmas, *Swindon Advertiser*, 21 December, 2007.

Growing up Goan-British

1. Office for National Statistics website at http://www.statistics.gov.uk/default.asp
2. Survey on Race conducted by *She Magazine* and CRE, 2002. http://83.137.212.42/sitearchive/cre/publs/catalogue.html
3. Religious discrimination in England and Wales, Home Office Research Study 220 http://www.homeoffice.gov.uk/rds/pdfs/hors220.pdf
4. Fernandes E, *Holy Warriors*, London: Portobello Books Ltd., 2008, p 267.

Love, Friendship and Farewell

1. *The Kenya National Archives, Nairobi, Kenya, The Murumbi Africana Collection*, A Guide to the Collection of the correspondence and personal papers of Joseph Murumbi including a short biography, compiled by Reuben Owuor Magero, Officer-in-charge. 1980. Benegal Pereira made available to me Eddie Pereira's writings on Murumbi. Eddie and Murumbi were one-time fellow boarders. More intimate details of Peter and Ezalda's life together were provided by Jennifer Price-Pereira, Murumbi's half-neice. Eddie Fernandes made enquiries about the house in Guirim. See also Emergence of a Nationalist: An interview with Joseph Murumbi. Part II. By Anne Thurston. *Kenya Past and Present*. 1979. Issue Number 11.
2. Kenya murder trial of Joseph Bernard Potter, *TT*, November 6, 1929. Details about this episode were also filled in by Jennifer Price-Pereira.
3. Emergence of a Nationalist: An interview with Joseph Murumbi. Part II. By Anne Thurston. *Kenya Past and Present*. 1979. Issue Number 11. P 24.
4. Emma Gama Pinto's unpublished biography.
5. Criticism in India of Kenya rule, *TT* April 20, 1953
6. Emma Gama Pinto's unpublished biography
7. Mr Joseph Murumbi, *TT* Nov 21, 1953.
8. Rothmans Chief in Kenya, *TT* Oct 26, 1966.